YEAR OF THE
GATOR

YEAR OF THE GATOR

FLORIDA'S 1993 SEC CHAMPIONSHIP SEASON

JEFF SNOOK

Rutledge Hill Press
Nashville, Tennessee

Published in Nashville, Tennessee, by Rutledge Hill Press, 211 Seventh Avenue North, Nashville, Tennessee 37219.

Typography by D&T/Bailey Typesetting, Inc., Nashville, Tennessee.

Library of Congress Cataloging-in-Publication Data
Snook, Jeff, 1960–
    Year of the Gator : Florida's 1993 SEC championship season / Jeff Snook.
        p.   cm.
    ISBN 1-55853-320-6
    1. University of Florida—Football—History.   2. Florida Gators (Football team)—History.   I. Title.
GV958.U523S67   1994
796.332'63'0975979—dc20   94–21388
                                                                          CIP

Printed in the United States of America.

1 2 3 4 5 6 7 8 9—99 98 97 96 95 94

To Ferne and Eddie

CONTENTS

YEAR OF THE
GATOR

PREFACE AND ACKNOWLEDGMENTS

I T WAS ONE OF THOSE perfect fall afternoons in Columbus, Ohio. Sunny and cool; the leaves had finally turned that shade of orange that makes you thankful summer has come and gone.

September 30, 1972.

North Carolina versus Ohio State.

Archie Griffin, a freshman running back, took a pitch to the right side and . . . fumbled.

It was his first collegiate carry and my first football game at Ohio Stadium. I knew that day that I would never let myself drift too far from this great game. Sure, I could always buy season tickets. Or I could watch the game on television and put up with Keith Jackson. Or I could make a living out of it. The choice was easy. Why go to law school? The world already has too many attorneys.

One of the stories behind this book begins on September 10, 1992, two days before the Kentucky Wildcats were to visit Gainesville for the first game of the season. The Florida players were going through another hot, humid, sweaty practice.

It was an afternoon that would change the life of William Gaines.

During a routine, supposedly harmless, noncontact drill, Gaines fell to the ground clutching his right knee. Oddly, there was no pain, just an absence of feeling. The tendons and ligaments in his knee were torn. As the six-four, 293-pound defensive tackle lay helpless on the field, his mind was in a whirlwind of panic. What was going to happen to his football career? What were his pro chances now? Was it all gone?

It almost never began for Chris Doering. Growing up in Gainesville, his father on the faculty of the university, Doering had a dream—a simple, all-too-common dream. He wanted to play football for the Florida Gators.

He needn't be a star player like his idol, former Gators receiver Cris Collinsworth. He just wanted to wear the orange and blue, run through the players' tunnel onto massive Florida Field, and catch a pass or two.

But no college coach, including the coach of the team that mattered most to him, wanted Doering. He felt like the typical skinny kid in the corner of every playground in America, the kid nobody wanted when it came time to choose sides.

Being part of a team was never a problem for Monty Grow. His heartbreak was different. He had made the team but suddenly found himself suspended for reasons he couldn't comprehend. They were saying that he had violated the rules, that he had used steroids. They said he was a drug-user. And now he was just a bystander, just a spectator.

On September 11, 1993, another unwilling spectator sat slumped over in a chair outside the visiting team's locker room at Kentucky's Commonwealth Stadium. Terry Dean stared at his feet, shaking his head. His eyes watered; his voice wavered. "I don't know what to say," he said. "I guess I gave it all away." Dean had been pulled from the game after throwing his fourth interception. In his place, freshman Danny Wuerffel came off the bench to win the game with a twenty-eight-yard touchdown pass in the final seconds.

Three years of frustration from not playing and three years of anticipation had culminated in a three-hour nightmare. Florida had won, but Dean had lost. The job of starting quarterback was surely gone, at least for now. Would he transfer or quit football altogether?

To some this may be just a story about just another college football season. Nothing more, nothing less. I hope that you'll see this as a collection of stories about individual perseverance, an account of several comebacks from the depths of heartbreak and adversity to the heights of success.

William Gaines, a year after knee surgery, became a dominating defensive lineman. He was unblockable in the Gators' victory in the Sugar Bowl in New Orleans as the team climaxed the best season in University of Florida history.

Chris Doering won a spot on the team, then a scholarship, then some playing time. It was he who caught the winning touchdown pass in the Kentucky game. Reality had surpassed his dream.

Monty Grow found vindication, accomplishing what many thought impossible: winning an appeal to the NCAA for another season of eligibility. Even more important, he cleared his name and his reputation.

On October 30, Terry Dean came off the bench to help win a game. But it was not just any game. It was *the* game against rival Georgia. He reclaimed the starter's job, steered Florida past Alabama for the Southeastern Conference championship, and then guided the team over West Virginia in the Sugar Bowl.

As you read this book, I hope you come to understand the resilience of Gaines, Doering, Grow, and Dean. Perhaps you will feel the youthful energy and charisma of Errict Rhett, the competitiveness of Willie Jackson, or the unusual maturity of Wuerffel.

And that brings us to the biggest Gator of them all, head coach Steve Spurrier. You can't write about University of Florida football without writing about him. He *is* Florida football.

Spurrier has guided Florida football to new heights while overcoming the shadowy pall of NCAA scrutiny.

These are a few of the cast of characters who comprise the team that won a school-record eleven games, the second SEC championship in school history, and a first-time Sugar Bowl victory.

Maybe you will absorb a feeling for the nuances of the daily routine of a college football program. I also hope you relive the season one more time from a perspective closer to the practice field, the locker room, and the sideline.

It may have been just another football season to some; to others it is a microcosm of life. Facing adversity. Having to regroup. Struggling to overcome. And ultimately achieving.

Until the University of Florida wins a national championship, the 1993 team will be remembered as the greatest achievers in school history.

I would like to thank the University of Florida sports information staff for providing access to its library of photographs. Led by John Humenik and assistant athletic director Norm Carlson, this group consistently ranks at the top of its profession.

I also want to thank correspondent Matt Adams and Florida State beat writers Scott Tolley and Chris Talbott, for their contributions.

Here's to my late Uncle Paul, who let Dad and me use his season tickets now and then. He introduced me to the game.

To Auntie, God rest your soul. For all those days we played catch in your backyard and for attending every one of my games, rain or shine. Not a day passes when I don't remember your smiling face or your perfect personality.

To Ferne, for getting out of bed to fix me breakfast on all those cold winter mornings of yesteryear. For sacrificing so often so the family could have so much. For having the biggest heart a person can have, and mostly for sharing it with all of us each and every day.

To Eddie, for all the miles you crossed to and from work when I was a kid, and especially for all the seemingly endless hours on the job in between. Your sweat, pain, and determination put me through college. You taught me the work ethic of your generation, just as if it was nothing special. It was.

How can I put into words what you have meant to me? You are much more than parents. You are two of my best friends.

My final debt of gratitude goes to Anne for understanding when I pack my bags each Friday morning from September through January. For missing all the dinner parties simply because you don't want to go without me. For greeting me at the kitchen door on my return with a smile that makes me regret the time I was gone. For learning to like this game almost as much as I love it.

And, by the way, Archie Griffin rushed for 239 yards that day. Ohio State won 29–14. It was an unforgettable beginning.

1

A SWEET CELEBRATION

S TEVE SPURRIER PLACED HIS half-empty mug of beer on the table and raised a full champagne glass. His change of drinks was appropriate. This wasn't the time to raise just a cold one. This was a Dom Perignon kind of night. Surrounded by dozens of University of Florida officials and their wives, the Gators' head coach was about to toast the school's winningest football season ever. Everyone in Room 2910 of the New Orleans Hilton saw this as the end to a perfect night.

"Raise your glasses . . . whatever you have in your hand," he announced. "Hey, this is fun. We've come a long way this season. We got what we deserved. Here's to the Gators. Here's to eleven victories. Here's to winning the Sugar Bowl. Cheers!"

It was almost two o'clock in the morning of January 2, 1994. The college football season was over, but the party was just beginning. The Florida Gators had just whipped previously unbeaten West Virginia 41–7 in the Sugar Bowl and the euphoria filled the room like cheap perfume. No coach or wife was ready to sleep just yet. Who could sleep? There was too much to celebrate, too much to enjoy, too many plays to re-live.

A season of sixteen-hour days, sleepless nights, heartache, and ecstasy was over finally. But that wasn't what the party was about. In fact, the end of the season was the sad part. Teams prepare a whole month for a bowl game, not just one week as in the regular season. And a bowl is magnified. It's the last game the alumni remember.

While Florida's coaches and athletic officials celebrated at the team's hotel, most of the players were roaming Bourbon Street. Beer in hands, they were high-fiving their way from one bar to another, letting off steam after a long, hard season. The cold, misty night wouldn't bother them. They knew there would be no more 9:00 A.M. practices or film sessions. No more boring meetings. No more intense Tuesday practices. And they would miss it all for nine more months.

The illicit lure of the French Quarter had barely tempted them during the week before the game. They had remembered what had happened two years earlier when they played harder on Bourbon Street than in the Superdome, contributing to a 39–28 loss to Notre Dame. This time Florida took a businesslike approach before the game while West Virginia overindulged in buckets of beer and the city's most famous drink, the Hurricane. So now the Gators were making up for lost time. Their mission had been accomplished.

Back in the Hilton suite, the most unlikely of people joined in the celebration. Rick Flair, a former World Wrestling cult figure whose daughter attended Florida, stood smiling and laughing in the middle of a circle of people. His flowing white hair alone made him an attraction. Flair, who had watched the game from the sideline, was wearing a blue Gators sweatshirt and talking football strategy. Defensive ends coach Charlie Strong, a huge fan of big-time wrestling, which most people know is more acting than wrestling, stood in awe. Flair wanted to talk football. Strong, built like a weight lifter or big-time wrestler himself, wanted to talk wrestling. "Look at Charlie," defensive coordinator Ron Zook said. "He loves his wrestling. He's in heaven right now."

On this night and into the morning every Florida Gator was in heaven. The football team had made it an unprecedented night. The Sunshine State's largest university, situated in tiny Gainesville, gave birth to a football team in 1906 and had won only once on New Year's Day in all that time. That lone victory was twenty-seven years ago. The school had never even won a Sugar Bowl—the host bowl of the Southeastern Conference, of which Florida had been a charter member some sixty years earlier. But this trip to New Orleans turned into every dream come true. A win, as Spurrier had said, "would knock down a few more barriers." Everyone knew Florida had plenty of obstacles to overcome. While state rivals Florida State and Miami had been perennial national powerhouses since the early 1980s, it wouldn't be until this night that Florida would come close to that level.

Florida won eleven games for the first time ever and, ironically, the eleventh turned out to be the easiest. The team dominated the Big East champion Mountaineers, who were ranked third nationally (behind Nebraska and Florida State, who were squaring off in the Orange Bowl that same night) entering the game and had actually talked of winning the ephemeral national championship. After spotting West Virginia a 7–0 lead, the Gators scored the game's final forty-one points. It was nothing Spurrier, who brought a focused team to New Orleans on December 26, didn't expect. He knew his team had more talent than West Virginia long before he noticed the Mountaineers' party approach to the week before the bowl game. West Virginia had not been to a bowl in five years and it showed. He had seen the same signs in his team two years earlier. "I saw one of West Virginia's players on television early in the week saying, 'We've had a great time. We'll get ready for the game on Thursday and Friday.'" Even Spurrier, never to be confused with a workaholic, knew it didn't work that way. While West Virginia was looking for a national championship, realizing they needed a Florida State win over unbeaten and top-ranked Nebraska in the Orange Bowl, Spurrier figured it wouldn't matter what happened in Miami that night. He expected his team to win easily.

As he put down his champagne glass and grabbed his beer again, he remembered what West Virginia coach Don Nehlen had said earlier in the week. "You know, at one of those functions, Nehlen whispered in my ear, 'I hope you don't beat us too bad,'" he recalled. "I think he knew what was coming. We just had too many good players. They don't have anybody who will be in the NFL."

That is never the case with Florida, Florida State, and Miami. The state has more than its share of crime, citrus, great beaches, and most of all, football talent. Since Miami won its first national championship, beating Nebraska 31–30 in the 1984 Orange Bowl a decade ago on this night, the three schools had become a trifecta of football talent. They had a combined record of 287–68–5 (an 80 percent winning average) in that period. Miami had won four national championships. Florida State had a legendary coach in Bobby Bowden and had won an NCAA-record ten straight bowl games. If it hadn't been for the Hurricanes, Bowden and FSU probably would have had multiple national championships of their own.

But since the 1970s the University of Florida had managed to make the biggest blunders despite having the best intentions. The school's resources and alumni base are unparalleled in the state. While the university was successful in its academic accomplishments, usually placing in the top ten colleges in the nation by the number of National Merit Scholars on campus, and enrollment reached forty thousand, this degree of success never carried over to the football field. What hurt most was the fact that the program had suffered more than just losses on the field. The biggest loss, a loss of integrity, had given the football program a horrible reputation during the eighties.

The Gators had some fine talent under Ray Graves, who coached eight consecutive winning teams from 1962 to 1969. But even with Steve Spurrier himself at quarterback in 1964, 1965, and 1966, when he won the Heisman Trophy, the team always seemed to lose the one game it needed for either a conference championship or a berth in a major bowl. Losing big games was one thing, but cheating to win them became another. It all started in 1979 when the school hired Charley Pell as head coach even though Pell had been forced out at Clemson University for violating NCAA rules. It was said that Pell was as ethical as a used-car salesman, but this used-car salesman knew how to assemble football talent and that was all that mattered to Florida at the time. As Gators fans soon would find out, his methods hadn't changed when he arrived in Gainesville. After an 0–10–1 start, Pell put together 8–4, 7–5, 8–4, and 9–2–1 seasons from 1980 to 1983. Suddenly Pell was popular with everyone but the NCAA.

Three games into the 1984 season, Pell's unscrupulous approach caught up with him, and the NCAA placed the Gators on probation. Pell was fired, then handed the keys to a new Cadillac by Florida boosters. As he drove out of Gainesville in style, offensive coordinator Galen Hall moved into the head coach's office at Florida Field. Hall led the Gators to eight straight wins and a 9–1–1 finish. However, the Southeastern Conference championship—which would have been Florida's first—was stripped from the team because of the infractions incurred by Pell.

Through it all, Hall, a nice guy with a laid-back approach, earned a new contract and shed his interim status. His teams were explosive from 1985 to 1989, with such future NFL stars as Emmitt Smith, John L. Williams, Neal Anderson, Jarvis Williams, Louis Oliver, and Godfrey Myles leading the way. Quarterback Kerwin Bell, who would never stick to an NFL roster, rewrote the school's record book. The fun ended when the NCAA brought its cloak-and-dagger act to Gainesville again. This time, investigators determined that Hall had helped a player make a child-support payment, in addition to other minor rules violations. Hall denied the charge, but he was forced to resign following a 16–13 win at LSU, and the school found itself in the midst of another athletic scandal. That, coupled with an ensuing investigation by the NCAA and the Drug

Enforcement Agency of Norm Sloan's basketball team, helped label Florida as the Jesse James of college athletics. With the media discovering violations almost daily, the football team became a mental mess after a 6–1 start, losing four of its final five games. The program was at its lowest point ever. The NCAA had caught countless schools cheating over the years, but a school that continues to violate the rules and guidelines of the NCAA also cultivates a reputation as a habitual offender. Players looking toward a future in the NFL, like Smith, couldn't wait to leave.

So while Miami and FSU were loading up on talent and trophies, Florida was developing an intimate relationship with NCAA investigators. Only the football program at Southern Methodist University, finally given the so-called death penalty, had a worse reputation.

At the top of the crippled and shamed athletic department, director Bill Arnsparger was far from a shrewd businessman. He never realized his teams or coaches were breaking the rules unless somebody from the NCAA told him. Arnsparger, owning one of the game's most intelligent minds when it came to scheming defenses in either college football or the NFL, was born to coach. Few people understood why he traded in a headset and whistle at Louisiana State University for a suit and tie and a stuffy office at Florida. To his credit, he handled the dirty work, firing Sloan after the basketball program was also placed on NCAA probation. As for Sloan's replacement, Arnsparger hired Lon Kruger, one of the game's youngest and brightest coaches.

Arnsparger finally admitted he was more comfortable on the sidelines, but before he left to become defensive coordinator of the NFL's San Diego Chargers he made what was probably the most important hire in school history. Yet, in all fairness, it was a no-brainer. Steve Spurrier, the school's only Heisman Trophy winner, was also the most popular player in school history. After stops with the Tampa Bay Bandits of the short-lived United States Football League and later with Duke

University, Spurrier had shown he was every bit the coach that he was the player, perhaps even more so. His offenses were nearly unstoppable in both jobs, even though his teams were not talent laden. Plus, he had a reputation for integrity. Maybe most importantly, he was a Gator and not an outsider. He was the perfect choice. He was the only choice. Spurrier, whose Duke team was headed to the All-American Bowl in Birmingham, Alabama, had wanted the job ever since Hall had been forced to step down in October 1989. But after he accepted the job he wanted to delay the announcement until his team had played its bowl game. So after Duke had lost to Texas Tech on December 30 by the lopsided score of 49–21, Spurrier came home. The most important step had been taken in Florida's long, ardent climb from the valley to the summit of the football mountain. He would become Florida's eighteenth head football coach.

Nobody expected the Spurrier era to begin as well as it did. To begin the 1990 season, the Gators, wearing blue jerseys as they had before Pell arrived, routed Oklahoma State 50–7 on the new grass at Florida Field. They also won their next three games, including a thrilling 17–13 win over Alabama in Tuscaloosa, where Florida had not won since 1963. The sense of ecstasy, however, evaporated when the NCAA announced that the team would be placed on a year's probation for the infractions discovered a year earlier. Spurrier was furious. His Gators were off to a 4–0 start and ranked tenth nationally. Probation meant no bowl, no television, and no SEC championship. Again. After a 45–30 loss to Florida State in Tallahassee in Spurrier's first head-to-head meeting with Bobby Bowden, the Gators limped home with a 9–2 record. They would stay in Gainesville on New Year's Day. Spurrier was incensed about the penalties, but his appeal to the NCAA went nowhere.

To this day Spurrier fumes over the penalty assessed his 1990 team and lashes out at the NCAA whenever he can. "The NCAA punished them for being good, for being successful. They thought we were going to be a 7–4 or 6–5 team that didn't have a chance to win the championship." He contends that none of his players or coaches in 1990 had done anything wrong, and he's right. "These kids had nothing to do with any alleged child-support payment in 1986," he pointed out. Unfortunately, the NCAA enforcement committee wields a catch-all rejoinder by invoking the operative phrase "institutional control." According to the NCAA, the University of Florida lacked institutional control over its coaches and had to be penalized, regardless of who now coached or played at the university.

Nevertheless, Spurrier wasn't going to let a team go unrecognized that would have been SEC champions. He requisitioned first-place rings for his players, telling them, "The SEC didn't recognize you and never will, but you were the conference champions."

Three years later—following 10–2 and 9–4 seasons in 1991 and 1992—the Gators were celebrating their first New Year's Day bowl victory since Lyndon B. Johnson occupied the Oval Office. It was their first eleven-win season and their first Sugar Bowl victory. Given their recent calamities, was it any wonder that the night of January 1–2, 1994, was so special?

It wasn't a big surprise that Florida would finish 11–2 in 1993. In August, Spurrier and his players had expected even better. Loaded with talent, a result of three years of above-average recruiting classes, the Gators had finally put the stigma of NCAA probation behind them. Record-setting quarterback Shane Matthews had graduated, but Florida returned every other offensive starter. The defense had a solid and deep line, with eight players who could start at almost any program in the nation. Only one, tackle William Gaines, was a senior. The media unanimously picked Florida to win the conference's Eastern Division, but the sportswriters still selected defending national champion Alabama to win the conference.

As the Gators wrote their team goals before the season, for the first time in their eighty-seven-year football history, they listed the ultimate prize: the national championship. Since they would play Florida State and Tennessee at eighty-five-thousand-seat Florida Field, where they hadn't yet lost under Spurrier, their aspiration seemed reachable. Even the head coach felt giddy about 1993. "They've listed some pretty lofty goals," he admitted. "But if they work hard enough and things go right, it's not out of the question. We have the opportunity to do something that's never been done here. We've got a good chance." As optimism flowed like Gatorade after an August practice, the team even chanted "NC" following each practice. "We can win it all here," quarterback Terry Dean said in August. "Why not? We have everything it takes." Defensive end Kevin Carter said that it was time the program joined the ranks of Miami, Florida State, Nebraska, and Michigan. "We never seem to get the national attention here like some other schools," he said. "We want it."

Losses to Auburn and Florida State ended the dream of a national championship, but Florida would win its second SEC championship with a 28–13 win over Alabama in the conference's championship game. That game was less than a month before the Sugar Bowl, but the memory seemed like an eternity that New Year's evening in the Hilton in New Orleans. All the hours of coaching, the late meetings, the early wakeup calls, the endless watching of tape would be put on hold for nine months. Recruiting wouldn't start for two days.

Of all the happy people in the room at the Hilton, Ron Zook had to be the happiest and the most relieved that the season was finally finished. His defense had been criticized by the fans, the media, and Spurrier since the 41–34 victory over Tennessee in the third game of the season. Everyone speculated that he would either be fired or reassigned. It was a legitimate concern since Spurrier had a history of impatience with defensive coordinators. In fact, before Zook was named to the position in 1991, Spurrier had never had the same defensive coordinator for two consecutive years. But on this night, the Gators' defense swarmed West Virginia, allowing only a first-quarter touchdown and a total offense of 265 yards. It appeared he would make it to his fourth season. So Zook, an energetic guy who rarely sat still for more than a few seconds, darted around the room hugging and slapping hands with anyone in his path. He knew his job was secure for now. Or at least he had reason to believe it was. Athletic director Jeremy Foley, who had worked his way up from assistant ticket manager at the school in 1977 until he replaced Arnsparger in 1992, enjoyed watching Zook work the room. "You know, that guy can flat-out coach. . . . I don't care what anybody else says," Foley noted. "You know what else? He deserves more money and I am going to get it for him first thing Monday. He and his family went through hell this season."

Zook's wife, Denise, sat on a sofa a few feet away and smiled. She did not hear Foley or she would have smiled even wider, if that were possible. They had been married for thirteen years, and she had never seen her husband as miserable as he was earlier this season. Therefore, she too had been miserable. The family loved Florida and didn't want to leave. The final game probably meant more to Zook than to anyone else in the room. His future had been riding on the defense's performance.

In the corner of the room, tight ends coach Carl Franks, who had been with Spurrier since Franks had played fullback at Duke in the early 1980s, sipped a beer. He watched the room as if he were a player on the sidelines waiting to enter the game. Then a woman approached him and asked for an autograph. She fawned all over him before finally leaving. "Who the heck was that?" he asked. "Never saw her before." Apparently a fan had crashed the party.

Toast after toast, the laughter, the emotional release would last until almost sunrise, although Spurrier and his wife, Jerri, had left the party at 3:00 A.M. As the Sugar Bowl's winning coach, he had to face a 10:00 A.M. press conference. The lights from the television cameras would seem awfully bright after this night of revelry.

Spurrier walked in promptly at 9:58 A.M. with tailback Errict Rhett, the game's most valuable player, in tow to meet about seventy reporters. The coach grabbed a glass of tomato juice and stood behind the podium, soaking in the news that Florida State, an 18–16 winner over Nebraska in the Orange Bowl, had been voted number one. He would never say it, but the thought wrenched his stomach. He believed that Notre Dame, which also had only one loss but had beaten Florida State 31–24 in November, should have been number one. To think that his state rival not only had national bragging rights during recruiting season but had beaten Florida to a national title wasn't pleasant. FSU had not begun its football program until 1947. As usual, he used the poll controversy to let everyone know he was in favor of a college football playoff. "It will happen, and it will happen pretty soon," he said. Then he turned his attention to his team. "We didn't hit all of our goals. We didn't win them all. But our football program is in solid shape now. It was an interesting year. One I'll remember for a long time and one all Gators should be proud of."

Rhett, the team's most enthusiastic player, had gained 105 yards and scored a career-high three touchdowns against West Virginia. It was the perfect ending to a career in which he became the school's all-time leading rusher. The NFL was next for him. Asked about capping his career this way, he glanced at the ceiling and grabbed his head. "You just wouldn't realize how much work goes into a season like this. We started back in January, a year ago, to get to this point. All the sweat and blood . . . I'll miss everyone . . . the coaches, my teammates. Man, this season just blew by like the wind."

2

A ROUT AND
A MIRACLE

WHILE THE FOOTBALL SEASON never begins officially until early September, the Southeastern Conference kicks off its season with a huge media gathering in early August. One by one, coaches face hundreds of reporters spewing the same boring rhetoric as the year before. Several of the SEC's head coaches are Paul "Bear" Bryant disciples and, intentionally or not, it seems they sound more and more like the Bear each year. One rough, gravelly voice after another penetrates the huge theater at the Birmingham Sheraton Civic Center as reporters yawn and look forward to the weekly golf outing.

So coaches like Spurrier and Auburn newcomer Terry Bowden, son of FSU's Bobby Bowden, are a welcome relief to the media. They are quotable and interesting and usually give reporters something to write about. But they are truly outsiders to the Curley Hallmans, Gene Stallings, Ray Goffs, and Jackie Sherrills of the SEC, although Sherrill always generates a story.

On this day Spurrier raised everyone's eyebrows by promoting Terry Dean's ability for All-Conference honors before a single game had been played. "Terry Dean is one of three quarterbacks capable of being named All-Conference this season," he said, referring to Georgia's Eric Zeier and Tennessee's Heath Shuler. Some may have thought it was a bold statement, but then those would be people unfamiliar with Spurrier's history. He had coached three Duke quarterbacks to the All-Atlantic Coast Conference team, and his only starter at Florida, Shane Matthews, had been named to the All-SEC team for three consecutive seasons.

Spurrier then rambled on about the team's deep defensive line, the talent-laden corps of wide receivers, linebacker Monty Grow's return for a fifth season of eligibility after an NCAA suspension, and his bigger, stronger players. He had noticed that his linemen had been pushed around at times during the 1992 season and that they also weren't the best-conditioned team. He had to do something other than rely on the intense Florida heat and humidity to condition his players naturally. So he had hired strength coach Rich Tuten, a barrel-chested, no-nonsense conditioner from North Carolina. After an off-season on Tuten's program of weights and conditioning, Spurrier saw a new team in August. "Coach Tuten has made a big difference," he commented. "We are stronger and in better condition—almost everyone. We may have tired in some of those games last year in the fourth quarter. I don't think that will happen now."

On August 11 the players showed up for media day appearing a little bulkier and stronger than when they had left Florida Field in the spring. It was time for Dean's first session with the media and he didn't disappoint anyone. "Coach told me to watch what I say," he started and then promptly forgot. "I'm a guy who says what he feels, I guess. Anyway, I know I'm the best quarterback here and nobody's taking my job." He then went on to describe what he says on the field and how he baits defensive players.

At lunch Spurrier talked of how he had a staff of joggers. Led by the head coach, who runs every day at noon, it seemed most of Florida's coaches kept in shape. "We had our twelve-minute run for the players and five coaches ran," he added. "Coach Zook led everyone with seven laps."

Then Spurrier talked about his players. "The biggest difference this year is the number of players we have. We have never had a lot of solid backups before. I am hoping this defensive line will be the strongest ever." A reporter asked if his redshirt policy had changed. Redshirting refers to a school's declaring a freshman or an injured player ineligible for a season without losing a year of eligibility. Spurrier, unlike Florida State's Bobby Bowden, favored the policy. Bowden had lost too many juniors to the NFL to hold them back. "We hope a player realizes the importance of getting a degree from the University of Florida," Spurrier answered. "The odds of making it in the NFL aren't that good anyway." In other words, most of Florida's freshmen, unless they could play right away, would be redshirted.

Even though it was Florida's first game in what his players believed would be an unprecedented season, the team was not fired up to play Arkansas State on September 4. Arkansas State, which until a year ago had played in a division lower than major college football, was coming off a 2–9 season, and coach Ray Perkins had left to become Bill Parcells's offensive coordinator with the New England Patriots. Everyone, even they, knew this would be one of those one-sided, boring games. In fact, *Sports Illustrated* had rated Arkansas State 106th out of 106 major college teams. "I would say that is an astute observation," first-year coach John Bobo said seriously. "It shows somebody did their homework. I wouldn't expect us to be ranked anywhere else." But Arkansas State needed the money and would take home $175,000 for the game against Florida. "How else can I look at it?" Bobo asked. "A game like this can buy us the facilities we need." The practice of scheduling a weak team here and there is common in college football, especially in the SEC since 1992 when the conference expanded to twelve teams. Teams in financial need will travel

GATOR BAIT

Arkansas State ball carriers spent most of the season opener being crushed in the backfield. Here Jason Bartley (45) and Henry McMillian (60) usher a helpless Indian to the turf.

to a large stadium and sacrifice their dignity to take home $175,000 or $200,000. It's as if every school with a large stadium buys a win or two each season. During the 1993 season, Auburn had Samford and New Mexico State, Alabama had Tulane and Louisiana Tech, Ole Miss had Northern Illinois and Tennessee-Chattanooga, and Florida engaged poor defenseless Arkansas State.

The Gators rode a number nine national ranking and an eighteen-game home winning streak into the game. The players spent the week giving their usual These-guys-can-beat-us-if-we-don't-watch-out routine. "There have been bigger upsets in college football," guard Jim Watson noted. "Anyway, it will

GATOR BAIT

Willie Jackson crosses the goal line on a forty-yard touchdown pass from Terry Dean, giving Florida a 24–6 halftime lead.

be great to hit somebody besides ourselves." That would be the gist of it. By early September, the players were tired of seeing the same old faces across the line of scrimmage. Two-a-day practices in the heat and humidity of Florida are slightly less fun for players than pulling an all-nighter for a calculus exam. Arkansas State would provide a break from all that for three fun hours. "They didn't have a great year and everybody knows that," Dean observed. "We should score every time we touch the ball. I worry about not scoring on that first drive. But like I said, we should kill these guys."

When Florida punted after its first three plays and Arkansas State scored to take a 6–0 lead, the only thing that appeared dead were the Gators' emotions. But Dean soon got hot, completing eleven consecutive passes as Florida rallied for a 24–6 lead. He completed sixteen of twenty-two passes for 237 yards and two touchdowns before being relieved by backup quarterback Danny Wuerffel, a redshirt freshman, who completed his first career pass for twenty yards to Chris Doering. He also would throw two touchdown passes. The game ended with a final score of 44–6 and Dean, usually outspoken but always extremely bright (a 4.0 business student) was subdued. "It was hard to get fired up for these guys," he admitted. "We came out dead." Before leaving Florida Field, Arkansas State nose guard Ed Rufus got in a parting shot: "I wasn't impressed with Florida. We weren't intimidated by the crowd or the noise. They won't win the SEC."

Meanwhile, Florida had a sprouting quarterback controversy. Spurrier tried to quash it as he met with sports reporters after the game, saying, "Don't even ask me who's going to be the quarterback. Danny played well, but Terry Dean still is our quarterback." At least Dean hoped so. He had agreed with Spurrier's comments in Birmingham, figuring he would give Shuler and Zeier a run for All-Conference honors. He knew Spurrier's offensive system well by now. After all, he had the physical tools: six-foot-two, 205 pounds, strong, and a great arm. He was faster than most quarterbacks, but he had relied on his speed too often in practice for Spurrier's liking. The coach consistently yelled at him to stay in the pocket and find the open receiver rather than scramble. "I remember being intimidated by him when I got here because I would run out of the pocket for twenty yards in practice and he would come and yell at me," Dean recalled.

After the Arkansas State game, Wuerffel stood against a wall outside the locker room and enjoyed the moment. He was a shy, religious kid who always said "yes sir, no sir." It was a contrast to the outspoken Dean, who declared before the season that no quarterback would take his job. "If I can't hold it, I don't deserve it," he commented. "It's my job . . . no one else's." This was the first time Wuerffel had spoken with a group of reporters since signing with Florida. Some didn't even know who he was since he wasn't wearing a jersey. One writer took him for linebacker Jim Bates. "You must have me confused," Wuerffel answered. "Happens all the time." He went over and told Bates, who had a pretty good chuckle over the confusion.

Spurrier just shook his head when asked about the team's performance. "I really don't know what you get out of these games," he answered. "We gave Arkansas State some money to take home and we played all of our players. Other than that, we just needed to get this game out of the way and start preparing for Kentucky."

The next morning the telephone rang at the Spurrier residence, a sprawling home in the countryside west of Gainesville. It was Steve Spurrier Jr., a receiver at Duke. The younger Spurrier had caught a pass in the school's 45–7 loss to top-ranked Florida State. "He was all excited because he caught a pass near the end of the game," Spurrier remembered. Tapes of FSU's games are shown on Sunday nights in Florida, so Spurrier watched the entire game that night to see his son's catch.

When the rankings were announced on Sunday, Florida had jumped from number nine to number eight. That afternoon Spurrier claimed that the first game hadn't been a total waste of time, saying, "I think we got the first-game jitters out of the way. We learned that we have some offensive linemen on the second team who are close to the [quality of the] first." He chuckled when the discussion turned to Arkansas State's passing attack. "We tried to figure out if they threw any passes between the hash marks," he noted. They hadn't.

On Monday he was rolling his eyes at the Wuerffel-versus-Dean controversy stories in the newspapers. A day earlier, the

Kansas City Chiefs had beaten Tampa Bay in Joe Montana's debut as a Chief. Spurrier asked redshirt quarterback Brian Shottenheimer, whose father, Marty, coaches Kansas City, "What were Joe's stats?" Told fourteen of twenty-one, Spurrier turned and looked at Dean. "You were sixteen of twenty-two and they are writing like you had an average day. You had a better day than Joe Montana."

Now that Dean had seen Wuerffel under game conditions, he took the struggle for the starting quarterback's job seriously. He told some reporters, "I think the competition will bring out the best in me, but coach said it was my job. Hey, I was happy for [Wuerffel]. It wasn't like I was rooting for him to throw an interception."

After a rainy Monday night practice, Spurrier stood in the tunnel to the Florida Field locker room and offered a small group of sportswriters a brief lesson. "Did you guys know you can punt the ball any time? You can catch a pass, run downfield, and punt it. You can catch a kickoff, run twenty yards, and punt it. But why would you want to?" he asked with a sly smile. Turning to leave, one of the writers questioned if Dean was having to look over his shoulder now that Wuerffel had played well. "I don't think he will if you guys would stop writing about it," Spurrier answered. But he did announce that David Swain would start at center in place of Gantt Crouch, because Crouch had blown some assignments in practice.

The ensuing week was anything but relaxing. Everyone knew Kentucky would be a real test, especially with the game being played at Lexington. Furthermore, in three years under Spurrier, the Gators weren't the best road team, winning only nine of seventeen games. Under coach Bill Curry, the Wildcats—previously called the Mildcats—were getting better each year. Curry, who had played for the Green Bay Packers under Vince Lombardi and for the Baltimore Colts under Don Shula, had coached at Georgia Tech and Alabama before arriving in Lexington. Since Spurrier had come back to Florida, however, the Gators had beaten Kentucky by scores of 47–15, 36–27, and 35–19. He spent the week trying to get his players to forget those easy victories as well as Kentucky's 12–22 record in three years under Curry.

Besides the usual incentives, Spurrier had his own reasons for wanting to beat Kentucky. He had coached under Pepper Rodgers at Georgia Tech in 1979. When Rodgers was fired, Curry was hired. Curry chose not to keep Spurrier on as offensive coordinator, and Spurrier never forgot the snub. While Florida was pounding Arkansas State, Kentucky was beating Kent State 35–0. Curry had hired former LSU head coach Mike Archer to coach his defense, and it appeared the Kentucky defense had improved significantly.

"That's the best-looking team at Kentucky since I've been here," Spurrier said on Tuesday. "Some people are picking them to go to a bowl game."

Archer had worked earlier at LSU as an assistant to the master defensive strategist Bill Arnsparger, ironically the Florida athletic director in 1989 when Spurrier was hired. So when Curry needed a defensive boss, he called Arnsparger. "Bill, did he really do all those defenses then or did you?" Arnsparger replied, "Mike can coach. He knows how to stop the option." Curry was sold. He was tired of Kentucky fans putting down his teams and focusing entirely on basketball season. "We want to give the fans something to talk about over the summer besides basketball recruiting," he said. "We think we are a little better. We are bigger, we are faster, and we are more confident in our program." Spurrier also pointed out the financial commitment Kentucky had made to its football program by building an $8.5 million indoor practice facility.

What money can't buy, however, is healthy players. "We have three safeties out this week," Curry announced. "The worst team to play in a week like this is Florida."

Unlike Spurrier, it didn't take warm weather and golf to lure Chris Doering to Florida. He grew up in Gainesville, spending each Saturday at Florida Field with his father, Paul, a chemistry professor at the university. With his father's connection to the university, he also was allowed to attend several practices. The kid idolized former Florida receiver Cris Collinsworth, who later starred with the Cincinnati Bengals. Furthermore his resemblance to Collinsworth was amazing. Doering looked like him, ran like him, dressed like him, and played the same position. He had the same tall, thin frame. Collinsworth was listed at six-foot-four, 192 pounds at Florida; Doering at six-foot-four, 193 pounds. It was as if Collinsworth had been reincarnated for a second career with the Gators. "He's been my hero since I was five years old," Doering explained. "I've always tried to pattern my play like his."

Doering led the state in 1990 in touchdown receptions as a senior at Gainesville's P. K. Yonge High. He thought it would be enough to become a Gator, but on the night before national signing day, Florida recruiting coordinator Jim Goodman called with the bad news: there would be no scholarship for Doering. He ran into his bedroom, where Collinsworth's posters still were taped to the walls, and cried himself to sleep. Paul Doering couldn't stand by and do nothing, so he called and sent faxes to dozens of recruiting coordinators. Only one, Florida State's Ronnie Cottrell, offered an invitation for a tryout but stipulated there would be no scholarship. Players without scholarships are called "walk-ons," who sometimes are treated no better than water boys.

Still, it was Doering's only chance. He visited FSU's Tallahassee campus and enjoyed his meeting with Bowden and the other coaches. When he later attended a Florida-Florida State baseball game in Gainesville that spring, the realization hit him: he would be playing for the rival of the team he always loved. "I had always hated FSU, and here I was at this baseball game trying to root for them," he recalled. "I just couldn't do it."

Chris Doering called Goodman and talked him into a tryout. Doering would still be a walk-on, but at least he would be a walk-on for his beloved Gators. He would wear orange and blue and run through the same Florida Field tunnel where his idol, Collinsworth, had once run.

Two years later, after trying to get noticed on the scout teams and after an impressive spring game, Doering was called into Spurrier's office. The coach had a scholarship offer for him. "I waited a long time for it," Doering recalled. "It was a dream come true."

September 11 was a cool night in Lexington, and Doering's dream was about to get much better. But dreams sometimes follow nightmares, and the first half was frustrating for the Gators. Dean threw four interceptions, although at least two were not his fault, as Florida struggled to a 9–7 lead.

Finally, Spurrier had seen enough. He replaced Dean with Wuerffel, who picked up where Dean left off, throwing three more interceptions. Kentucky had a 17–9 lead by the fourth quarter. While Dean was despondent, Wuerffel remained cool despite throwing some wobbly, ugly passes that were mercilessly plucked out of the sky by Kentucky defenders.

Florida's championship hopes were slipping away with each errant pass. Wuerffel finally threw a nineteen-yard touchdown pass to Doering with 7:36 remaining. "Here I was just happy to be playing, and I score my first-ever touchdown," Doering said. Wuerffel's two-point conversion pass to senior Willie Jackson tied the game. Kentucky came right back, however, driving to Florida's eight-yard line. With 1:23 remaining, Juha Leonoff, a walk-on kicker from Finland, made a twenty-five-yard field goal to give the Wildcats a 20–17 lead as more than fifty thousand Kentucky fans celebrated.

The Gators had entered the game a two-touchdown favorite and now their conference championship ambitions, not to mention their national championship aspirations, were about to end in a shocking upset. "I was thinking how crappy the plane ride home was going to be," guard Jim Watson recalled. "Here it was my senior year and I was thinking, 'Here we go again, another 1–1 start.' You think about stuff like that."

Jim Watson, starting his third season at right guard, usually had the best one-liners in the Florida locker room. Trailing Kentucky 20–17 with seconds remaining in the game, he was beginning to dread the flight home.

UNIVERSITY OF FLORIDA SPORTS INFORMATION

After senior Harrison Houston returned the ensuing kickoff to the forty-two-yard line, Florida moved to Kentucky's twenty-eight with only seventeen seconds remaining.

Commonwealth Stadium was rocking with Wildcat fans who thought they were about to enjoy their finest football victory in at least ten years. One incompletion later, Wuerffel overthrew Doering over the middle. The errant pass actually benefited Florida because had Doering caught the pass, the clock would have expired. Eight seconds remained, time enough for two plays at best. Receiver Jack Jackson came back to the huddle and suggested Wuerffel fake toward him to the right and throw back across the middle to Doering on a post pattern. Archer's defense had two safeties in the middle of the field.

When the play started, one safety went left to cover Jackson; the other went right. Wuerffel dropped back and couldn't believe his eyes. Doering had broken free down the middle. The pass landed softly in his hands at the goal line. As the referee signaled touchdown, Florida players piled on Doering in the end zone. "I was thinking I was going to get crushed," he remembered. The clock showed two seconds remaining.

At the other end of the stadium a fan yelled, "He caught it!" But sitting in seats near field level, Paul Doering and his wife couldn't tell who caught the ball until another fan told them that it was their son. Frank and Nancy Dean were sitting next to them. They were happy for the Doerings and Florida's amazing 24–20 victory but miserable for their own son.

"As great as we felt, we felt sorry for them," Paul Doering reflected. "I could tell what they were going through. For us, it was the greatest night, but for them, it had to be a nightmare."

Minutes later, as dejected Kentucky fans abandoned the stadium, Doering and Wuerffel stood next to each other, talking with reporters. Wuerffel's buzz haircut was soaked with sweat, and both players had tears in their eyes. "It still hasn't sunk in," Wuerffel said. "I just feel blessed. I can't believe it. I really can't. Tell me what happened again." He turned and hugged Doering.

"The ball seemed like it hung in the air forever," the sophomore wide receiver explained. "First, I didn't think I would play much. Then I played. Then I didn't think I would catch many passes, and I caught my first touchdown. Now this."

Spurrier, still stunned like a kid looking over a new bike on Christmas morning, didn't say much. He probably couldn't find the words to convey his relief. "We really didn't deserve to win this one," he commented. "Gosh, that was wild at the end there."

Watson, a chubby offensive guard who emits a huge smile, a bright personality, and the best lines, shook his head. "The kid with the golden arm found the kid with the golden hands," he announced.

Athletic director Jeremy Foley compared the catch with Spurrier's famed field goal against Auburn in 1966 and quarterback Kerwin Bell's 1986 run that defeated Auburn 18–17. "It has to be one of the biggest plays in Florida history," he said. The plane ride home wouldn't be crappy now.

In the losing locker room, Curry was shocked. He had never experienced a loss at Kentucky, perhaps anywhere, as tough as this one. He also knew he couldn't let his pain show or it could ruin his players' outlook for the remainder of the season. "We didn't finish the job," he concluded. "You can't come within seconds of finishing the job. We have to finish the job to become a good team." Archer's hiring didn't look like such a bright move on this night.

One Florida player suggested, "They should have had five defensive backs in the end zone." Spurrier added, "Yeah, you would think they would guard the end zone better." The final play illustrated the importance of coaching. Spurrier and his players had somehow believed they could pull it out. Archer had his defense in a two-deep zone instead of putting three or four defensive backs in the end zone.

"I thought with eight seconds left they would go for the win," Archer explained. "If our safety reads it, and without looking at the tape it's hard to say, but he wasn't in position to make the play. They executed, we didn't. That Number 28 killed us."

While Doering was basking in the glow of his newfound stardom and while Archer was learning his name in addition to his jersey number, Dean was miserable. He never envisioned being benched two games into his first season as a starter and he didn't know if he would play again. He wanted to cry too, but for a vastly different reason than Wuerffel and Doering.

Lost in the euphoria of the Wuerffel-to-Doering miracle was the performance of the Gators' defense. It says something to win a game in which you throw seven interceptions, but Florida held Kentucky to thirteen first downs and 251 yards of offense. "Sometimes people forget about the defense in a game like this," Ron Zook commented. "But we threw seven interceptions and we won the game. We stopped them when we had to. That's what's important."

With the biggest conference game of the season, Tennessee at Florida Field, looming before them the next week, the team now had a huge quarterback controversy. It was every coach's nightmare.

Spurrier prides himself on developing quarterbacks, so seven interceptions in a game meant that he wasn't teaching them well. "Maybe they were trying to look off the defensive backs too much and not concentrating on where they were throwing," he speculated on Sunday afternoon. When would he name a starter for the Tennessee game? "What time's the game?" he quipped, adding, "Probably Wednesday or Thursday." Dean's problems were his biggest worry. "I certainly didn't want it to go like this," he said. "I was hoping Terry would breeze through the season."

Quarterback controversies divide teams. That was the bad news. Tennessee was coming off a 38–6 pounding of Georgia and talking about a national championship themselves. That was worse news. The game probably would determine the season for both teams, picked in the preseason to battle it out for the Eastern Division title. Nevertheless, the Tennessee game seemed a year away for Doering.

The next morning, Paul Doering ran up and down Atlanta's Hartsfield Airport between connections looking for any newspaper he could buy. "Already read the Kentucky papers," he said excitedly. Fans were introducing him to other fans as "Chris Doering's dad." Suddenly, the younger Doering was a big man on campus in Gainesville. Girls smiled at him. Professors knew his name. He received dozens of congratulatory calls. *Sports Illustrated* wrote a short story on him, but what he was waiting for was a call from Collinsworth—which

 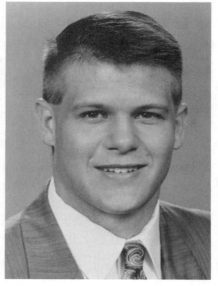

UNIVERSITY OF FLORIDA SPORTS INFORMATION

The real battle for the job as Florida's quarterback began in the wild 24–20 win at Kentucky. For Terry Dean (*left*) and Danny Wuerffel (*right*) the competition wouldn't end until late November.

he missed. Fortunately his answering machine recorded the call. People sent him tapes of the play. "I've already watched it a hundred times," he admitted. "My roommate is getting sick of it. He said, 'Chris, just think how different it would be if you would have dropped that pass.'" The thought made Doering cringe.

It was something the former walk-on that nobody wanted didn't have to think about.

3

SPURRIER THE LEGEND

I T WOULD HAVE BEEN DIFFICULT for Steve Spurrier to understand Chris Doering's path from obscurity to stardom. He was everybody's All-American coming out of Science Hill High in Johnson City, Tennessee. He had been a superstar in every sport he played since the first grade.

Stephen Orr Spurrier was born April 20, 1945, in Miami Beach, the son of Presbyterian minister J. Graham and Marjorie Spurrier. The family moved to Athens, Tennessee, then to Newport, then to Johnson City. He became a local hero. He was All-State in basketball, football, and baseball, but almost every college wanted him as a quarterback. Alabama and Mississippi were the front-runners to sign Spurrier, and each had a legendary coach, Bear Bryant and Johnny Vaught, respectively.

On a routine recruiting visit to Florida, Spurrier played golf at the university course. It was December 1962. "I thought, 'Gosh, here it is freezing up north and you can play golf down here,'" he recalled. "I fell in love with Florida and thought I could spend a lifetime here."

It didn't hurt that Florida coach Ray Graves, unlike Bryant and Vaught, had a passing offense. Plus, like Spurrier, Graves had been a preacher's son and also was from Tennessee. Spurrier became a Gator.

With his first pass, a fifty-six-yard completion against Southern Methodist in 1964, Spurrier instantly became a star at Florida. It was the beginning of a record-breaking career. He not only won the Heisman Trophy in 1966—the only Florida player ever to do so in the sixty years of college football's most prestigious award—he also won the hearts of every Gators fan.

Spurrier not only had the athletic ability to win football games, he demonstrated the kind of competitiveness that is unique to sports' superstars. He had the leadership of a Johnny Unitas, the versatility of a Steve Young, and the fire of a Dan Fouts. He would never become the pro quarterback to match any of those three, but he was unsurpassed as a collegiate quarterback.

During Spurrier's senior season, as the Gators were on their way to an Orange Bowl berth, he worked his special magic against Auburn. That afternoon Spurrier completed twenty-six of thirty-five passes for 349 yards and three touchdowns, and he had punted seven times for a 46.9-yard average. With two minutes remaining in the game, Florida and Auburn were tied, 27–27.

On fourth-and-long, with the ball on the twenty-three-yard line, Coach Graves pondered his options. He didn't believe his place kicker could convert the field goal attempt, but he had to kick the ball. Spurrier walked up to him and said, "Let me give it a shot." He had attempted only three field goals all season and hadn't made one since the first game. Graves went with his quarterback. The forty-yard kick split the uprights, making Spurrier an instant legend. Bill Clark of the *Atlanta Constitution* wrote, "Spurrier, with his hands tied behind his back and facing a firing squad, would be favored to escape." Graves said in retrospect, "You just knew if anybody was going to make that kick, it would be Steve Spurrier."

Since the Heisman Trophy ballots were due to be cast soon, the timing was perfect. As Spurrier's kick cleared the goalposts, sportswriters were mentally writing his name on their ballots even though Purdue's Bob Griese had had a good season too. Norm Carlson, Florida's long-time sports information director, had waged a consistent and effective campaign to writers in the South. Some say that Spurrier's receiving the Heisman remains a sore spot to this day with Griese, a two-time winning Super Bowl quarterback, a member of the Pro Football Hall of Fame, and current ABC football analyst.

Spurrier's wife, Jerri (the two met in college and married before his senior season), once remarked that the memory of that field goal is something that never fades with people. "The thing that people remember most in all the years of all the plays and all the things he did was when he kicked that field goal," she said.

His NFL career never matched his collegiate highlights, although that didn't erode his status as a living legend in Florida. The San Francisco 49ers made Spurrier the third pick of the 1967 NFL draft, but he soon found himself behind a guy named John Brodie. He played his final season in the NFL with the Tampa Bay Buccaneers during their initial year in the league.

As much as he was born to play, Spurrier picked up the skills of coaching immediately. Stops as an assistant at Florida in 1978, Georgia Tech in 1979, and Duke from 1980 to 1982 enabled him to study under head coaches Doug Dickey, Pepper Rodgers, and Red Wilson. Every head football coach since the game became more sophisticated in the so-called modern era, whether it be at the pro or college level, holds an expertise on one side of the line of scrimmage. Few know defense and offense equally well. This is especially true with Spurrier, who has become one of the game's most brilliant offensive coaches in the past fourteen years. In fact, there are few, if any, on the college level who can match his ability to teach and develop an effective offense; there may be few NFL offensive coordinators and head coaches on his level too.

Spurrier's fascination with diagramming what he calls "ballplays" and his imaginative way of doing it started in 1979 when Rodgers allowed him to be his offensive coordinator for a few games. His official title was quarterbacks coach. Through trial-and-error he refined his offensive approach as an assistant under Wilson at Duke. His basic belief is that there is a pass route that will work against any defense, whether the defense be in a blitz, a two-deep zone, a three-deep zone, and especially man-to-man coverage. It's the quarterback's responsibility to see that route before he takes the snap from the center or early in the play. This theory doesn't hold up if the offense sends only one or two receivers into the secondary for each play, but Spurrier's system usually employs four or five receivers on each play. By recruiting more than the usual number of talented receivers, the system can produce mismatches since most college teams have only two or three good defensive backs.

Notre Dame coach Lou Holtz once said, "If you want to write a history of football's formations, get a Florida playbook. In watching Florida, you are seeing the most sophisticated offense and passing attack in college football." Of course, Holtz said that before his team defeated Florida in the 1992 Sugar Bowl. A large part of that victory was Holtz's knowledge that Spurrier would forgo the running game and depend entirely on his passing attack should the Gators fall behind. Defensively, the Irish used three or four players in their pass rush and dropped everyone else into zone coverage.

The running game behind this offensive philosophy is limited to a tailback, who gains most of his yardage on the sprint draw. Utilizing this system, Spurrier's teams have produced four All-Conference quarterbacks, three one-thousand-yard rushers, and hundreds of broken offensive records. For instance, Shane Matthews, Florida's starting quarterback from 1990 to 1992, holds fifty-seven school records. At the same time, tailback Errict Rhett twice has rushed for a thousand yards or more.

"If the defense puts eight men on the line of scrimmage, we'll throw it over their heads," Spurrier explained. "If they drop six men deep, we'll throw underneath or run it. There's a play that should work for every defense."

Spurrier, who scoffs at the three-yards-and-a-cloud-of-dust attitude that dominated the Southeastern Conference for decades, often has said he thinks of new plays while he takes his usual jog at noon. He has diagrammed them in the dirt and on paper napkins. Ben Bennett, a Duke quarterback in the early 1980s, refers to him as "the Genius." Matthews added, "I don't know how he does it or where he comes up with the plays he does."

The source may not be as important as the results. Since Spurrier arrived, the Gators have scored more than thirty points in twenty-eight of forty-nine games and more than forty points in fourteen games. While he often preaches balance, his offenses have tilted toward the pass, averaging 310 yards passing in his eighty-three games as a collegiate head coach.

At times this has put significant pressure on Spurrier's defenses simply because his offense scores quickly, rather than running out the clock with a time-consuming drive utilizing running plays. It didn't take Ron Zook long to discover this precarious truth. In his first game as Spurrier's defensive coordinator, the Gators were flying up and down the field in a 59–21 win over San Jose State. Zook, who came from Ohio State, was accustomed to long offensive drives that gave him time to make defensive adjustments. "Damn, everything moves so fast here," he said. "We would just get over there on the sideline and, boom! we would have to go back in the game because we had scored again."

The Spurrier offense, tagged "the Fun 'n' Gun" in 1990 by *Gainesville Sun* sportswriter Mike Bianchi, has put the coach in awkward situations when his team has built a big lead late in the game. No coach wants to run up a score and embarrass the other team, but keeping it down has been difficult at times simply because the basis of Florida's offense is built around throwing the football.

"I'm going to let the backup players play and run the offense," Spurrier has said often. "I am not going to put them in there and tell them to hand off on every down. If we are way ahead, we are still going to throw because that's our game." The only thing Spurrier said he would stop short of doing if he had a big lead would be calling a time-out so the team could score.

Ironically, Florida State's Bobby Bowden and Miami's Dennis Erickson also have been caught in this no-win situation during their careers. The fine talent in the state has something to do with it; the schools' backup players are much better than many teams' starters.

Spurrier never envisioned that his first head coaching job would be in pro football, but the fledgling United States Football League tossed him his big chance in 1983. He was recommended to the late John Bassett, owner of the Tampa Bay Bandits franchise. Starting from scratch, Spurrier made the team an instant winner with his pass-frenzied offense. Tampa Bay had a 35–19 record over three seasons, including two playoff appearances, before the league folded. It was just the experience he needed to get the attention of athletic directors and NFL general managers. Spurrier badly wanted to fill the Buccaneers' opening the next year, but team owner Hugh Culverhouse hired Alabama coach Ray Perkins instead. Ironically, when Steve Sloan left Duke to become athletic director at Alabama after Perkins's departure, the domino effect reached Spurrier. Duke named him head coach.

By winning at a basketball school with tough academic standards, Spurrier would prove he was qualified for almost any job. Everything went as planned. His teams won twenty of thirty-four games with less-than-stellar talent in three seasons at Duke. He was named the Atlantic Coast Conference's Coach of the Year twice, although that did little to improve his status of playing second fiddle to basketball coach Mike Krzyzewski.

Anyone who knows Spurrier knows he doesn't want to play behind anyone. Naturally, that made Florida the perfect place for him to coach. Every sport in the Sunshine State takes a back seat to football. Spurrier would be bigger in Gainesville than Krzyzewski ever was at Duke. That is, if his teams won.

UNIVERSITY OF FLORIDA SPORTS INFORMATION

Steve Spurrier, the 1966 Heisman Trophy winner, was, is, and probably always will be the biggest Gator of them all.

Getting the job was his greatest obstacle. At the same time the university was trying to overcome the obstacle of NCAA scrutiny and probation.

Finally the dark clouds over Gainesville parted on the last day of 1989. Who better to coach the Gators than this favorite son of the university, already a proven coach? The timing couldn't have been better. Despite Florida's program's having reached a new low and being placed on probation, the Gators' run-oriented offense was boring fans to tears. Not even Emmitt Smith, now widely regarded as the best runner on Sundays, could save the team. In a crushing 10–7 loss at Auburn, Florida quarterback Donald Douglas completed seven passes. Six were to Auburn players.

"Our goal is to become the best football program in this state," Spurrier claimed. Such a goal would sound reasonable if the state in question were Montana or North Dakota or even Texas. But Miami had won national championships in 1984, 1987, and 1989. Florida State contended for the same crown annually and had one of the game's best coaches in Bowden. To his naysayers, Spurrier replied, "Why shouldn't we be the best? We have the most alumni, the best resources, the finest academics. There is no reason we can't have the finest football team." One of his immediate goals was to raise the team's graduation rate. "We're cheating our players and ourselves if we don't try to do that," he said.

Across the country that night, in Phoenix, Bowden was putting his Seminoles to bed before a Fiesta Bowl meeting with Nebraska. He knew Spurrier was getting the job and he also knew the Florida-Florida State rivalry was about to get hotter, if that were possible. "He's the perfect choice," Bowden said. "They won't regret it."

Four seasons later, the Gator faithful haven't. In fact, all Gators fans hold their breath each time an NFL owner or general manager announces a need for a new head coach.

NFL owners love Spurrier's offensive style, knowing it would fill the seats of their huge stadiums. When Spurrier accepted the Florida job, he turned down overtures from the Phoenix Cardinals, who hired Joe Bugel, and the Atlanta Falcons, who hired Jerry Glanville. Denver owner Pat Bowlen called following the 1992 season. Spurrier declined.

What the public and few Gators fans fail to realize is that Spurrier probably wouldn't accept an NFL coaching position until his teams have won a national championship or two for the university. Steve Spurrier is many things, but he is not a workaholic. He loves the college schedule, where coaches can vacation following recruiting season and during the summer. NCAA athletes are limited to twenty hours of practice each week. In the NFL's off-season, there are drafts to prepare for, minicamps to run, fall camps to organize, and personnel decisions to make.

Who would have time to play eighteen holes? Which brings up Spurrier's favorite hobby. Then again, labeling golf as Spurrier's hobby is similar to saying music was Elvis's hobby. By July of each off-season, Spurrier's handicap is around scratch. Not bad for a full-time collegiate coach who often brags that no player has ever beaten him on the golf course.

Coaches in the NFL, where the workaholics thrive and forty-hour weeks are reached by Wednesday, enjoy a rare tee time for benefit outings only. Coaches like former Washington Redskins coach Joe Gibbs used to spend nights on cots in their offices. Anybody who knows Spurrier would gasp if he spent a night on his office couch. "I don't think you have to drill your players for endless hours and watch tapes over and over and over again and spend eighty hours a week in your office," Spurrier said. "You would get stale. Some guys can do it, but I am not one of them."

Furthermore, there is nowhere Spurrier would be more secure than in Gainesville, Florida. He is more recognizable and more popular than any other figure in the state, perhaps excepting Bowden, Don Shula, and singer Jimmy Buffett. With the high school talent in the state, Spurrier knows that he will always be successful at Florida. NFL fans are short on patience and tolerance, and the talent pool is distributed equally in the draft.

Once hired, Spurrier immediately made changes at Florida. He had the artificial turf at Florida Field ripped out and replaced with natural grass. He toughened penalties for missing class. He revived the Gators' use of blue jerseys for home games.

Without his ever having coached a game at his alma mater, every button Spurrier pushed generated magic. Even his first recruiting class was a good one, although put together on short notice from January 1. The magic quickly translated to the Gators' on-field performance, even without Emmitt Smith, who left school early to join the Dallas Cowboys. Florida won its first five games under Spurrier and finished 9–2 in 1990. NCAA probation, however, prevented Florida's claiming the conference championship, but Spurrier ordered conference championship rings for his players anyway.

The Gators won ten games for the first time ever the next season and their first outright SEC championship, but they fell to Notre Dame in the Sugar Bowl. In 1992, Florida won nine more, including a 27–10 win over North Carolina State in the Gator Bowl, the school's first bowl victory in four years. As effective as he had become on the sidelines, Spurrier wasn't known to be elegant or captivating in front of a microphone. At times, in all fairness, his foot-in-mouth clumsiness was nothing more than a result of his competitiveness.

Before the 1993 season, he grabbed the whole state's attention at one of the Gator Booster gatherings in Miami. Florida had dropped Miami from its schedule when the SEC announced in 1990 it would expand to twelve teams and each would play eight conference games instead of seven. The Gators, wanting to play six home games each season in newly expanded Florida Field to keep the athletic budget in the black, had to drop either Florida State or Miami. The Florida-Florida State rivalry was untouchable and probably always will be. The Gators could have opted to continue to play Miami home-and-home but that meant forfeiting a home game every other year. Instead, they dropped the Hurricanes entirely.

You would have thought the governor had said that he planned to ban air conditioning in August. The uproar from Hurricanes and Gators fans continues to this day. In Coral Gables, the University of Florida is now referred to as the "Chicken Gators" school.

The thought his team would purposely avoid a specific team, especially a state rival, boiled Spurrier's blood. Few subjects riled him as much as this did. Near the end of the 1991 season, the SEC champion Gators were headed to the Sugar Bowl. The opposing berth had not then been determined, but playing Miami in New Orleans was an impossibility. The Hurricanes were staying home to meet Big Eight champion Nebraska in the Orange Bowl for the national championship. The Sugar Bowl committee, realizing 10–1 Florida had no chance for the national championship, wanted to book Notre Dame to ensure a good television audience.

That didn't stop Spurrier, however, from saying that he wanted to play Miami in the Sugar Bowl. Before the bowl bids were announced, Spurrier told any reporter with a note pad that the so-called Chicken Gators wanted to face top-ranked Miami. And they wanted them bad. The gauntlet was laid down.

Miami soundly defeated Nebraska 22–0 to win its fourth national title; Notre Dame, a team with three losses and a poor defense, rallied to embarrass Florida 39–28.

Many think that Spurrier challenged Miami because he already knew there was no way the Hurricanes would turn down a more lucrative Orange Bowl bid and a chance for the national championship to play a thousand miles from home. He probably also knew the Sugar Bowl wanted Notre Dame. "How did I know all that?" he asked. "I just wanted to play Miami and I thought Miami would want to play us."

In June 1993 Spurrier was at it again. As head coaches go, he is an average speaker. But in Florida, next to Bowden, who comes on to an audience like a Billy Crystal or a Robin Williams with a clipboard, Spurrier is just another rah-rah guy. He tells the orange-and-blue clad audience what they want to hear for ten to fifteen minutes and then heads for the door. Who can blame him? Booster outings grow tiring, and Spurrier would rather avoid them altogether. But he realizes that, like recruiting, they are a part of his job as head football coach.

This time he told the Miami booster group that the Gators had a plan to meet the Hurricanes in a preseason game in Joe

Robbie Stadium in August. He said the proceeds would go to Hurricane Andrew victims.

Reporters promptly called athletic director Jeremy Foley and Miami athletic director Dave Maggard. Neither had a clue what Spurrier was talking about. There were no such plans. Sports columnists ripped Spurrier again for his loose tongue.

Under NCAA and SEC rules, such a game could not be played for several reasons, the first of which is that a team is allowed to play no more than thirteen games in one season. With the possibility of the SEC championship game on the schedule, Florida could never add another game. Also, there are no such things as preseason games between NCAA schools.

Spurrier claimed that he was quoted out of context, and he looked worse when he lashed back at the columnists' criticisms. He attempted to explain: "I only said we were looking into the game and that I hoped it could be played somehow."

In August 1993 Spurrier criticized Jacksonville's attempt to receive an NFL franchise, saying the state had enough pro football with the Miami Dolphins and Tampa Bay Buccaneers. Town leaders and those behind the bid to the NFL, later to be proved as visionaries when Jacksonville was awarded a franchise in December, suggested that Spurrier should mind his own business.

Despite his years of dealing with the media—as a player, a professional coach, and a college coach—Spurrier has never understood how most reporters respond to his offbeat comments. After quarterback Shane Matthews had thrown five interceptions in a 30–6 loss at Mississippi State in 1992, Spurrier gave him a week off from interviews. It was understandable. Matthews was a fine kid who didn't deserve the white-hot spotlight of criticism, even on a five-interception night.

"He needs to be by himself and not be asked about all the interceptions and such," Spurrier explained. "Shane's just been taking on too much. He'll be fine."

Matthews—honest, sincere, and modest—didn't mind talking to reporters. He wasn't extremely talkative, but he answered every question, even following that miserable night at Mississippi State.

The next Saturday, Matthews came back strong, completing twenty-five of thirty-seven passes for 285 yards and two touchdowns in a 28–21 win over LSU. What did Spurrier say when he started his postgame press conference? "We would have scored another one earlier if our quarterback hadn't checked off that one time." Spurrier was upset that Matthews had changed a running play at the line of scrimmage to a pass pattern. A freshman offensive lineman jumped, and the Gators were hit with an illegal procedure penalty.

So after the game, the reporters didn't ask Matthews about his comeback or his 285 yards or his twenty-five-of-thirty-seven day. They asked about the audible. Matthews was dumbfounded. Spurrier had contradicted himself. He had tried to take the pressure off Matthews the week before, but five days later he threw his star quarterback to the wolves and publicly questioned his judgment. Some players, particularly defensive players, came to resent their coach's public criticism. "It's as if the guy never made a mistake in his life," one defensive back complained. "We aren't all Heisman Trophy winners."

Spurrier's gaffes aren't limited to football. He was in West Palm Beach in April 1991 during the time of the controversial William Kennedy Smith rape trial. The trial, televised live daily, was a major conversation piece in Florida. Smith is a nephew of Sen. Ted Kennedy. The state attorney whose office was prosecuting Smith was David Bludworth, a Florida alum who had helped recruit Spurrier to the ranks of Gatordom in 1963.

Spurrier had played golf that day with Bludworth. When he stepped to the podium in front of about five hundred school boosters that night, he said, "I have a good joke for you that my old buddy David Bludworth told me today: 'How did William Kennedy Smith get that girl to go home with him that night? He said, "You either go with me or I'll let my uncle Teddy drive you home."'" Many in the audience gasped. Some laughed. Most were shocked. Bludworth, redfaced, stood in disbelief. This wasn't a football coach telling an off-color joke in the locker room. He was standing before an organized banquet. Again, several columnists blasted Spurrier, who later apologized for the joke. "Yeah, I never should have told that one," he admitted later.

Still, these were relatively minor gaffes. It's not as if he had skirted the NCAA rules and guidelines as his predecessors had. Considering what Florida had been through in the 1980s, school officials knew there were worse things than having a coach with loose lips. Most schools would roll out the red carpet for a coach like Spurrier, even with his mouth as part of the contract. Playing by the rules isn't the name of the game. Winning by the rules is. And Spurrier takes care of that part as well as any coach in college football.

"One thing about Steve," said Norm Carlson, an assistant athletic director at the school, "he's never boring."

4

A ROCKY TOP FEELING

EVERYONE—FANS, MEDIA, coaches, and players—realized what the Tennessee-Florida game meant: the winner of the game pretty much owned the SEC's Eastern Division and would have to suffer a total collapse to lose it. But that's exactly what had happened the previous year when Tennessee lost consecutive games to Arkansas, Alabama, and South Carolina after trashing the Gators 31–14. Coincidentally or not, the Volunteers' losing streak corresponded with head coach Johnny Majors's return from heart surgery. Phil Fulmer, who had coached the team to a 5–0 record, was suddenly very popular.

While Florida won the division because of the Volunteers' collapse, though they eventually lost to Alabama in the inaugural SEC championship game, Tennessee fans and boosters were grumbling about Majors and his conservative coaching approach. Finally, he was forced to leave the university prior to the Vols' appearance in the Hall of Fame Bowl, and Fulmer was appointed as the new head coach. It was a bitter departure. Majors, now the head coach at Pittsburgh, accused Fulmer of orchestrating his removal to get the head coaching job.

Knoxville returned to normalcy when Fulmer's team easily beat Boston College in the Hall of Fame Bowl. In the spring he engineered an excellent recruiting class. It was clear that the Volunteers' program, which Majors had overseen since 1977, wasn't going to fade into mediocrity any time soon. At the start of the 1993 season the Vols had beaten Louisiana Tech 50–0 and Georgia 38–6, eliminating the Bulldogs, who had lost to South Carolina the week before, from the Eastern Division race. The third game of the season was to be a match between titans.

Before the 1990 season the Tennessee-Florida matchup wasn't much of a rivalry because the teams didn't play each other every year. The expansion of the SEC, which added Arkansas from the Southwest Conference and South Carolina from the Metro, changed everything. The conference now comprised two six-team divisions, and Tennessee and Florida were sent to the Eastern Division, along with Georgia, South Carolina, Kentucky, and Vanderbilt. Division teams would play each other every season without exception.

Florida's biggest rival in the conference, Georgia, had tended to have roller-coaster seasons since Vince Dooley left coaching to become the school's athletic director, up one year and down the next. South Carolina's program hadn't recovered from coach Joe Morrison's fatal heart attack in 1989. Kentucky was considered by most people as a basketball school, but it had hired one of the game's finer coaches in Bill Curry. Vanderbilt was, well, Vanderbilt. Its academic standards were higher than every other SEC school and that alone distinguished Vandy's recruiting priorities from other regional schools like Louisville, Tennessee, Georgia, Georgia Tech, Auburn, and Alabama.

It appeared that the Vols and Gators would battle annually for the top slot in the division. It was as if two bullies had been placed in the same schoolyard after years in separate neighborhoods. All the ingredients existed for a new rivalry.

In his first game against Tennessee in 1990, Spurrier's team was whipped 45–3 at Knoxville in what would be Florida's only SEC loss of the season. The next year at Florida

Field, the Gators avenged themselves with a 35–18 win on their way to their first SEC championship. In 1992, with Coach Majors in the press box as an observer following his surgery, Tennessee routed Florida 31–14. All three games had been won by the home team and none were close.

In burgeoning rivalries, if the players don't quickly learn to dislike each other, the fans will. This happened immediately between Florida and Tennessee. It also didn't hurt that Spurrier had grown up in Johnson City, Tennessee, and that former Florida coach Doug Dickey was now Tennessee's athletic director. As Spurrier walked off Neyland Stadium's artificial turf following losses in 1990 and 1992, Volunteer fans heckled him and mocked the Gator chomp. It seemed there was no team Tennessee loved to beat more than the Gators, especially now that Spurrier was head coach.

Florida football fans, meanwhile, were developing a reputation as the nastiest and most disrespectful in the conference. They would throw things at the opposing bench. Fights would break out. Any fan wearing the visiting team's colors was sure to be accosted. Most of the perpetrators were intoxicated students and most of the problems occurred at night games when they had had the entire day to indulge in their favorite beverage, which wasn't Gatorade.

As at any school, 90 percent of Florida's fans are courteous to their visitors. Yet no fans received as much abuse in Gainesville as did those adorned with Volunteer orange. Not even Florida State fans. Serious altercations during the 1991 game in Gainesville resulted in the introduction of an SEC rule mandating that visiting fans sit behind the visiting bench, creating a buffer zone.

Fan interaction is but one facet of a school rivalry. Individual games in a rivalry are usually distinguished by a touch of scandal. An incident before the 1991 game heightened Tennessee's contempt for the Gators and particularly for one of the assistant coaches.

Florida defensive coordinator Ron Zook had been Majors's secondary coach at Tennessee from 1984 to 1986. Jack Sells, a fellow assistant coach and a close friend of Zook's, worked at Tennessee at the same time. After Zook had gone on to other coaching posts with Virginia Tech and Ohio State, Sells was forced to resign when the NCAA discovered some minor rules violations. By several accounts Sells was a scapegoat. One way schools satisfy the NCAA when violations are found is to fire the coach involved, extenuating circumstances or not. Once an assistant coach is branded a violator by the NCAA, it is next to impossible for him to find another coaching job, especially during the prevailing climate of athletic reform being monitored by university administrators. Zook saw what happened to Sells, and both men nurtured their own resentments of the athletic politics of Rocky Top land.

Prior to the 1991 game, Sells faxed Zook some plays and formations from Tennessee's old playbook. An employee of the Knoxville copying store, an avid Volunteers fan, stumbled upon the material after Sells had left the building. He alerted the media and "Faxgate" was underway. All that was missing were Woodward, Bernstein, the FBI, and the CIA. Tennessee fans were outraged. Spurrier made the matter worse by denying that any Florida coach had received information. Then, following the game, he admitted that Zook had received the material but said it was "nothing beneficial," just a few newspaper clippings. The truth is, since assistant coaches change jobs almost as regularly as used car salesmen, the practice of sending friends helpful information is as common as bowl games on January 1. Dickey knew that and refused to press the issue with then Florida athletic director Bill Arnsparger. Not that Tennessee fans cared. They cried foul, instantly turning Sells from an unknown former assistant coach into a notorious villain wanted statewide. He was punched at a bar because of the incident.

On the Sunday before the 1993 Florida game, Fulmer, a guard at Tennessee from 1969 to 1971 and an assistant under

Majors for thirteen years, rekindled the two-year-old fire. He boasted to the media, "We had information like a playbook, not the whole playbook . . . on Florida last year." Asked where and how it was obtained, he snapped, "That's privileged information." Spurrier, to his credit, dismissed it as no big deal.

The intensity of the two teams grew all week long. "Yeah, it's gotten to the point where there's a little hatred there," Florida wide receiver Jack Jackson conceded. "I'll admit that. Most of the guys would."

The crowd noise at Florida Field is usually off the scale at games like this. There are no official rankings of what school has the loudest football stadium, but Florida's ranks near the top. Of course, the loudness depends on what kind of season the home team is having. For instance, the noise at LSU's Tiger Stadium once registered on the school's Richter scale. Now the place is easily confused with the school library. The other so-called Death Valley in Clemson, South Carolina, is truly noisy. And Auburn's Jordan-Hare Stadium would rank toward the top of the list. Size doesn't really count in terms of the amount of noise generated on autumn Saturdays on the college campuses across the country. The University of Michigan has the nation's largest stadium, holding 105,000 fans, but a game at Ann Arbor is a day at the opera compared to most stadiums in the South. And Florida and Tennessee own two of the loudest in college football.

"Hopefully, our team will be as ready as the fans," Spurrier commented. Fulmer didn't sound too worried about the expected noise. "I don't know how to solve it," he said. "There's only a limited number of things you can do. We'll put eleven players on the field and they'll put eleven on the field."

Spurrier didn't want to hear coaches blame the noise for losses. "We put up with it on the road . . . at places like Neyland Stadium and it always seems to be louder when the Gators play," he added. "You could tell on the tapes that Georgia could not hear anything last week. It now seems accepted when you go to another team's stadium that noise will be a part of it. I think Tennessee realizes we have a stadium that is a tough place to play just like we realize they have one."

Noise or no noise, it looked more and more as if Florida would have to play the game without its best receiver. Willie Jackson, who had led the conference in receiving the previous two seasons, sustained a deep knee bruise when he scored the tying two-point conversion against Kentucky.

On Tuesday the players were putting the game in perspective. It didn't take an engineering major to do that. The SEC's Eastern Division champion was going to be decided on Saturday and everyone knew it. Each player chose his own specific motivator—revenge, rivalry, importance, bragging rights, or national rankings (Tennessee was number five; Florida had dropped to number nine). Each was legitimate.

"Georgia's got two losses already," wide receiver Jack Jackson observed. "It looks like it will be between us and Tennessee again."

"This is the one we've looked forward to," linebacker Monty Grow asserted. "It's the biggest game we're going to play, . . . at least as far as the SEC East is concerned. We don't need to get in a room and tell each other how big this game is. We all know without saying a word."

Spurrier agreed but still wanted to send a message to his team in case the worst happened. "It's not the end of the season for the team that loses it. But the games will get bigger for the team that wins it."

What bothered Spurrier as much as anything from the team's first two games was the unusually high number of penalties levied against the Gators. Florida had been the most-penalized team in the conference since he arrived in 1990, and it appeared that wouldn't change this season. As with most penalties, the infractions during the first two games were mostly mental lapses. A defensive tackle would jump offsides when all he had to do was concentrate on the football in front of him. A defensive back would forget to turn his head as the pass arrived, bringing a pass interference call. The newest way to lose fifteen yards, "the celebration rule," could have cost Florida the Kentucky game had there been more time on the clock after Doering's winning touchdown. Officials were schooled to flag any prolonged or contrived celebration, especially early in the season to get the message across.

On the other side of the line, Zook was upset with free safety Lawrence Wright, who drew a fifteen-yard taunting penalty following an interception against Kentucky. Wright had run alongside the Kentucky sideline, showing the Wildcats the football. "We can't have that in any game," Zook protested. "I guarantee you he won't do it again. But it was his first college interception. If the knucklehead had just come to our sideline like he was supposed to . . ."

Spurrier added, "I have told them: 'You don't have a right to celebrate and taunt. You don't have a right to jump offsides. You don't have a right to push and shove after a two-point conversion.' If some of our guys played as hard as we celebrate, we would be OK. Some players just grow up thinking that is the way you are supposed to act."

The celebration phenomenon had filtered from the NFL to college to the high school level. After seeing Lawrence Taylor dance following a quarterback sack on Sunday, a college player would imitate him the next Saturday. Then a high school player, watching both levels of play on television, would do it the following Friday night.

To curb his players, Spurrier initiated what he called the Stupid Penalty Club. Violators would run extra sprints following Monday night practices. "Penalties make us look like stupid coaches. Everybody sees them and says, 'Hey, those coaches have no control over their players.' They're right. That's the way it looks."

Asked if the surviving team from Saturday's game had a chance at the national championship, Fulmer bristled. "It's too early in

YEAR OF THE GATOR

the season for that," he snapped. "I haven't heard any of our players mention it. They know better." In fact, several Volunteers had mentioned it following the thrashing of Georgia. Tailback Charlie Garner had acknowledged, "It's in the back of our minds. We'll work hard to win the SEC championship and then the national championship."

Florida and Tennessee each had made the national title their goal before the season and were two of maybe seven or eight teams that had the talent to pull it off. Talent wins titles, but talent also needs a certain degree of luck, especially in the close games. Alabama had proved that the year before.

Spurrier decided who would be his starting quarterback on Monday. On Tuesday he still hadn't announced it. "I've got an idea what direction is good for both of our quarterbacks. There's a good chance both of them will play." When would he announce his choice? "We might go until Friday before we tell," he answered. "I want them to have a week in peace."

Spurrier was asked if he would ever turn to third-stringer Eric Kresser. "No. He's that far behind." Kresser, a quiet, polite redshirt freshman with the strongest arm on the team, felt that he deserved a chance after watching Dean and Wuerffel throw seven passes to the wrong-colored jerseys the week before. After Monday night's practice, he commented, "I thought I was capable. I was coming on at the end of the summer and all of a sudden, the reps stopped." Repetitions, or "reps" to the players, are snaps taken in practice. They are a backup quarterback's best friend, but Kresser wasn't getting them, and now he was hinting at transferring. Spurrier, who thought that Kresser hadn't picked up the offense, admitted that transferring probably would be best. Kresser's father began to call other schools to see if his son was wanted. "He's got one of those fathers who is living through his son's achievements," Spurrier concluded.

If Tuesday's weekly meeting with the media was any indication, Spurrier had chosen Wuerffel. Wuerffel met with reporters; Dean did not. "I am approaching it like I did the last two games," Wuerffel said. "Whether you are on the first, second, or third team, you go into it as if you are the starter. Then if you do get in, you'll be ready. Anyway, he told us both to be ready. It's not my call or my decision. It's a tough call, but it's not mine—thank goodness."

Whichever quarterback started would have to put the Kentucky game behind him. Because he threw the winning touchdown, perhaps Wuerffel's three interceptions were being overlooked while Dean's four were being scrutinized. "It's like shooting a basketball," Wuerffel explained. "If you shoot an air ball, you come back and shoot again. There are bad shots and bad passes." Spurrier loved that kind of attitude. Wuerffel never got down, never gave up, and it paid off against Kentucky.

By Friday afternoon, Spurrier's own anxiety had peaked. He was obviously uptight following the usual Friday walkthrough practice at Florida Field. He trotted off the field toward the tunnel to the locker room, not wanting to stop long to talk to reporters. Sometimes he would linger with the reporters and even joke with them or give a short lesson on the intricacies of the game. He quickly announced his decision: Wuerffel. Then he admonished the beat writers for making such a big deal about who would start at quarterback. "You all don't write much about who should start at center," he submitted.

Centers don't throw touchdown passes or interceptions, date cheerleaders, or win Heisman Trophies like the one Spurrier had in his den. Of all people, the head coach realized that. He said that Dean "probably" would play too. "I just feel this is the way we should go right now, . . . then I'll call the rest of the game by feel." Asked if he would evaluate the position series-by-series, he snapped, "What do you want me to do, tell you my game plan?"

Spurrier ran off, and the sportswriters were left to discuss his obvious but rare nervousness. So much was riding on this game, and the game was riding on his decision between Wuerffel and Dean. What if Wuerffel crumbled under the pressure? He was only one year out of high school.

Knowing what intrigue could do to a quarterback's mind, Spurrier had told the quarterbacks of his choice on Monday. He instructed them to keep mum, but Dean told a reporter on Tuesday that he thought Wuerffel would start the game. That didn't please the head coach, not that Dean cared at this point. Dean understandably was disappointed, and he immediately contemplated quitting. Then he considered transferring to a Division II school where he could play next season. His parents talked him out of each option and summoned the minister from the family's church in Naples. He drove to Gainesville to counsel Dean. So the team's quarterback situation was this: the starter was a redshirt freshman while numbers two and three were considering transferring.

Like Dean, Zook had his own problems. Tennessee fans hated him and he felt likewise. That wasn't the problem. This was his game to be emotional, his game to let all those personal feelings out. That wasn't a problem either. Tennessee's explosive offense, led by quarterback Heath Shuler, had the capability to go up and down the field on anybody. That was the problem. The thought would give any defensive coordinator a headache.

"Heath Shuler does so many things," Zook observed. "He's one of those kids who everybody looks to when things are going bad. He's just a winner."

Shuler hadn't thrown much in 1992 and was known more as a double threat who could run the football as well as he threw it. In 1993 he would become more of a dropback passer, the kind of quarterback that the NFL loves. Shuler knew what awaited him and his teammates in Gainesville. "I think they may have been looking ahead against Kentucky and focusing on this game," he said. "I am sure they can't wait until we get there. We've spent all week preparing for the noise."

By Saturday morning Spurrier was more relaxed as he left a team meeting at the Holiday Inn West, where the team stays the night before home games. Zook followed him out the door but paced nervously as Spurrier stopped to talk to a sportswriter. "A great day for football," he said, glancing at the clear blue sky. "Hope Gators fans are ready. . . . I think we're ready to play a good one."

It was a great start for the Gators, who jumped to a 21–0 lead behind Wuerffel, who was flawless. He threw touchdown passes of eight yards to Aubrey Hill and seventeen yards to Doering before Errict Rhett scored on a one-yard run. It looked like another rout was underway, but it turned out, as expected, that Tennessee, specifically Shuler, was too good for that.

The Volunteers bounced back with a fifty-four-yard scoring pass from Shuler to Cory Fleming. Then, with fifteen seconds remaining in the first half, Shuler rolled right, avoided two defensive linemen, and heaved a desperation pass into the end zone. Billy Williams leaped and took it out of the hands of five-foot-nine cornerback Anthone Lott, falling back into the end zone for a touchdown.

As the Volunteers celebrated on their way to the locker room, trailing only 21–14, Florida's coaches screamed at the officials. A twelfth Tennessee player had failed to get off the field at the snap of the ball. Fulmer was wrong; his team wouldn't play with eleven players. The 85,247 fans, the second-largest crowd in stadium history, and the national television audience sensed this game was just heating up.

"That gave us a big lift . . . you could just feel it on the sidelines," Fulmer recalled. "We felt our receivers could get by their secondary guys. It worked."

The momentum Tennessee gained was immediately lost on the second-half kickoff. The Volunteers fumbled and Wuerffel passed thirty yards to Harrison Houston for a 28–14 lead on the next play. Houston made a remarkable catch by spinning around to his left to make an over-the-shoulder grab

Chris Doering was basking in the glow of the spotlight before the Tennessee game. During a three-game stretch—Kentucky, Tennessee, and Mississippi State—he caught twenty-one passes and scored six touchdowns.

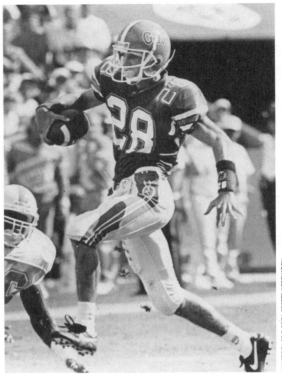

UNIVERSITY OF FLORIDA SPORTS INFORMATION

at the goal line. "What a catch!" Wuerffel said. "It wasn't a great pass. He just made me look good on that one. I owe him."

The Gators continued to maintain at least a seven-point lead, but that didn't stop Shuler from impressing everyone. Late in the fourth quarter a thunderstorm drenched Florida Field as Shuler rolled left and threw five yards for his fifth touchdown pass, getting the Vols to within seven points, 41–34, with 1:46 remaining.

The rain was pouring out of the sky and suddenly things didn't seem so great to Spurrier. The Gators' defense was being shredded. Shuler had completed twenty-five of forty-one passes for 355 yards and five touchdowns, and the Volunteers' offense had been unstoppable. Tennessee was only an onside kick, a touchdown, and a two-point conversion away from pulling off a comeback victory. But as the rain fell harder, the Gators covered the kick and ran out the clock. Minutes later the players sang the school's alma mater with the crowd as they did following every home victory since Spurrier had become coach, but the coach didn't feel much like singing. He went to the locker room and lashed out at his players.

"We could have scored fifty or sixty points . . . we left too many points out on the field," he implored before turning to his defensive backs. "You have to play smarter than that. If we are going to be a championship team, we can't allow them to come back that easily. They threw it right over our heads all day. We played too tight, obviously. You'd think with a 21–0 lead, we'd be [playing] back farther." He was relieved and upset at the same time. Spurrier had wanted to beat the Volunteers badly, not just by seven points.

Zook was worried. His defensive backs appeared as if they had not practiced at all. "They just haven't played much . . . remember they're redshirt freshmen," he explained. "They are trying and playing hard . . . they just need time to develop, but unfortunately, we don't have much time. They have to get better. They just got beat deep. I kept telling them to stay back, stay back. But we played pretty well outside of the big plays."

Lott, cousin of NFL great Ronnie Lott, took the blame for three Tennessee touchdowns. "I gave them eighteen points," he said. "Without that, it's a blowout." Lott was too willing to martyr himself. On Shuler's long throw before the end of the first half, it was Lawrence Wright who missed his assignment by staying too close to the line of scrimmage. Yet to the fans and announcers it looked like the coverage was Lott's responsibility.

Overshadowed by the defensive disappointments was Wuerffel's performance in his first career start. He had completed nineteen of thirty-eight passes for 231 yards and three touchdowns. More important, he was the winning quarterback although Shuler had the better game. "Overall, it was a pretty doggone good performance," Spurrier said of Wuerffel's day. "He made some big throws out there."

GATOR BAIT

One of the rare times Tennessee quarterback Heath Shuler didn't have time to throw the ball. Linebacker Ed Robinson tackles Shuler as Kevin Carter (57) approaches. Shuler threw for 355 yards and five touchdowns.

As he left Gainesville, Fulmer and his team knew that they needed help to get back in the SEC Eastern Division race. "Florida's on top in the East, and somebody has to beat them for us," he admitted.

While Florida was winning on the field, the fans were unruly in the stands. Tennessee fans always see the worst side of Florida Field. Athletic director Jeremy Foley's office was bombarded with irate phone calls and letters. Volunteers fans had faced it all this time. They had been spit upon, cussed, pushed, shoved, and punched. There was even a report of a Florida student relieving himself in a cup and then throwing the parcel of unpleasantness into a section of Tennessee fans. "This thing is on the verge of being like a soccer match in Europe," Tennessee fan Ron McMahon wrote to the *Gainesville Sun*. "In my fifty years of traveling across the country to watch games, I've never seen anything like it. The language and vulgarity were just brutal."

Sixty-one fans were ejected for throwing things at the visitors. Part of the problem is that Florida allows fans to leave the stadium at halftime and return. Over the years students developed a tradition of visiting a nearby bar, downing a few

Errict Rhett found running room against Tennessee, rushing for 147 yards and two touchdowns in the Gator's 41–34 victory.

To cornerback Anthone Lott the 41–34 victory over Tennessee felt like a loss. He had a tough day with Heath Shuler and the Volunteers' talented receivers.

quick ones, and rushing back to the stadium for the second-half kickoff.

Foley called Dickey to apologize. "I just told him we were committed to correcting the problem," he said. "We'll set up a meeting with student affairs to talk about this. We certainly don't condone it. It has detracted from an important win."

Another Tennessee-Florida meeting was in the books as the rivalry had taken another step toward some wacky level of maturity. And the Volunteers and Gators had one more reason to dislike each other.

5

SHERRILL COMES TO TOWN

T
HE DAY AFTER THE EMOTIONAL win over Tennessee, Spurrier and his coaches looked forward to having an off week. Off weeks in college football mean that no game is scheduled to be played. On Saturday, that is. Florida always plays on Monday nights.

Called "Monday Night Football," just like the namesake it precedes on national television at 9:00 P.M., the Gators' version starts about 7:30 and runs right up to the kickoff of the NFL version. Most of the younger players who don't get to play on Saturdays get a chance to impress the coaches with their skills during the Monday scrimmages. "That's what it's for," Spurrier explained. "We don't want these guys sitting around for a year or two without gaining experience or getting hit."

Hitting is the name of the game in Monday Night Football. There have been fights, players carried off, and the usual head-ringing, jarring tackles that coaches call "decleaters," meaning the ball carrier had his cleats separated from the grass.

The competition gets so fierce that the starters and second-teamers gather to watch after they finish running their mandatory sprints around the practice field. They yell and scream for their side of the ball. The teams are simple: offense versus defense. On this night, minutes before the Broncos and Chiefs were about to square off in Kansas City, freshman running back Terrence Foy was decleated. Starting defensive end Kevin Carter threw back his head. "Ouch!" he shouted. "The perfect hit."

With a week to prepare before hosting Mississippi State, the Gators were 3–0 and far from perfect. "We need the week off right now," Spurrier commented. "We can heal and we have to [keep] those defensive backs from letting people throw it over their heads."

Terry Dean, battling with depression over losing his job, impressed Spurrier in Tuesday's practice. "Terry's handling it as well as could be expected," he observed. "I am proud of the way he is adjusting. We still feel we have two good quarterbacks." Again, Spurrier noted that Dean might play the following Saturday. "There are some things I've got in mind for him, but I wouldn't want it to be in the newspapers." Dean had heard the same thing the previous week; then he sat by the water cooler for four quarters, never having a reason to put on his helmet.

As they had for Tennessee, Florida players had revenge on their minds the following week, too. Mississippi State had embarrassed the Gators 30–6 on a Thursday night ESPN game in Starkville the year before. It was the worst game of quarterback Shane Matthews's record-setting career. Matthews, who had grown up in Pascagoula, Mississippi, was intercepted five times.

"It seems we play one lousy game each year and that was it," Spurrier recalled. "Gosh, that was a long night." The loss was the team's worst of the season, although the score was just 13–7 early in the fourth quarter and Florida was threatening. But with the ball inside the Bulldogs' ten-yard line, an offensive lineman jumped early and later Matthews was intercepted. Spurrier remembered that there was more to it than that. "One of their linebackers hollered 'Hut, hut,' and we jumped," he remembered. "Is it fair? I guess it is if you can get away with it."

Guard Jim Watson had no excuses. "They just lined up and whipped our butts last year," he grimaced.

"They really embarrassed us on national television," recalled wide receiver Jack Jackson, also from Mississippi. "I know most of those guys and I am always rooting for them, but once they got ahead they just talked the whole game. They wouldn't shut up." Jackson remembered how Mississippi State fans had given Matthews and him the one-finger salute before the game, and it wasn't that they were saying the Bulldogs were number one.

Jackson wanted to win this game more than anybody else in the Florida locker room. Those in his hometown of Moss Point had ridiculed his choice of college, then they rubbed it in even more after the 1992 game. "I took a lot of flak for coming here," he admitted. "All of my high school coaches are graduates of Mississippi State."

After Mississippi State had lost two of its first three games, including home games to Memphis State and LSU, Jackson predicted, "They're probably pointing fingers at each other by now. That's a characteristic they've had over the years."

As Monday came, Jackson thought of his former teammate, Matthews, now a third-string quarterback with the Chicago Bears. "I want to go out and redeem Shane and myself this week," he promised. "They all told us we should have stayed in-state."

Despite their poor start to the season, Mississippi State was becoming a force again in college football. The Bulldogs had been less than mediocre for a decade, not having played in a major bowl since 1981. That all changed when Jackie Sherrill moved to Starkville in 1991. Sherrill had won a national championship in Pittsburgh and then turned Texas A&M into an annual Southwest Conference championship contender. He left

College Station, Texas, with the NCAA on his rear bumper. The Aggies were on probation, and Sherrill was suddenly out of the coaching business.

Two years away from football had made Sherrill hungrier than ever to return. He got the chance when Mississippi State's president and athletic director had had enough of losing. After getting assurances from the NCAA, they hired Sherrill before the 1991 season. A rag-tag outfit with a 5–6 record the year before had won seven games and played in a bowl game in Sherrill's first season. In 1992 the Bulldogs again had won seven and played in another bowl.

Sherrill had taken the state by storm, literally. He had openly feuded with Ole Miss coach Billy Brewer. But nobody outside of Mississippi paid much attention to him until he had a bull castrated in front of his players to motivate them prior to playing the Texas Longhorns. "It was educational," he said. "I wanted to show them how a bull becomes a steer." Animal rights' activists all over the nation criticized him on that one. Suddenly, tiny Starkville, Mississippi, thirty miles west of the Alabama border, was on the college football map and everyone wanted to know the real Jackie Sherrill.

"I guess there is a mystique there," he admitted. "People want to get inside my head. They want to know me, but I don't want them to know me. All they need to know are my football teams."

Sports Illustrated had published a feature on Sherrill before the season, detailing his affinity for clowns and dressing up with makeup and an orange wig. "I read it one time and then put it away," Sherrill said. "It was just the writer's perception. It's not me."

A change on Sherrill's staff didn't bode well for Florida. Offensive coordinator Watson Brown had left to join Oklahoma's staff. Under Brown the Bulldogs ran the option and emphasized a power running game. Florida's defense could stop most running teams, and this would be the perfect

MISSISSIPPI STATE SPORTS INFORMATION

Mississippi State head coach Jackie Sherrill administered the Gators' worst beating a year earlier. His first trip to Gainesville wouldn't be so pleasant.

week to face such an offense, considering the secondary's troubles. As it was, though, new offensive coordinator Bruce Arians had installed a pro-style, drop-back passing offense. Option quarterback Greg Plump was benched, and strong-armed Todd Jordan was the starter. The six-foot-five Jordan was averaging thirty-one passes per game. "He's a tall guy with a good arm," Arians commented.

On Monday the Gators received some good news of their own when Willie Jackson claimed that his knee would be ready by Saturday. "No doubt about it," he said. "I'll play. I just have trouble cutting on it right now." The next day, Jack Jackson, no relation to Willie, separated his shoulder when he slammed into a goal post in practice. He stood to miss the one game he had anticipated all year.

Spurrier was unhappy with the number of penalties Florida had accumulated: fourteen for 115 yards. The Stupid Penalty Club would expand this week. Reminded that he had drawn a fifteen-yarder for throwing his visor and cursing at an official just before the first half ended against Tennessee, Spurrier answered, "That's not in the rule book. I am going to look that one up. Anyway, it's not a stupid penalty when there's two seconds on the clock and you're at your own twenty."

Now that Wuerffel's performance against Tennessee seemed to put the quarterback controversy to rest, at least temporarily, much of the focus turned to the secondary. The Gators' defensive backs, particularly Lott, played terribly against Shuler and the Volunteers and they knew it.

Spurrier diagnosed the problem as a combination of too little pass rush and poor coverage. The first part was a mystery since Florida had returned eight good defensive linemen from the 1992 season. Most teams struggle to find four, but the Gators were among the deepest teams in the country at the position.

"We weren't getting there at all in the fourth quarter against Tennessee," Spurrier complained. "William Gaines is the only one getting anything done."

Everyone admired and respected Gaines for the way he had come back from a nasty knee injury. In an August practice before the 1992 season he had crumpled to the ground screaming. The ligaments in his right knee had torn completely during a noncontact drill. He returned for ten plays in the Gator Bowl, but nobody thought he would ever return to his old form.

The Gators' defensive scheme—an eight-man front with only three defensive backs—was also being scrutinized by the sportswriters. Coincidentally or not, the team has been one of the best in the nation against the run and less than average against the pass.

"Our coverage and our scheme will work if they stick to their assignments," Spurrier said. "It's a different one on each play. We spent five days with the Arizona coaches this summer. They play the same scheme, and their defense is one of the best in the country."

But Arizona doesn't play an eight-man front; Arizona plays a standard 4–3 scheme. "Heck, it isn't the scheme that has made us successful," Arizona defensive coordinator Larry MacDuff remarked. "We just have some great players. Coach Spurrier and [Arizona head coach] Dick Tomey played golf, and the assistants compared notes and worked together."

If Spurrier had been on the links during the meetings, he could easily have overlooked the intricacies of Arizona's defense. Nevertheless, the Florida defensive backs were the target of his criticism, even when he explained, "It's coaching. You tell the players what to do, but if they don't go do it, it's coaching. How many of you writers even noticed we had two safeties on the field for the whole fourth quarter?"

Spurrier occasionally quizzed beat reporters during his Tuesday meetings with the media, hinting that they knew little about football. As former Chicago Bears coach Mike Ditka once commented, "Everyone learns to write by the third grade, but most of us go on to bigger and better things."

Reporters aside, the target of Spurrier's wrath after the narrow escape over Tennessee also included Zook. With the 21–0 lead, he claimed that he had told Zook to play "softer," meaning the defensive backs should play deeper. For some reason, the defensive backs didn't get the message. They certainly didn't play as if they had the message. "I know one thing," Spurrier warned. "We are going to get better or we are going to play different people." Michael Gilmore, an honor student but not very big for a free safety at five-foot-ten and 175 pounds, recalled that the game plan was to play Tennessee's receivers tight, "but it opened up holes deeper."

This was one of those weeks that make assistant coaches wish they had chosen some other career. Zook, an excellent defensive back at Miami University from 1972 to 1975, had screamed, ranted, raved, consoled, instructed quietly, and encouraged his players, but the defensive backs still didn't make the plays. "I kept telling them, 'Stay deep, stay deep . . . don't let them get behind you,'" he explained. "Those plays have to be corrected. They will be. Hey, if it's the biggest problem on this team, then we're in good shape. Nobody talked much about the defense when we beat Kentucky with seven interceptions." Then he predicted, "Mississippi State will go deep on us after the problems we've had. What's the game plan? Keep people loose."

While Lott was taking the heat for three of Tennessee's touchdowns, Zook admitted that Shuler's touchdown with fifteen seconds remaining in the first half was safety Lawrence Wright's responsibility. "He was screwing around near the line of scrimmage and Anthone just hustled back to the ball. He made a great play just to get there."

Like a true defensive back, Zook tried to deflect the media criticism away from his players. "I've been there before. It's not my first time and it won't be my last."

While Florida was off that Saturday, giving the players a chance to watch other games on television, the biggest news in the college football world was a rash of on-field fights. Duke and Virginia clashed. So did North Carolina and North Carolina State and Colorado and Miami. Spurrier had tried to fly to Charlottesville, Virginia, to watch Duke and Steve Jr. play. The airlines canceled his connection from Charlotte, and he returned to Gainesville when he realized he wouldn't arrive in time for the kickoff. Like his old man, Steve Jr. was no fighter. "Bubba said he was over there on the sideline watching it," Spurrier said. "But he started and caught five balls. Anyway, it's amazing all those fights happening in one week. It's like one team watched one fight on television and said, 'Hey, it's OK to fight.'"

Spurrier pointed out that none of his teams, at Duke or Florida, had ever been in a brawl. Then he jabbed at the fans.

"The only negative about our stadium is the unruly fans who turn on the visiting team's fans. It's hurting our reputation and our image."

The Mississippi State game would ensure that Spurrier would have other worries by Saturday night. It would be the shootout of the SEC season, at least in terms of yards, if not points. In what was once labeled as a conference of boring run, run, run, and run again football, this game resembled something right out of the Western Athletic Conference. If the crowd didn't know the familiar uniforms, the 84,738 fans at Florida Field might have thought they were watching Brigham Young and San Diego State.

Jordan started the game by tossing a fifty-two-yard touchdown to Chris Jones, who had beaten cornerback Eddie Lake badly. Lake had missed the Tennessee game with an injury, so this was his indoctrination to the defensive backs' woes. Wuerffel responded with two touchdown passes to Doering, who lined up as a standing tight end. Spurrier figured he would be mismatched with a linebacker, and he was right.

Trying to motivate Errict Rhett, Spurrier benched the All-Conference tailback after he had dropped two passes and gained only five yards on four carries. The score was 14–14 at the half. Jordan had passed for 168 yards, Wuerffel for 240. But the fans had not seen anything yet.

As the second half began, Jordan passed deep to Eric Moulds, who bobbled the ball while cornerback Larry Kennedy tried for the interception. The ball bounced back into Moulds's hands and Kennedy fell down. The result was a sixty-three-yard touchdown. Kennedy had been in single coverage, and on the sidelines Spurrier was livid with Zook.

Jack Jackson, who wouldn't let his sore shoulder keep him out of the game, then got his revenge and turned the game around on the next play, taking the kickoff at the goal line and heading down the left sideline. He cut right and saw an open field. He was gone. Touchdown. One hundred yards. "I'm glad it came against Mississippi State," he remarked. "I wanted to show the people back home what they missed out on. Now I can go home and hold my head high."

The nightmare continued for the Gators' secondary as Jordan and the Mississippi State receivers continued to frustrate their efforts. Doering would catch one more touchdown pass to make the the final score 38–24, but the Florida locker room was almost as sullen as if the team had lost. Jordan had completed twenty-four passes for 405 yards.

Spurrier was furious. "Coach Zook . . . he's going to stay . . . so our players are going to have to get better or we'll get some freshmen back there," he said. "Great teams don't let this happen. Gosh, good teams don't let it happen."

Standing in the middle of the locker room where he talks to reporters following every game, Zook looked as if there had been a death in the family. He was frustrated, angry, and puzzled. With each probing question, he became more agitated as the crowd of sportswriters swelled around him. "Write whatever you want. I can coach. I know I can coach," he asserted. "I will get it fixed. There's nobody tougher on me than me. I will replay this game a thousand times tonight and tomorrow."

It would be worth a thousand headaches. Jordan may have been impressive, but Wuerffel was awesome. He completed twenty-seven of forty-one passes for a conference and school record of 449 yards. Four weeks earlier he had figured he would be holding a clipboard for the season. Now he was holding two of the most prominent records in college football. "I am not much for records," he commented, sitting on his locker stool. "The record that counts is four and oh. That zero part is the most important thing." Dean, whose locker is next to Wuerffel's, had already left. For the second consecutive week, he didn't need to shower.

Facing page: Danny Wuerffel, only a redshirt freshman, was simply brilliant against Mississippi State, setting a new school record for passing yardage.

About a screen pass away, Rhett had his share of reporters to face, too. He had bounced back in the second half to gain 117 yards on fifteen carries. "I never questioned my ability, but I was upset. I thought I should be in there helping the team," he said. "They were playing the run in the first half."

In the visitors' locker room, Sherrill wasn't exactly gracious. "They won the game . . . they didn't dominate the game. There's a big difference," he noted. "Of the two quarterbacks, you would say Jordan played better. It's just that the other guy has better people around him catching the ball. Our defense just got tired in the fourth quarter."

Nobody was more tired than the Florida head coach. The defense's play took him back to his days at Duke. "I hate to go back to the old days, but then they used to run it down our throats. Now they throw it over our heads. I've got a feeling we are going to play in a lot of these games."

Foley, the school's athletic director, walked into Spurrier's interview room. "I told Jeremy when they hired me that we would set a lot of records here," Spurrier joked. "But we're setting them on both sides of the ball."

Despite the fourteen-point win, Spurrier was agitated with the officials about two calls. Mississippi State's Scott Gumina muffed a punt return at the five-yard line, picked up the ball in the end zone, and started to run. He was tackled one yard deep in the end zone, but officials ruled the play a touchback and awarded Mississippi State the ball at the twenty-yard line. Spurrier blew up and the fans booed. In the NFL, the play would have been ruled a safety. Yet, according to NCAA rules, the officials made the correct call. It is a strange rule and one that needs to be corrected, but, nevertheless, a rule is a rule.

The second incident happened when Wuerffel suddenly shifted from under center into the shotgun formation on fourth-and-two at Mississippi State's thirteen-yard line.

University of Florida Sports Information

Defensive coordinator Ron Zook's days were work-filled and his nights were sleepless following the Gators' victories over Tennessee and Mississippi State. The secondary was playing poorly, and Zook was on the hot seat.

Mississippi State jumped offsides and the Gators believed they had a first down. The officials, however, called an illegal procedure penalty, costing Florida five yards. Again Spurrier tossed his visor and argued while the fans booed even louder. And again the officials were correct. An offensive player cannot simulate the snap of the ball by shifting with the intent to draw the defense offside. The NCAA had put that one on the books three years earlier. The officials' job was to interpret whether Florida tried deliberately to draw Mississippi State offside or actually shifted into the shotgun to run a play. This one was clear.

Maybe arguing with the officials was just a needed diversion from his own troubles. Florida's defense was struggling, and Spurrier suddenly realized the team might not have the defense necessary to win either a national championship or even the conference championship.

It had all looked so promising in August. Nine good defensive linemen returned, and yet there had been practically no pass rush in the first four games. The inside linebackers had great potential, but they were young. Two of the three defensive backs were redshirt freshmen who were playing like redshirt freshmen. Throughout the past two weeks Spurrier had spent much of his time ping-ponging back and forth when he talked about the secondary's problems. At times he said that the defensive backs were playing lousy and something had to be done. At other times he said that the media were making too much out of the big passing games by Tennessee and Mississippi State.

The day after the Mississippi State game, he told reporters, "We really didn't play that bad on defense, and we had a better effort than we did against Tennessee. Most of our players were in pretty good position. I just think we have been unfortunate, too. Every time the other quarterback throws deep, he puts it right there. Really, it wasn't that bad. Heck, we forced nine punts. We never forced nine punts at Duke."

Pressed about his comments after the game when he remarked that it was time to put some freshmen out there, he said, "I guess that was frustration. We haven't given up on these people yet. They are our best players. I am not sure what Coach Zook wants to do." Zook, however, hadn't changed his opinion, although he was getting somewhat edgy with the constant probing by reporters about his scheme, personnel, and coaching. He would continue to put the best players he had on the field. "These players can play. I know they can," he contended. "We have to correct their mistakes. We will correct them."

Spurrier awakened Sunday and watched the tapes of the Mississippi State game, after which he defended the defensive coaches. "I thought Coach Zook had a good game plan and called a good defensive game," he observed. "We just did not cover the long ball as well as we needed to."

He said that part of the problem was that the defensive backs were underestimating the speed of the opposing receivers. "And a combination of not turning and running and getting back," he added. "Of course, Larry Kennedy was in perfect position and tried to go for the interception." This especially infuriated Spurrier since defensive backs are taught to knock the ball down forty yards downfield. An interception that far downfield is no better than a punt.

Another part of the problem, although Spurrier refused to recognize it, was his quick-strike offense. Using a no-huddle offense, Florida scored on possessions of 2:02, 1:55, 1:41, :17, 1:59, and 3:33, thus sending the defense right back onto the field. Usually, a team that punts nine times, as Mississippi State did, would score no more than fourteen points.

With a game at LSU ahead, improving the secondary increasingly became the team's priority. LSU quarterback Jamie Howard had passed for 339 yards a year earlier as a freshman, but Florida had held on for a 28–21 win. The game didn't appear to be much easier because it was on the road. Florida was 11–8 on the road under Spurrier, contrasted with a perfect 21–0 record at home.

"LSU's having their problems," Spurrier noted. "But it's never easy to play in Baton Rouge . . . especially if we don't cover anybody. I got a feeling we are going to be playing a lot of these games."

Still, his team was 4–0, in first place in the SEC's Eastern Division and ranked fifth nationally. With those numbers, times should have been more pleasant around Gainesville.

6

JOY ON THE BAYOU

WHILE THE SECONDARY WAS struggling, the offensive line was performing almost perfectly. Some coaches have suggested that the best way to judge an offensive line is to examine the offense's statistics. Florida had scored forty-four, twenty-four, forty-one, and thirty-eight points and was averaging 503 yards per game, ranking second nationally. The quarterbacks had been sacked only twice, each time for holding the football too long. Florida had gained 619 yards the previous week against Mississippi State. It was obvious the offensive line was winning the battle in the trenches.

"These guys don't get their names in the newspaper, but they deserve to get the credit," Spurrier said. "That was probably the best the offensive line has played since we've been here."

Another way to gauge the effectiveness of the offensive line is to ask the quarterback how he feels the morning after the game. Wuerffel, who dropped back to pass forty-one times against Mississippi State, noted, "I woke up and felt great. That is the true test. It's really something to sit back there and have time to see what happens downfield."

The man responsible, offensive line coach Jimmy Ray Stephens, had discovered another plus: the second-team line was almost as good as the first. Backup left tackle Jeff Mitchell, right guard Donnie Young, and right tackle Anthony Ingrassia could have started for most teams. And everyone knew centers Gantt Crouch and David Swain were in a dead heat for the starting job.

So Stephens had no reservations putting the second team in the game, even if the outcome was on the line or the offense was in the "red zone," inside the opponents' twenty-yard line. The previous offensive line coach, Rich McGeorge, who had left to join Don Shula's staff with the Miami Dolphins, had preferred to stick with the first-teamers throughout the game.

"When a running back has been in there the whole game and a fresh line comes in, he'll know a hole will be there," Young promised. "Coach Stephens does more rotating and that's good. You used to be nothing but a 'second-team guy' and that's it. Now everybody keeps from getting down because they aren't playing."

All the backups loved the system. "Before, you didn't want to go in when you were up by twenty-five points in the final minute," Jeff Mitchell observed.

Stephens, a center at Florida from 1972 to 1976, had been a high school coach for most of his career. He had turned around a Fort Walton Beach team from 0–10 in 1986 to 10–1 the following year. His team won the Class 4A state championship in 1991 behind a quarterback named Danny Wuerffel, and he was credited with Wuerffel's unusual ability as a freshman to read defenses. "He taught me the intricacies of the passing game," Wuerffel noted. "What to look at, what to look for, how to read what the defense is doing or disguising."

Spurrier had noticed Stephens's coaching talent for years but never had the chance to hire him until McGeorge departed for Miami. "The guy can flat-out coach," he said.

Throughout the history of football, offensive linemen have had two things in common: they stick together and they love to eat. Stephens's offensive linemen were no different, gathering at Sonny's Barbeque each Sunday night. Why Sundays? For one thing, the team always had the day off. For another, Sundays were all-you-can-eat-chicken nights. Imagine the look on the cooks' faces when five or six college guys averaging six-foot-four and 289 pounds came trudging through the door.

"Sunday is our favorite day," observed offensive tackle Dean Golden, who has the mean look of a bouncer at one of the roughest biker bars. "We're just a bunch of hogs."

"Once in a while, we'll go to a spaghetti place for a buffet," Mitchell added. "Ingrassia always eats the most anyway, but when it's spaghetti . . . look out!"

Speaking of hogs, Chris Doering, a sophomore, was getting a complex. He had caught twenty-four passes and scored six touchdowns, a good season for most college receivers. Senior Willie Jackson, the conference's leading receiver in both of the previous two seasons, had only sixteen receptions and had scored one touchdown, although he missed the Tennessee game with a knee injury. Jackson had caught only three of Wuerffel's twenty-seven completions against Mississippi State a week earlier, and Doering noticed he wasn't real happy.

"I don't want people to think I am trying to hog the ball or be a superstar or anything," Doering contended. "If I was a senior and I had three catches, I might be upset, but he's still our best receiver. I don't really feel guilty . . . it's not like I am telling Danny to throw it to me."

He didn't need to. Wuerffel was smart enough to realize that Doering was getting single coverage, usually by a bigger and slower linebacker who couldn't keep up. He also roomed with Wuerffel on nights before the games. Naturally, roommates communicate a little better than other teammates. Wuerffel and Dean had roomed together until the starting job became a hot topic and Spurrier thought it best to separate the pair.

On Monday, Spurrier had decided to move receiver Shea Showers to free safety. Showers was buried on the team's receiving depth chart. "He had a lot of interceptions in high school," Spurrier commented after practice. "It was kind of his idea. Shea wants to get out there and play, and we can use him."

The next day at his media luncheon inside Florida Field, Spurrier announced that the starting lineup would remain the same. "We think the guys we have back there can play," he added. "Coach Zook has seen them make the plays during the spring game and in practice. We just need to make them in the games."

LSU's Tiger Stadium, once among the toughest in the nation for a visiting team, now was a pussycat's den for most good teams. Death Valley, as it once was called, was a thing of the past in Baton Rouge. After four consecutive losing seasons, including a school-worst 2–9 season in 1992, attendance was down. Only 57,316 had showed up for LSU's 38–17 victory over Utah State the previous week while some fans and boosters were asking third-year coach Curley Hallman to resign. Until he did, they swore they wouldn't return to Tiger Stadium. LSU was 2–3, but they had beaten Mississippi State 18–16 on the road.

"We're fighting to rebuild," Hallman explained. "When you are winning, you are packing the stadium. When things aren't going good, certain individuals will not come. That's just the way it is."

The morale of the LSU players apparently wasn't much better. "Once something bad happens, the guys get down immediately," receiver Eddie Kennison remarked. "That will set us back the rest of the game. The guys have been having losing seasons and we have to get in the spirit of winning again."

In the aftermath of Florida's two previous games, you would expect the next opposing quarterback in line would be looking up his school's passing records. LSU's Jamie Howard, however, had other ideas. Like completing a pass. He had completed five of twenty-seven passes in a 24–0 loss at Texas A&M and nine of thirty-six in a 34–10 loss to Auburn at home.

Fourteen-of-sixty-three wasn't going to scare many defenses, including the Gators'.

The A&M and Auburn games had to be two of the worst performances by a quarterback in the same season. A year ago, as a freshman, Howard had appeared to be a legitimate NFL prospect. "I had to adjust to throwing the football again after baseball," noted Howard, a minor-league pitcher in the Atlanta Braves' farm system. "Right now, a baseball scout would be more impressed with me."

After viewing tapes of Shuler's and Jordan's big days against the Gators, Howard refused to get excited. "I was surprised they spread them out so well," he observed. "But they are going to be ready after having that many yards thrown against them. I don't think for a minute that we're in for an easy night."

Zook wouldn't be in a better mood until his defensive backs started improving. On Tuesday, he shook his head, saying, "Sometimes it looked like we were robots out there. They can't play like that. You have to play loose. After watching the film for the third time, I left thinking that we were the unluckiest team I've ever been around."

By Wednesday, Spurrier saw his defensive backs playing better in practice. Coaches have always preached that you play the way you practice. Apparently, Florida's defensive backs had not yet come across that proverb of football.

"That's the frustrating thing," Spurrier said. "We have seen them play a lot better in practice than in the games. Larry Kennedy is a third-year starter and he hasn't played the way he is capable."

Spurrier was also worried about the weather. Forecasts for game time predicted heavy rain for Louisiana. "In a drizzly rain, we're OK," he noted. "Heavy rains make it sloppy for everybody."

The game would be played at 7:30 that evening so ESPN could televise it nationally. The Gators had to leave Florida to get any attention this week, anyway, since Miami and Florida

State were playing in Tallahassee. The state's newspapers and radio talk shows virtually ignored the Florida-LSU matchup.

While the team worked out at Tiger Stadium on Friday afternoon, Wuerffel felt a twinge in his back. The pain wouldn't go away, and doctors told Spurrier his quarterback was having back spasms. He didn't tell the reporters about Wuerffel's problem.

With the evening starting time, Florida's players and coaches were able to watch Florida State beat Miami 28–10 during the day. That was fine with them. They wanted the Seminoles to be fat, happy, and overconfident when they arrived in Gainesville in late November. As Florida State celebrated on television, the Gators headed off to Tiger Stadium.

Contrary to the midweek forecast, there were no clouds in sight. It was warm, too, a perfect night for football. Even on the bus ride Spurrier didn't know who his quarterback would be. After getting a good rubdown and throwing on the field, Wuerffel told Spurrier he was ready. As it turned out, Florida could have put any of the team's student trainers at quarterback and beat LSU.

Andre Lafleur kicked a twenty-nine-yard field goal early in the game to give the Tigers a 3–0 lead and plenty of hope. Wuerffel then lofted a beautiful thirty-nine-yard touchdown pass to Jack Jackson to begin one of the greatest mismatches of the season. Wuerffel, sore back and all, was flawless, completing fourteen of eighteen passes for 221 yards and four touchdowns. After completing eleven in a row, with the score 37–3 in the third quarter, Wuerffel headed to the bench at Spurrier's orders. There was no use having a starter injured on a night like this. That was the plan, but the reality was that linebacker Monty Grow jogged to the sideline with his right forearm limp at his side. His arm was fractured.

Dean replaced Wuerffel and passed thirty-four yards to Sorola Palmer, a Louisiana native, for another touchdown. It was the latest of the Gators' lightning-quick scores, using only

:06, 2:57, 1:44, :54, :43, and 1:16 on six scoring drives. Eight of the team's touchdown drives for the season had taken less than a minute. "It just seemed like every play worked tonight," Wuerffel observed.

Florida also was practically penalty free for once, committing only six infractions for forty yards. Maybe the lectures were soaking in, or else running sprints for the Stupid Penalty Club weren't as much fun as they were cracked up to be.

With the score at 51–3, Eric Kresser, the third-team quarterback, changed a running play at the line of scrimmage into a passing play. He completed a long pass to set up third-string tailback Terrence Foy's six-yard touchdown run with 1:38 remaining.

"He was eager to make something happen and to make that check," tackle Donnie Young noted about Kresser. "When he came back to the huddle, he said, 'Coach Spurrier's mad at me.' I had to chuckle at that. So we let Terrence Foy run it in for the score."

Spurrier wouldn't stay angry for long. He was relieved the lowly Tigers didn't shred his defense. Yet he almost felt sorry for LSU and Hallman; the 58–3 loss was the worst in LSU history. As the two coaches met at midfield after the game, Spurrier apologized. "It's not a real good feeling when you beat somebody that bad," he commented, standing outside the locker room. "LSU is struggling . . . we all know that. It's not easy for me to win like this, either."

When told it was LSU's worst loss in history, resulting from the final touchdown, he added, "Well . . . we weren't trying to do that. We were just trying to win a ball game."

For the first time in three games, Florida won without the defense apologizing to anyone. This time Zook's boys were punishing and relentless. Freshman Darren Hambrick, just four months out of tiny Dade City Pasco High School, replaced Grow and intercepted two passes. LSU had only fourteen first downs, 263 yards, and didn't sniff the end zone even once. "I am really proud of our defensive team. We had a couple of big interceptions by Darren Hambrick and Lawrence Wright when the game was close," Spurrier added.

Outside the locker room, some players wondered aloud if Grow would get his job back when his arm healed. Hambrick was that impressive. "I think this young guy can play," junior cornerback Larry Kennedy said. "You'll be talking to him a lot." Hambrick stated, "I really didn't think I'd play much this year, but I knew I was ready. I just wanted to get in there. I had played OK in practice and I wanted to step on the field during a game. I've heard freshman-this and freshman-that, and I was tired of it."

Rhett, who gained only seventy-five yards, a poor night for him, loved seeing the freshmen and sophomores contribute. "A lot of young guys played and were able to score touchdowns," he noted. "Everybody played and had fun, so I don't care about my stats. It was easy."

Even though nothing had seemed to come easy for Zook this season, this game was as pleasant as a picnic on the beach at sunset. LSU's offense never had a chance. As he exited the locker room, he showed little emotion and began to deliver the usual straight-faced postgame evaluation. Someone asked, "Ron, show some emotion. Aren't you even happy?" "Hell yes," he replied, breaking into a huge smile. "I can't tell you how happy I am. I can't tell you how excited I am for these players."

Of course, as usual in football, when one coach is happy, another is miserable. By the end of the game, fewer than five thousand LSU fans had remained. Most stayed just to gather around LSU's tunnel that leads to the locker room in order to give Hallman a piece of their mind. Obscenities and insults fell out of the sky like a hundred punts at once as he walked by, never raising his head.

"This is a very embarrassing evening for anyone associated with LSU," he remarked in his Texas drawl. "It's a very testing time for our young men. They whipped us in every category. I don't think they quit . . . but they are battered and beaten mentally, not physically."

LSU SPORTS INFORMATION

Most of LSU head coach Curley Hallman's time in Baton Rouge had been miserable, but no moment was as horrifying as the 58–3 loss to the Gators. The loss was LSU's worst ever.

When asked about Florida's final touchdown, Hallman said there was nothing wrong with it. "It's a waste of energy to say someone ran the score up on you," he replied. "You've got eleven players on the other side of the ball, and their job is to score seven. I don't have any problem with that."

It was one of those games you had to feel sorry for the losing players. To practice the long hours during the spring, summer, and fall must have seemed worthless to them now. "I'll never get used to what happened tonight," commented senior quarterback Chad Loup, who replaced Howard in the second half. "We're really hurting right now."

Emotionally, the Gators didn't need an airplane to fly home in the wake of their most lopsided win in five years. They were already sky high. The next day they would be ranked fourth nationally, behind Florida State, Alabama, and Notre Dame. It was their highest ranking since 1985.

Suddenly the Southeastern Conference looked very strong. Three teams—Alabama, Florida, and Tennessee—ranked in the top ten while Auburn had won all six of its games to jump to number nineteen. The Tigers were next for Florida. "We won't beat Auburn by fifty-five points," Spurrier said. That, it seemed, didn't even need to be said.

7

HEARTBREAK ON THE PLAINS

L EGEND HAS IT THAT AUBURN'S former mascot, the War Eagle, dates back to 1864 and a Civil War battlefield in Virginia. An Auburn student had been wounded that day, and when he regained consciousness and looked around he saw nothing but dust, dirt, bodies in butternut brown uniforms, and a tiny baby eagle. The student recovered from his wounds and also nurtured the fragile eagle back to health, bringing it back to the plains of Auburn when he was sent home. Twenty-eight years later the man attended Auburn's first football game with the eagle watching next to him. After the school scored its first-ever touchdown, the eagle suddenly took to wing and soared above the field, and the fans yelled, "War Eagle!"

Fact or myth, Auburn officials have canonized the story as the origination of the battle cry. The school later changed its mascot to Tigers, but whatever they were called—War Eagles or Tigers—they almost always defeated the Florida Gators on the plains. Auburn had beaten Florida twenty-two times in twenty-seven games at home.

During Spurrier's time as head coach, however, Florida had been a perfect 3–0 against Auburn, including a 31–10 win at Auburn in 1991. Pat Dye, Auburn's long-time coach from

1981 to 1992, was one of those men whom you either loved or hated. There was no in-between. Of course, Auburn fans loved him, and Alabama fans hated him. Auburn's players were even more passionate for the man: they worshiped him.

Florida State coach and Birmingham native Bobby Bowden was one of those who had his differences with Dye. FSU and Auburn had played in 1985, 1986, and 1987 and in the 1989 Sugar Bowl, with the Seminoles winning all but the 1985 game when Bo Jackson ran wild. The schools had two games in 1990 and 1991 remaining on a contract when the SEC announced its plans for expansion. To accommodate the new format each SEC team would be dropping a home-and-home series. Florida dropped Miami. Florida State had been invited to join former Southwest Conference member Arkansas as the two teams that would push the SEC's membership to twelve. When FSU chose to join the Atlantic Coast Conference instead, the SEC brethren felt betrayed. LSU athletic director Joe Dean advocated a ban against scheduling Florida State in any sport—men's or women's.

So when Bowden took his Seminoles to Auburn in 1990, hard feelings were already in place. Florida State jumped to a 17–7 halftime lead and were driving for another score when one of Bowden's famed fumblerooski's backfired. Auburn's Stan White, a freshman quarterback, then led the Tigers on a furious comeback, resulting in a 20–17 upset. Dye later claimed the Seminoles "played dirty" and took cheap shots at Auburn players. Then Auburn announced it would not return to Tallahassee the next year for the final contracted meeting.

That started a brief Bowden-Dye feud that eventually burned out when Dye hired Bowden's son, Tommy, as his offensive coordinator in 1991 after former Heisman Trophy winner Pat Sullivan left to become head coach at Texas Christian.

Regardless of how anyone felt about Dye, they all agreed he knew how to coach college football. He had taken the Tigers to four SEC championships, more than any other school in the 1980s. When he was forced to resign during an NCAA investigation of alleged rules violations, the Auburn community felt as if there had been a death in the family. Following a 21–0 loss to eventual national champion Alabama in 1993, Dye broke into tears and announced his retirement.

Tommy Bowden, too, was without a job when Dye resigned. The Tigers were coming off 5–6 and 5–5–1 seasons; Alabama had just won a national championship and consequently owned the state's recruiting rights. It grew worse when North Carolina State coach Dick Sheridan turned down Auburn's offer to succeed Dye.

In the mother of all ironies, Auburn found the answer to its problems up the road in Birmingham, at tiny Samford College. Terry Wilson Bowden, the third of Bobby's four sons, had prepared his whole life to interview for such a job. He had learned not only his coaching but his communication skills from his father. And if people thought Ronald Reagan was the Great Communicator, they had never met the Bowden family.

Terry Bowden attended law school at Oxford, not to learn law or to become a lawyer, a judge, or a professor, but solely to have a more impressive coaching résumé. "I thought someday it might impress the right people and give me an edge for a job," he said. To illustrate how calculating he is, when Auburn's search committee contacted him for an interview, Bowden tried to learn something about each member of the committee just to have something to discuss with each. It worked. "When I left the interview, I called my wife and said, 'I just gave the interview of my life . . . if I don't get this job, it wasn't meant to be,'" he recounted.

It was meant to be for Terry Bowden to be Auburn's twenty-fourth head coach on December 17, 1992. It also meant that the Florida Gators now had to face two Bowdens every season.

At first, the Tigers didn't take to the new ways of the new coach. Bowden was just thirty-seven years old, but his discipline seemed old-fashioned to most of Auburn's players. Unlike Dye, he wouldn't allow them to wear earrings. Unlike Dye, he wouldn't allow them to have beards or mustaches. Unlike Dye, he wouldn't allow another sport to interfere with spring practice for a player. Nobody was exempt. Coaches also could not wear cowboy boots or jeans, which had been Dye's favorite apparel during the week.

"With the amount of media coverage we get, this university is seen through these players," he contended. "Love is important, but on fourth-and-one you need discipline."

Bowden played no favorites. Orlando Parker, the team's leading receiver in Dye's final season, wanted to skip spring practice to run track. Bowden told him to practice football during the week because he was an Auburn student on a football scholarship. Parker could run track on Saturdays. "He would say I kicked him off; I would say he quit," Bowden asserted. "Hey, if you can't get along with me, you can't get along."

Bowden's situation was nearly the opposite from Spurrier's when Spurrier took over at Florida. Spurrier was the popular legend returning to save the sinking ship. Bowden was a pirate.

Offensive tackle Wayne Grady compared things to a broken marriage. "It was like when your dad or mom marries a new spouse," he said. "We were all here in the first place because of Coach Dye."

What was peculiar was the fact that Bobby Bowden allowed his Seminoles to wear whatever they wanted: earrings, beards, or slogans shaved in their hair. Usually, a son takes a more modern approach than the father. "This isn't Florida State," Terry Bowden said. "Those things aren't right for Auburn University. Here, they would consider [Bobby Bowden] *undisciplined*."

Bowden took no prisoners when it came to recruiting. When he accepted the job, he called FSU recruiting coordinator Ronnie Cottrell and told him to stay out of Alabama. He wasn't joking. When he went head-to-head with the Seminoles for Lewis Battle of Roanoke, Alabama, he referred to his father's seniority by telling Battle that Florida had a mandatory retirement age of sixty-five. Bobby Bowden was sixty-three.

"I told him, 'I hope you are going to play the first two years 'cause old Dad's going to retire at sixty-five,'" he recalled. Battle now plays collegiate football as an Auburn Tiger.

Bowden did take his father's advice before naming the most important assistant coach for most staffs—a defensive coordinator. "He told me one of the best ones he had ever faced was already at Auburn," Bowden said. Wayne Hall was Pat Dye's right-hand man and one of the nation's best at preparing defenses and teaching fundamentals. But now that his friend and mentor was no longer head coach, would Hall want to stay and coach under a man six years his junior? After all, Auburn had interviewed Hall for the head coaching job and turned him down.

"I didn't think he would stay, but I met with him and told him I wanted him," Bowden declared. Two days later Hall decided to stay. "I love the place," he said. "Where would I go anyway?"

Hall chatted with Dye, who remained at the school as a fundraiser, several times every week. "His health is better than ever," he announced on the Monday before the Gators were due in town. "Most people don't know this, but the man had liver cancer. Fortunately, the chemotherapy got it all."

Hall loved going against an offensive mind like Spurrier's. He figured the Gators wouldn't be patient on offense, and Auburn could force a few turnovers with a good pass rush.

He chuckled about his relationship with Bowden. "He's easy to work for," he said. "But we haven't lost yet. Then I'll really know what he's like."

It was obvious that Bowden's disciplined formula and his emphasis on running the football were working for Auburn, which had won all six of its games. In recent years, Dye had let the offense get too complex. Quarterback Stan White, who had upset Bowden's father's team three years earlier, had taken a beating and looked confused when he tried to read defenses during his sophomore and junior seasons. The Tigers had one of the nation's best running backs in James Bostic, so Bowden built the offense around him, not White.

Again, it was an un-Bowden-like approach. "My ego's not big enough to think I am as good as Bobby Bowden," he commented. "As far as I am concerned he is the best in the business. This is a very conservative approach to complement the defense and the kicking game."

It was something Spurrier should have thought about while his defense was struggling. Even Hall admitted that. "Some guys just like to look good by throwing the ball all over the place," Hall said. "If you go 6–5 and throw a lot of passes, you look better than if you go 6–5 and have a boring offense. Perception sometimes is everything."

In August, Bowden had claimed he would be happy with a 6–5 record in his first year. He said he only wanted improvement, even if it was only a one-game improvement; Auburn had been 5–6 the year before.

With six victories already under his belt, he laughed, "That doesn't mean I'll be happy if we lose our last five games." As good as they were, the Tigers wouldn't be seen by the nation, since the NCAA had placed them on two years' probation before the season. The school had a choice of which year to take the one-year television ban. "We had to get it out of the way," Bowden claimed. "You can't recruit if players think they're not going to be seen on television."

He leaned back in his massive modern office and gazed at his huge desk. The Oval Office may not be as large or as plush. Bowden chuckled at the thought that this office was four times the size of his famous father's. "Dad couldn't believe this place when he first saw it," he said. "This is some room, isn't it? But you know, I still think of this as Coach Dye's office."

Dye even had an escape stairway built off the rear balcony. To escape from what? "The media," Bowden observed. "He thought of everything. Pat Dye built this place. Sometimes I get sad thinking he'll never sit in here again."

The sadness never lasts. Coaching is a fleeting business, even for a man like Dye. In the 1980s, as the post–Paul "Bear" Bryant era began, Dye could have run for governor and won. That's because Ray Perkins and Bill Curry coached at Alabama. Bowden gazed out his huge windows onto Auburn's practice field, where his team would begin preparing for Florida in less than two hours.

"I told these players to just believe in me," he added. "They had given so much and gotten so little in return. I wanted them to give me a chance, to see what would happen."

Tommy Bowden walked into the office, asking his brother about some tickets for friends. Terry had retained him, not as offensive coordinator but as quarterbacks coach. "I run the offensive show," he claimed. "I am like Dad that way. But I'll tell you one thing, Tommy Bowden is twice the coach I am. That man went through a lot the last few years here."

Bowden turned his attention to Florida. The game was bigger to him because of his roots. "I saw my dad lose to them six straight years," he said. "It ate him up. You don't think this game is big to me?"

Stan White, criticized by the media and booed by the fans in recent seasons, felt like a new man in Bowden's system. The emphasis on the running game had taken pressure off of him. Still, he didn't want anybody to get the impression that Bowden had waved a magic wand for the Tigers suddenly to become winners. Sitting on a couch outside the team's cafeteria, he reminded some reporters that Auburn would always have talented players regardless of who was sitting in the head coach's office. "Coach Dye didn't leave the car with an empty gas tank," he concluded.

The Gators may have forgotten that fact the week before the game. They had trounced Auburn three straight years, and players usually carry over a feeling of what to expect from season to season. They knew that the Tigers were 6–0, but Auburn had yet to meet a team with a winning record.

On Monday afternoon Spurrier was concerned that left tackle Reggie Green, a hulking six-foot-six, 300-pound sophomore, would miss the game with a sprained right ankle. "The trainers said we should keep him out of practice," he warned. "We won't know until late in the week."

Another slight off-the-field distraction warranted an investigation. Gerald Owens, a Florida State defensive lineman, had been declared an ineligible player by the NCAA in August. This week he announced plans to file a suit against Florida. Owens had signed a letter of intent with Florida in 1988, when Galen Hall was coach, but contended he had never attended classes. Florida officials reported that he did attend courses in the fall of 1988, meaning his five years of eligibility had expired. Owens also claimed that Florida defensive line coach Jerry "Red" Anderson, a former Gators player and a teammate of Spurrier's from 1964 to 1966, had given him six thousand dollars during his recruitment, which Anderson denied. Owens also alleged that Florida had no interest in his eligibility at FSU until the Gators coaching staff had heard that he had played well in the Seminoles' 1993 spring game.

Meanwhile, Florida athletic director Jeremy Foley was organizing a massive telecast of the Auburn game at Florida Field. He had to secure permission from the NCAA to show the game on closed-circuit television since Auburn was on probation and could not appear on television. Foley hired a company to place a giant Jumbotron screen in the south end zone of Florida Field.

The next day, Tuesday, when Spurrier joined a conference call with the Alabama media, Bowden was in the conference room below his office. He listened as Spurrier intoned, "It should be a game to remember for a long time."

Bowden followed him and spoke with his usual machine-gun pace. "Florida is more talented than us. We'll have to play our best. Can we beat them? No, if talent is the only factor. Right now, we are just a good football team playing great football. Can we play with them? Can we stay with them? I don't know. We have everything to gain and nothing to lose. We aren't ranked number four in the country. They are."

That was Bowden's way of placing the pressure squarely on Florida's shoulder pads. When he had finished, Auburn athletic director Mike Lude announced the Auburn Loyalty Fund, a money-raising campaign to replace the revenue lost for not appearing on television. Auburn had sent letters to ten thousand season-ticket holders asking for a hundred dollars each.

On Thursday, Spurrier said the pregame buildup for the game of unbeatens was overshadowing the game that would be on television, Tennessee at Alabama. The two games guaranteed that the state of Alabama would be the focus of college football for the weekend. "One of those teams has a loss," Spurrier noted, getting in a jab at the Volunteers. "The battle of the unbeatens will be in Auburn."

Spurrier denied that Florida, now 5–0, was overconfident. "The only time to get full of yourself is January 2," he said.

Auburn wouldn't have to wait until then. The Tigers' probation would prevent their season from extending into December. A bowl berth, which would have been wrapped up by beating Florida, was prohibited. "You know though, it really has brought this campus and the players together," Bowden observed. "Everyone expects them to win, not us."

Spurrier usually regarded point spreads as entertainment only. "I wouldn't think we would be favored by much," he suggested. His team was favored by seven points. "We know it will be the loudest place we will play all season. It should be an exciting game. Too bad it's not on television."

He was right on both counts. It was loud and it was exciting. If the 85,214 fans at Jordan-Hare Stadium were polled, many might have said that it was the most entertaining game they had ever seen.

At first it appeared the Gators would run away with the game, jumping to a 10–0 lead and threatening to score again. Wuerffel then dropped back from the Tigers' ten-yard line and made the biggest mistake of his season. He threw to the right, into the hands of defensive back Calvin Jackson. Jackson took the pass at the four-yard line and started to run down the left sideline. With each step the roar of the crowd crescendoed. By the time he reached the end zone, the stadium was shaking. Spurrier was furious. He had wanted Wuerffel to throw to the left to Chris Doering. Instead, Wuerffel misread the hand signal from the sideline and was trying for Willie Jackson on the right.

As he had shown against Kentucky, the interception didn't rattle Wuerffel. He shrugged if off and passed twenty-three yards to Aubrey Hill with only thirteen seconds remaining in the half to give the team a 27–14 lead. The crowd was silent now. Wuerffel had passed for 252 yards and Errict Rhett had rushed for 129 in the first half. Foley walked through the press box, beaming at the news that eighty-five hundred fans were at Florida Field watching the game in the rain. The school had spent $65,000 on the project and needed eight thousand fans to break even. "I'll bet they're having a great time down there in the rain," he said. "That would be almost as much fun as it is to be here."

Bowden told his team in the locker room, "Don't quit trying. Don't stop. Something good is going to happen. Trust me." Somehow he was right. It seemed Florida was one play from knocking Auburn out of the game. One play from turning this game into another rout like the lopsided affair in Baton Rouge a week earlier. But that one play never happened.

Auburn drove to the Gators' ten-yard line early in the third quarter, but defensive tackle Mark Campbell sacked White and then Scott Etheridge missed a thirty-five-yard field goal. Florida still had momentum; the Gators still controlled the game. Florida moved to its forty-nine-yard line. Facing third-and-one, Wuerffel's pass to Harrison Houston was knocked down. A completion here and an ensuing touchdown would have put Auburn away for good. But from that point on little went right for the Gators.

White threw a twenty-three-yard touchdown pass and was driving the Tigers again as a wild fourth quarter was about to begin. On fourth-and-one at Florida's four-yard line, tailback James Bostic took a pitch and ran left. Florida linebacker Dexter Daniels shot through a gap and had him by the jersey three yards deep into the backfield. Just as it appeared that Florida had held, Bostic broke loose and trotted into the end zone. Auburn led 28–27 and the stadium was rocking again.

Hall knew Spurrier well. He had predicted that if the game were close or if Florida were trailing, Spurrier would be impatient and neglect the running game. He was right. After Rhett broke a sixteen-yard run to Auburn's thirty-two-yard line, Auburn called a time-out. Hall ordered a blitz, thinking Spurrier might try to score on the next play. As Wuerffel dropped back, he was hit from the left but still tried to loft a pass downfield. "Harrison was open and it would have been a touchdown," Wuerffel would say later. Cornerback Chris Shelling intercepted the wobbly pass and ran sixty-five yards to Florida's nine-yard line. On the next play, receiver Frankie Sanders scored untouched on a reverse. Now the score was 35–27, and Jordan-Hare was in a frenzy.

But again Wuerffel showed the poise he had demonstrated in the Kentucky game. It was the main reason Spurrier loved the kid. He never panicked. He never yelled at his team-mates or screamed for protection in the huddle. He just calmly called the plays. He threw a thirteen-yard touchdown pass to Jack Jackson and then a soft, touch pass to Willie Jackson for the two-point conversion.

The score was now 35–35 with 5:44 left. Suddenly the overcast skies unloaded a constant drizzle. The Florida Field fans were also being rained upon several hundred miles away. In all fairness, the lords of football decided that the Auburn fans might as well be wet, too.

What followed was the most controversial play of the season. On third-and-eight at Auburn's forty-two, White passed to the left sideline for Sanders, who was straddling the white sideline chalk and the green grass of the playing field. As the ball whizzed over his head, free safety Lawrence Wright hit Sanders from behind, causing the Auburn receiver to plow into Coach Zook, taking him to the turf. The crowd roared and field judge Bill Bowdoin threw a yellow flag and signaled a personal foul on Wright. Spurrier argued, but Auburn now had a first down and a chance to win the game with a field goal.

With 1:21 remaining, Auburn faced a fourth-and-three at Florida's twenty-four. Etheridge, a 148-pound kicker, trotted onto the field with his kicking tee. He had won several games in the last minute for Pat Dye, now he would do the same for Terry Bowden in the biggest game of the new coach's life. His kick was perfect. Several Florida players fell to their knees while Auburn's fans went wild. White, the holder, turned to Etheridge. "I love you! You're the best kicker in the nation!" he screamed.

When it was finally over, the Tigers hoisted Bowden on their shoulders and carried him onto the field. He was pumping his fist like a boxer who had just won the heavyweight title. Zook started to walk to the locker room. "Was that a good call on

ED JONES/AUBURN SPORTS INFORMATION

Auburn tailback James Bostic breaks through a hole against the Gators. Moments later he eluded the grasp of linebacker Dexter Daniels on a four-yard run that gave the Tigers a 28–27 lead.

the penalty?" someone asked. He just stared blankly, never responding. The Gators trudged to the locker room like zombies.

Fifteen minutes later, Spurrier emerged and tried to speak over the Auburn band with his hoarse voice. "I hate for it to be decided on a close call like that," he began, referring to the penalty on Wright. "I am not going to stand here and say it was a bad call for you guys. But our guy hit Frankie Sanders as the ball got there."

Wright was sitting on the team bus when assistant sports information director Joel Glass climbed aboard. "Get out here, you have to talk to the press about this," he urged.

Terry Bowden replaced legendary Pat Dye and guided the Auburn Tigers to a perfect 11–0 record. His biggest victory came in a 38–35 shocker over the Gators.

AUBURN SPORTS INFORMATION

Wright couldn't believe it. The secondary had been picked on earlier and was told to become more aggressive. Now they were being penalized for being too aggressive. And the penalty wasn't just fifteen yards; this was the season. No team wins a national championship with one loss anymore.

"Everybody thought it was a bad call," Wright noted, wiping the sweat off his forehead. "That's the consequences when you play in somebody else's house. I was just trying to make something happen and I would do the same thing all over again."

About thirty yards away, Sanders sat down on a cement wall outside Auburn's locker room and laughed about the play. "I think it was a good hit," he said. "The ball was just an inch off my fingers. I still didn't know if we were going to win after that." His opinion that he didn't think a penalty was justified was stunning. Most players never disagree with an official's call when it helps their team.

Bowden's game plan had worked perfectly, although it never would have generated the win without the two interceptions. He had wanted to use his running game in the first half, hoping to stay close. But Auburn was behind by thirteen points. He would let White throw for most of the second half. His quarterback finished twenty-three of thirty-five for 267 yards and no interceptions. "It was the perfect game plan," White commented. "We wanted to run to set up the pass, but we almost got too far behind."

Bowden was inside a trailer, addressing the media. "I wanted so much for these players to feel the good part of college football," he announced. "They haven't felt that for a while. All I can say is that this is a big day for Auburn."

Across the way, Rhett was sitting on a folding chair. The whole scene was a nightmarish deja vu to him. Five years earlier, Rhett and his West Hollywood High team had led Fort Lauderdale Dillard High by a score of 19–0. Dillard had James Bostic, who had broken free of Dexter Daniels to give Auburn the 28–27 lead. Dillard also had Calvin Jackson, who had intercepted Wuerffel for Auburn's first touchdown. And Dillard had Frankie Sanders, whom Wright had hit on the crucial penalty. Dillard rallied to beat Rhett's team 20–19 on that night five years earlier.

The Florida running back had just gained a career-high 196 yards on twenty-two carries. Yet he was miserable. "It's ironic," Rhett observed. "It's just like high school all over again. I've known those guys all my life. Some of them live down the street from me. Now they've got bragging rights. I'll never get the chance to play Auburn again. It hurts. It doesn't matter how many yards I had, we didn't win. It was my last chance to beat them. This one will last forever. God, we should have put them away."

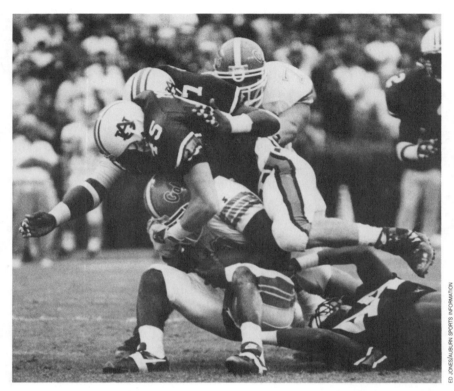

One of the rare times Errict Rhett was swarmed under at Auburn. He finished the day with a career-best 196 yards on twenty-two carries.

Spurrier knew the same thing. He brushed off questions about losing a possible national championship. "Our first goal is to win our division," he replied. Now he just wanted to get the heck out of Auburn and get home. The flight was short, but it must have seemed like it took forever. All coaches relive every play gone bad during the days following a loss. Florida had a week off before meeting Georgia. That meant Spurrier had even more time to relive the final crucial plays of the Auburn game.

There was one he couldn't ignore. Sunday morning, when he watched the tape of Wright's penalty, he was more convinced than ever that it was an unjustified call. "I don't think it should be called in that situation unless it is obvious," he commented. On Monday, he called Bobby Gaston, a friendly insurance executive and the conference's supervisor of officials. "Have you seen the tape yet?" Spurrier asked. Gaston hadn't. Since Auburn's games were not televised, he had to await receipt of the tapes. "If [Spurrier] calls, I know he has a problem," Gaston said the next day. "He isn't just calling to chat." Gaston had warned his officials to take into account the score and time of the game when making judgment calls. "I've told my guys over and over again to use good horse sense when it gets down to the critical point of the game," he said. "If it's going to be pass interference, it had better be a good one." Now Gaston was worried that Bowdoin had blown the call. But even after the express packages arrived, the tapes still weren't there.

Spurrier tinkered with the defense again in the meantime. This time he moved wide receiver Aubrey Hill to free safety and backup running back Tony Davis to strong safety, or "bandit" back as Florida calls the position. "These guys are tremendous athletes and we've got to get them on the field," Spurrier stated. "We didn't move them just for show . . . we expect them to play a lot for the rest of the season." Davis wasn't exactly pleased. "At least he let us know in advance, which was nice," he said. "And at least I am out there on the field," Spurrier concluded. "We don't really ask them, 'Do you mind switching positions?' We don't worry about their feelings in times like this."

Finally, Gaston received the tapes on Thursday. He saw the play from two angles. After reviewing both repeatedly, he announced, "It's in the eyes of the beholder on this one. This is strictly a judgment call. I can see why he called it. I really can. He thought the foul was there. I don't think the defensive back made any attempt to let up. It was a hard lick one and a half to two steps after the ball went by."

Spurrier didn't see it that way, but he knew his opinion didn't count for much. Winning every game takes some luck, and Florida ran out of it at Auburn. War Eagle luck had triumphed. Spurrier was right on one count, it was a game to remember, although that was no consolation. It was time to get ready for Georgia.

8

THE HATED BULLDOGS

THE TWO WEEKS BETWEEN the Auburn and Georgia games seemed to last forever for the Gators. Most coaches and players look forward to off weeks following a win or when minor bumps and bruises need a little extra time to heal. But only one thing atones for a loss, especially a heartbreaker like the defeat at Auburn, and that is playing another game and winning it.

Tennessee was shadowing Florida closely. The Vols had tied with Alabama and also faced an off week, licking their wounds before facing South Carolina. But Florida held a half-game lead on the Volunteers. The Gators could afford to tie another game to make it to the conference championship game in Birmingham, but a loss would put Tennessee in control. "It doesn't look like Tennessee is going to lose again," Spurrier noted. "So we've got to win 'em all."

On Sunday morning, eight days after the Auburn game and six prior to the meeting with Georgia, Spurrier let the team and the media know that he was no longer coaching just one side of the football. He would become more involved with the defensive planning and decisions on personnel. Many saw this as Spurrier's blaming the defense and

Zook for the Auburn loss. But if there ever was such a thing as a total team loss in which the kicking game and both offense and defense contributed equally, it was Florida's loss at Auburn. Since the game was not on television because of Auburn's probation, only the fans at the stadium saw the game.

Two plays accounted for a twenty-eight-point swing in Auburn's favor. Both were offensive plays: Wuerffel's interceptions. Essentially, the Gators' defense gave up twenty-four points, not thirty-eight. If Wuerffel had thrown touchdown passes instead of interceptions on those two plays (receivers were open on each although there was no pass protection on the second), Florida would have won 49–24. A rout. A whipping. All because of two plays.

"I am responsible for the defense," Spurrier announced Sunday. "I have more to say over there, and we are trying to challenge them to play better. I want these players more accountable to me. We won't play the same coverages or the same people we have been playing, but I am not going to give away our game plan."

Reminded of Wuerffel's interceptions and the subsequent Auburn points, he replied, "You get to the point where you run out of patience. We didn't put the new guys over there just to practice."

By Monday the Gators were ready to play Georgia right then and there on the practice field. As rivalries go, there are mild ones and some that turn hot and cold from year to year. Michigan and Ohio State respect each other. UCLA and USC have to share the same city, even if it is as large as Los Angeles. Oklahoma and Nebraska even get along at times. Texas-Texas A&M comes close, but for the most part, Florida-Georgia or Georgia-Florida, depending on which side of the border you call home, is not a friendly rivalry. It is rarely even respectful. The forthcoming game had all the ingredients necessary for a nasty football game, plus a little honest hatred.

The two schools have never agreed on much, including the win-loss record of the seventy-year-old series. Or is it seventy-one years old? Florida officials contend that the first game played in 1904 was played by a club team from Gainesville. Georgia counts it as a 52–0 victory. Florida does not count it as a meeting.

Nevertheless, the schools have met in Jacksonville's massive Gator Bowl on the banks of the Saint Johns River since 1933, except for 1943 when World War II prevented the two schools from playing football. While Florida was a willing participant, Georgia has owned the series, winning forty-three of the seventy games. Or forty-four of seventy-one if you go by Georgia's records. The Bulldogs always found a way to beat the Gators, even when they had less talent, even while they were on losing streaks, even when Florida was loaded. Even when Florida was number one, the Black-and-Red usually left Jacksonville with a smile on their faces. Florida fans departed year after year with a fresh taste of crow.

From 1964 to 1966 the Spurrier-led Gators won only once, 14–10 in 1965. During Spurrier's senior season, his Heisman Trophy–winning season, Florida entered the game with a perfect 7–0 record, but Georgia won 27–10. Some Gators watchers believe Spurrier wants revenge each season for that 1966 defeat. "Georgia beat him his senior year, and he looks back and gets fired up for this game," guard Jim Watson noted.

In 1975 Florida had a 7–1 record and a good shot at its first conference championship. The Gators were dominating the Bulldogs but only had a 7–3 lead in the fourth quarter. Georgia executed a tight end pass from Richard Applebee to Gene Washington for an eighty-yard touchdown to win the game. It was the Bulldogs' only first down of the second half.

The next year Florida had a 6–1 record and led 27–13 at the half. Georgia won 42–27.

In 1982 Herschel Walker left his large footprints all over the Gators in a 44–0 rout. That was a Florida team that entered the game with a 5–2 record and hopes for an SEC championship.

In 1985 the Gators had won at Auburn 14–10, knocking future Heisman winner Bo Jackson out of the game, and arrived in Jacksonville with a 7–0–1 record. They were ranked number one by the Associated Press for the first time in their history. The final score was Georgia 24, Florida 3.

Yet none of those defeats were as bad to Florida fans as what is known as the Lindsay Scott Game. In 1980 Florida had a 21–19 lead, and Georgia had the ball on its own seven-yard line late in the game. Some Gators already were celebrating what would be a 7–1 start to the season. Then Georgia quarterback Buck Belue dumped a short pass to Scott over the middle. Scott ran to the left, cut down the sideline, and continued running. He never stopped. The result was a ninety-three-yard touchdown.

Tickets are split fifty-fifty between the two schools, with the stadium divided into four sections, two for Florida fans, two for Georgia. If there is any single factor why this series has been so heated and so intense, this has to be it. More than forty-one thousand Florida fans travel to Jacksonville. And more than forty-one thousand Georgia fans do the same. They share the same hotels, restaurants, and bars. In the usual home-and-home rivalries of college football, most opposing fans don't mix. Therefore, it is much easier not to get your face rubbed into an embarrassing loss. Unfortunately for Florida's fans, the games aren't played in Athens, Georgia, or Gainesville, Florida. Every year there have been fistfights, drunken verbal battles, and insulting slogans painted on car windows.

Wuerffel remembered his first exposure to the series with the 1992 bus ride to the Gator Bowl: "It seemed every group of fans we passed were saluting us as number one. But each group was using a different finger." All the pushing and shoving is not exclusive to the fans. Georgia and Florida players battle between the whistles or under the piles where no referee can see. Following the 1992 game, Florida quarterback Shane Matthews lifted up his jersey to display a bite mark in his back the size of an apple. The dental imprint matched the choppers of linebacker Randall Godfrey. "That's why they call them the Bulldogs—they bite," Spurrier told Matthews. "If you can't get ready to play in that atmosphere," Spurrier warned his team, "then you just can't get ready to play."

When Spurrier arrived at Florida in 1990, Georgia had won fifteen of the previous nineteen meetings. He heard the normal complaints from fans and boosters about wanting to move the game from Jacksonville. That bothered him, but not as much as the myth that Georgia had won because they had "wanted it" more than Florida.

"It had gotten to the point that Georgia fans, players, and coaches regarded the Gator Bowl as their home stadium for the annual game with the Gators," he wrote in his book *Gators*. That galled Spurrier. Last time he checked, Jacksonville was a city in F-L-O-R-I-D-A. The place was called the *Gator Bowl*. Since then he has repeated his stance a million times: Florida should hope, pray, and beg to keep the game in Jacksonville; it should never be changed.

Spurrier's biggest job at Florida was changing the mindset, the psychology, and the mental barriers that every Gators team had adopted for years. They had never beaten Georgia, so why did they think they ever would? When the players arrived as freshmen, they heard how Georgia had dominated the series. Then they watched upperclassmen fall into the inferiority trap, which suppresses any confidence built up during the season. If the Gators fell behind Georgia early, a here-we-go-again attitude took control.

In the terms of Florida football history, the Gators' 38–7 trouncing of the Bulldogs in 1990 in Spurrier's first season as head coach was one of the biggest wins ever, if not the biggest. It erased the barriers and it sent a message to Georgia, too, that times were a-changin'. Following the 1990 game, Spurrier's Gators have never lost to Ray Goff's Bulldogs, with wins of 45–13 in 1991 and 26–24 in 1992.

The 1992 game was especially notable for the Gators, since they did to Georgia what had been done to them dozens of times before on the same field: they upset the better team. The Bulldogs had entered the game with a 6–1 record, and tailback Garrison Hearst was in the running for the Heisman Trophy. Florida, which had been destroyed by Mississippi State and Tennessee, held on to win by two points. Hearst was limited to forty-one yards.

After the game, Florida's players and Georgia's fans came together in an ugly confrontation. Several of the players gave a Heisman Trophy pose and then fell to the ground, mocking Hearst. Some taunted Georgia's sections. Then bottles flew from the stands like confetti during a ticker tape parade, only bottles hurt more than confetti. For a few minutes, it appeared that a riot might break out as Georgia fans tried to get to the field to wring a Gator neck or two. "They started the whole thing," Watson explained. "We were celebrating with our fans as we always do, and they came down there and started saying stuff to us."

It didn't hurt that Spurrier and Georgia coach Ray Goff didn't get along. What started their differences isn't known, at least by anyone other than Spurrier and Goff. But the fact is that it seems to get worse each year. Goff and Spurrier are the Hatfields and the McCoys all rolled into one neat coaching feud.

Spurrier was tired of seeing recruiting publications that touted Goff's classes as superior to his. Following Florida's 45–13 victory over Georgia in 1991, he decided to sink the hatchet a little deeper. "I keep reading how Florida always had the better players but Georgia always wins all the games because they want it more," he noted. "According to *Georgia Football Report,* Georgia has more talent than we do. They have finished first in recruiting the last five years. If they are that good, you have to wonder what happened to them after they got to Georgia."

A few reporters immediately scurried to the Georgia locker room to get Goff's reaction. He fumed and started to head toward Florida's locker room to confront Spurrier when he changed his mind. The anticipated confrontation would have to wait for another day.

The next year, Spurrier reported Goff to the conference office after the Georgia coach made one visit more than was allowed per recruit. The student, linebacker Dexter Daniels, was from Valdosta, Georgia, and he eventually signed with Florida. Goff was furious, citing a gentlemen's agreement that conference coaches contact the violator first to work out such a difference. "I wasn't here when they made that gentlemen's agreement," Spurrier retorted. "I never knew about it, not that I would have stuck to it anyway."

Following the 1992 season, Goff apparently vented his frustration about Spurrier to a friend, saying that he wished the two of them could have a few minutes alone in some back alley. This wasn't that inflammatory and nobody who knew anything about the two coaches ever doubted that Goff would say something like that. Of course it was picked up by a sportswriter and was printed as factual. When asked about it, Goff replied, "I won't say I said it and I won't say I didn't. But if it was said it wasn't said at a public affair. No writer heard me say it." Not exactly a strong denial. "Unfortunately," he continued, "a lot has been made about Coach Spurrier's relationship with me, or lack thereof."

At his Tuesday media luncheon Spurrier was asked why he didn't get along with Goff. "I don't know," he remarked. "He must be saying funny things about me." The room broke into laughter. Spurrier smiled broadly and ran his hand through his hair before breaking into laughter himself.

Ironically, Spurrier's and Goff's backgrounds aren't very different. Each quarterbacked at the school where he now coached, although Spurrier was more honored and successful. Spurrier was more popular in Florida than Goff was in

Georgia. Spurrier is also more secure as head coach. Florida would never think of running him out of Gainesville. Goff, after a 1–4 start in 1993, was as popular in Athens as Sherman was in Atlanta. Then again, maybe they weren't alike after all.

One thing was for sure, the old head-knocking Georgia-Florida games of the past were becoming a distant memory. Saturday's game appeared to be a matchup right out of the Pac Ten or the Western Athletic Conference. There would be plenty of passing. Georgia quarterback Eric Zeier had passed for 544 yards against Southern Mississippi, 379 against Vanderbilt, and 425 against Kentucky in the three previous games. After starting 1–4, the Bulldogs were riding a winning streak that evened their record. That alone provided the confidence and momentum they needed to beat Florida, which had dropped to number ten in the Associated Press poll after the loss to Auburn.

In these last three games, Goff and his offensive coaches had decided to scrap the running game almost completely. For comparison, when Goff played quarterback at Georgia his statistics were amazingly tiny next to Zeier's gaudy numbers. He passed for 322 yards in 1976 when he was named the SEC's Player of the Year. Zeier had done that in one half of one game this season. "We haven't gone into a game thinking we are going to throw it forty or fifty times," Goff noted. "It's just worked out that way for us."

Spurrier told Zook to have his defensive backs play deep. If in doubt, just turn and run. "They certainly will throw it a lot against us," he said. "The guy is really hot and they're going to go with the hot guy, not the running game," Zook added. "Their strength supposedly is our weakness."

By late Monday afternoon, defensive end Cameron Davis, who hadn't played much in his collegiate career, leaked Spurrier's new defensive scheme to the media: the Gators planned to use at least four and sometimes five defensive backs against Zeier and Georgia, instead of the usual eight-man front. They had worked on the new coverages during the off week, but Spurrier didn't want anyone to know about the change until game time.

Spurrier was in his office when he learned that Davis had discussed the new defensive strategy with the press. Slamming his pencil down on his desk, he lashed out, "Shit! That's the damn problem around here. We let the players talk to the press before we coaches talk to them! Well, I can put a stop to that." This, on top of having to suspend reserve linebacker Anthony Riggins for making obscene gestures to the crowd at the Auburn game, made for a grouchy head football coach that day.

Then a sportswriter entered Spurrier's office wanting to do a story on the Gators' unbalanced offense. Florida had a run/pass ratio of 35/52 at Kentucky and 27/50 at Auburn. In the other four games, they had a perfect 142/142 ratio. Was that just coincidence?

"No, we probably have gotten a little lopsided in some games," Spurrier responded. "But it's easy to look back after a loss and second-guess plays and think about what you would do different. I do it after every loss."

Florida was averaging forty passes per game, which would shatter the school's season record. Spurrier had called five running plays on twenty-eight plays on Auburn's side of the field. Five of twenty-eight. Those plays, along with a scramble by Wuerffel, gained 74 yards (12.3 yards per carry). "I call the plays by feel or by what the defense is doing," Spurrier explained, defending his methods. "I guarantee that if we score, the run/pass ratio doesn't look so bad."

Errict Rhett, for one, agreed that the offense was too dependent on the pass. After Monday night's practice, he stopped in the O'Connell Center parking lot and rolled his eyes at the subject. "You know I'd get in trouble if I said what I really feel," he told a sportswriter. "Hell yes, we should be running the ball more. We would have beaten Auburn by two touchdowns. I want the ball as many times as they want to give it to me. Just give me the damn ball. I wish somebody would tell him that."

The next day, Georgia and Florida were relaying their thoughts on who had the advantage in the Gator Bowl. "We feel it's our second home," Florida offensive tackle Jason Odom said. "We love the place, why shouldn't we?" Watson said. "We haven't lost there."

Goff scoffed, telling the Florida media Tuesday afternoon, "That's where the game always is played and that's where we'll show up Saturday. I don't think it's a home field advantage for either team. Remember, that place has a special feeling for me because that's where I got the job." True, Georgia officials told Goff following the 1988 Gator Bowl against Michigan State that he would replace Vince Dooley. Goff then was the quarterbacks coach and his promotion surprised many who thought he wasn't ready to become a head coach. Goff got in one final shot at Florida: "I've had more success there than failure." Goff was 3–0 against the Gators as a player and 1–0 as a coach before Spurrier arrived. Now he stood 4–3 overall. By the same token, Spurrier was 4–2.

Georgia fans now started to complain about the problems they had encountered in Jacksonville since the 1990 game. Price gouging and poor stadium conditions headed the list. And the complaints grew louder and more frequent with each Bulldog loss to Florida. "They didn't complain about all that when they beat us ten out of twelve years," Florida assistant athletic director Norm Carlson observed. Legitimate or not, Jacksonville's merchants were being lectured by city officials who desperately wanted to keep the game in the Gator Bowl. The contract was set to expire in 1994. City officials went so far as to make sure that merchants displayed red and black when Georgia was the designated home team during odd-numbered years, even if the proprietor were a Florida

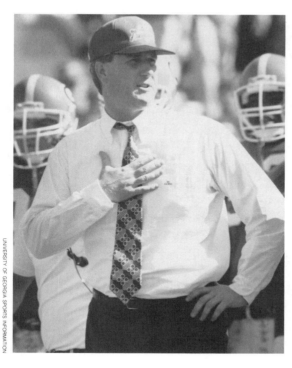

Georgia head coach Ray Goff and Florida's Steve Spurrier are not the best of friends. Thus far Goff's Bulldogs have not been able to beat Spurrier's Gators.

UNIVERSITY OF GEORGIA SPORTS INFORMATION

graduate. Similarly, orange and blue were to be shown when Florida was the home team during even-numbered years.

No chamber of commerce in the world, however, can control the weather. When players and fans awakened Saturday morning, they were in for a shock. A tropical storm had camped over Florida, and the rain poured out of the dark sky. This was no little drizzle; this was an old-fashioned constant downpour. On the fifteen-mile bus ride from the team's hotel to the Gator Bowl, Spurrier knew he had to change his game plan. It's tough to throw and catch in the wind and rain. He figured the game would ride on Number 33's shoulders. Rhett was thinking the same as soon as he peered out his hotel window. Whatever it took, including poor weather, he was ready to run with the football as many times as necessary.

Early in the game, Wuerffel wasn't loving the weather so much. Having problems gripping the wet ball, he started by completing only three of nine passes for thirty-seven yards. Two went through Georgia defenders' hands. Zeier, however, was hitting his receivers in stride. The rain was reduced to a constant drizzle by the second quarter, and by that time Zeier had thrown two touchdown passes to put Georgia ahead 20–13. Once when Wuerffel came to the sideline, Spurrier chewed him out: "Their quarterback's throwing it pretty well; can you do it?" Spurrier had seen enough; he pulled Wuerffel and put Dean in the game.

It was a new life for Terry Dean, even though he would spend most of the day handing off to Rhett. Yet he was effective when he did throw, especially on a perfect thirty-five-yard spiral that landed in Harrison Houston's lap for a touchdown that gave Florida a 23–20 lead. Rhett then carried the team on drives of 10:57 and 5:40 for a touchdown and a field goal and a 33–26 advantage.

With less than two minutes remaining, Florida had a chance to run out the clock by moving to Georgia's thirty-five-yard line. On fourth-and-three, Spurrier gambled and decided not to punt. But Dean's pass over the middle was batted into the thick mud. Georgia had to move sixty-five yards in 1:26 *and* score a two-point conversion for the victory. Would this be a Lindsay Scott finish all over again?

Zeier quickly led the Bulldogs to Florida's twelve-yard line. With five seconds remaining, he passed over the middle to a wide-open Jerry Jerman in the end zone. Touchdown! That's when the controversy started. Florida cornerback Anthone Lott, who had played poorly early in the season, had heard Zook screaming for a time-out before the play. The defensive coordinator realized that he had only ten players on the field. Lott asked the official for the time-out just as the ball was snapped and the official blew the whistle, but nobody heard it since 80,392 fans were screaming as if the game was

GATOR BAIT

Kicker Judd Davis didn't have many problems with the mud at the Gator Bowl; he converted all four field goal attempts despite the mire in the thrilling 33–26 win over Georgia.

coming down to one play. And it was. As Georgia's fans and players celebrated, officials waved the play off and awarded the time-out to Florida. Goff screamed at the officials and slammed his hat into the mud.

"In a situation like that, a defense doesn't always get the time-out," Zook commented. "It's not like on offense when you have the ball and can call it anytime you want. I am sort of surprised they gave it to us."

On the next play, Lott was called for pass interference in the end zone. Receiver Hassan Graham had caught the pass but landed out of bounds. The official on the play made no call. "He told me, 'Good play . . . game's over,'" Lott said. Another official on the sideline, ten yards away from the play, ran up and threw the flag. A game cannot end on a defensive penalty, so Georgia had one more chance to win the game. The ball was spotted at the two-yard line. The clock read :00. This one play and the ensuing two-point conversion, if Georgia scored, likely would determine the direction for each team's respective season.

In the shotgun as he had been all day, Zeier aimed at receiver Jeff Thomas, who had lined up in the right slot and had run a slant over the middle. The pass was slightly behind Thomas, who reached back as the football glanced off his finger tips and fell harmlessly into the mud. Zeier grabbed his head and fell to his knees. Spurrier pointed to the sky and ran off the field, stopping for the traditional handshake with Goff. Their hands touched in the blink of an eye. Nothing was said. The game said it all.

"It just seemed at the end that we were meant to win this game," Spurrier noted.

"It feels like we own them," Watson said. "I am sure they are sitting over there saying, 'Man, how did we lose this game?'"

Georgia's players and coaches thought they knew how: the official who allowed Florida to call time-out had taken it from them. "It's unfortunate that a game as good as this one had to come down to something so controversial," Goff said. "I am mad. I am sick. I am disgusted. I think they took it from us," linebacker Mitch Davis growled. "I am not willing to accept losing to them four years in a row. I want to go back out there and play another quarter. The refs made a mistake at the end of the game. You can't take away a touchdown from somebody with five seconds to go. I never wanted to win a game more in my life."

Zeier said that he had no doubts the Bulldogs would have scored on the two-point conversion had they scored the touchdown. "I think we would have won . . . in fact I know it," he claimed. Who was to doubt Zeier? He had set a school record by throwing sixty-five passes, completing thirty-six for 386 yards. Told of that statistic, Spurrier asked, "Did he throw it sixty-five times? Did we hold him under four hundred yards? How many times did we throw it?" Told twenty-one, he replied, "Gosh, that's the way Georgia used to play." Florida hadn't attempted so few passes since Spurrier had become coach. It wasn't that Father Time was changing Spurrier. Mother Nature forced him to change, but only for a day.

Like Zeier, Rhett had a record day, carrying a school-record forty-one times for 183 yards and two touchdowns. Forty-one carries means getting tackled forty-one times. As he sat in front of his locker, he ached all over. "Help me on with my coat," he asked. "I can't lift my arm." But it was that good, achy feeling every running back loves. "I think I could do this every game. I got stronger as the game went on. Forty-one times! Man, I didn't know I had that many. I am sleeping in tomorrow. This was my last time to play Georgia. You have to show the younger guys how big a game this is every year. All I know is that they've never beaten us since I've been here."

Next to him, Dean was getting reacquainted with the reporters. He had been out of the limelight since the Kentucky game. Now he was surrounded by television cameras and note pads again. And once again, there was a quarterback controversy. It wasn't as if he passed Georgia silly. But he was effective, completing eight of twelve for 105 yards. "When he told me to go warm up, I thought, Yeah, right, I'll get in the game," Dean said sarcastically. Spurrier had been telling him that for three years, and he usually never got in the game. "Then all of a sudden he said, 'Come on!'"

Errict Rhett ran a school-record forty-one times against the Bulldogs. His 183 yards, two touchdowns, and determination led to the Gators' fourth consecutive victory over Georgia.

Meanwhile, Wuerffel dressed quietly. "I don't think I played that badly, considering the circumstances," he commented. "I couldn't get a good grip on the ball. I don't know why he took me out . . . he never told me."

Spurrier didn't want to hear excuses. He said he changed quarterbacks because Dean threw well in warmups before the game and Wuerffel was complaining about the weather. "Terry's our quarterback. He's looked extremely good in practice, and he's had a great attitude," Spurrier asserted. "A lot of kids would have quit, sulked, or transferred."

If the three previous meetings weren't enough evidence, this game surely made everyone think that the momentum behind the series had changed Florida's way. The final few plays made it obvious. The Gators had beaten Georgia when they were a better team; this time they were a luckier team.

The next day, Spurrier addressed his up-to-the-minute quarterback situation: "My job is to put the best quarterback at the time on the field, so I watch them practice and watch them in warmups. Right now, I think Terry Dean is the best player we can put on the field." What was wrong with Wuerffel, who looked poised and unflappable earlier in the season? "I think his footwork is not as good as it needs to be. That's my fault. I've been coaching every dadgummed thing that moves instead of worrying about the quarterbacks. I've done a poor job with him the last couple of weeks. We have to realize he is a second-year quarterback, and he needs somebody with him every day, every minute in practice."

The officials would be a target of Spurrier's wrath for a second straight game, even though Georgia had the biggest complaint on the time-out call. Florida was penalized thirteen times for ninety-seven yards to Georgia's five for forty-six yards.

"It will make me sound like a crybaby, but all you have to do is look at the statistics," he stated. "Something's wrong there. Either we're the worst coaches in the country as far as teaching our players the rules or something's amiss." Spurrier added he would make a video of poor calls against Florida and send it to the SEC office. "Maybe a video will let the world know what is happening to us instead of me complaining all the time," he concluded. "I hate to complain."

Not that he had any reason. If there was any doubt before, there wasn't now: Spurrier was Georgia's main nemesis. He was 4–0 against the Bulldogs as a coach, and he loved the feeling.

9

FLORIDA'S MOST
VALUABLE PRANKSTER

ERRICT UNDRA RHETT WAS ONE of those kids your mother would have wanted you to avoid while you were growing up but your father would have loved. He was gregarious beyond his twenty-two years, owning a personality usually reserved for stand-up comics or public relations gurus. He wasn't just a college football superstar with an empty head or a shallow outlook, yet he had a lovable naiveté to him. He would lean over reporters' note pads and watch them write his words onto paper. "How do you decide where to put that comment?"

On the field he was the team's unquestioned leader and had been even when Shane Matthews was the record-setting quarterback from 1990 to 1992 and Rhett was an underclassman. He exuded all the qualities of every great leader, taking charge in the huddle when the offense was struggling, chewing out who needed to be motivated, and joking when the mood was morbid. He would lead by example in practice, working as if the Heisman Trophy or a national championship rode on each session. This was rare for most players, who regarded the long, arduous practices as tiresome and boring and yet a necessary evil of college football.

"Nobody practices harder than Errict Rhett," Spurrier often noted. "The guy runs out every play as far as he can run it . . . sometimes a hundred yards. He's always enthusiastic and just a fun guy to be around. All the players love him." And Florida's coaches loved the fact that all their players loved him. They knew that underclassmen would see Rhett's example and follow. It was like having another assistant coach at tailback.

Rhett said he developed his work habits simply because he understood how short life is, another rare outlook for a college student. "I tell the younger guys that if you don't give 110 percent, you'll regret it someday," he explained. "I just like to make practice fun."

Defensive end Kevin Carter, six-foot-five and 265 pounds, learned as a freshman just how much fun it was to try to tackle Rhett in practice. He ended up on his back one day, puzzled that the star tailback was taking the workout so seriously. When he saw young defensive players get run over by Number 33, he just chuckled and told them, "Errict Rhett will run over everybody on this team by the end of the season. It's not that you're special or anything."

Off the field, Rhett earned a reputation as the team's leading prankster. Nothing gave him a kick like the scare he could throw into unsuspecting teammates who wandered into his room, oblivious of his fondness for an eleven-foot boa named Bushwick. Rhett and a few teammates would rig a video camera aimed at the door. A player would walk in and someone would throw Bushwick around the hapless soul's body. Then Rhett and his buddies would spend hours watching the knee-slapping videotape. "I am sitting on his couch one night," Watson remembered, "and all of a sudden I feel this cold, clammy thing wrapping itself around me. Errict just laughed." Rhett also had an eighty-pound pit bull named Hard Time. Why Hard Time? "Because he gives all the other dogs a hard time," Rhett laughed. Made sense. Players would gather in Rhett's room to watch Watson and him wrestle. Watson tipped the scales at about 280 pounds. "We really go at it," Rhett commented. "It's to see who's tougher."

One day Spurrier couldn't figure out what was constantly beeping in his office. "I didn't know where it was coming from, and it was driving me crazy," he recalled. Finally, Carl Franks, then the running backs coach and now the tight ends coach, stopped by. When Spurrier told him of the noise, Franks asked, "Has Errict been in your office?" Rhett's beeper had fallen out of his pocket and rolled under Spurrier's desk. Spurrier wasn't amused. Rhett explained that he needed the beeper in case his family wanted to reach him. Once when Rhett was stopped by campus police for riding a bicycle without a light at night, he didn't have any identification but told the officer his name was John Smith. "I couldn't think of a name," he confessed. That has been his only brush with the law.

The media also was a frequent target of Rhett's gags, especially his knack for creating wild stories. Reporters would scribble down every word, thinking this Rhett guy was one strange character who made for an excellent feature, only to find out later that he was playing with them as he would a slow, overweight linebacker.

One time, when the subject was weight lifting, Rhett claimed, "I can bench press about 500 pounds." Few linemen in college football, or even the NFL, can bench press 500 pounds. Even though he has weighed 195–215 pounds during his career, Rhett did have the upper body of a weight lifter. He had virtually no body fat. But 500 pounds? He had a better chance of gaining 500 yards in one game.

Another time he told several writers that Hurricane Andrew, which destroyed sections of Miami and Homestead in the summer of 1992, had blown his home into another zip code. The hurricane didn't do much damage in West Hollywood, Rhett's hometown.

As a sophomore, Rhett told sportswriters that he rented cars and drove around the country when he became bored. He just had to get away from the pressures of football and driving hundreds of miles relieved his stress. He never figured that athletic department officials would read the story in the newspapers and check it out. Considering Florida's past troubles with the NCAA, they understandably were sensitive to any possible violations and they wondered where Rhett got the money to afford so many rental cars. There were no such rentals.

At the team's media day before the 1992 season, Rhett showed up wearing a gaudy bracelet with his first name spelled in diamonds. Asked the cost, he remarked, "It was about six thousand dollars, but don't print that." Someone did, and the athletic department scurried to find the truth again. It's amazing how cubic zirconia can fool the naked eye. The bracelet was worth about twenty-five dollars.

There's no illusion, however, about Rhett's ability. He always was a good athlete, especially when he wrestled at Hollywood's MacArthur High. He combined his agility and strength with his zaniness to win matches before they ever began. He would drink red fruit punch and let a little dribble down his chin. Then he would tell his opponent that he bit himself just to get ready for the match.

One time he did bite another wrestler, "because he put his hand in my mouth . . . even though I wasn't that hungry." To gain weight—Rhett wrestled in the heavyweight division—he ate potato chips. His junk food diet didn't prevent him from becoming a state champion.

"Errict Rhett just enjoys life," noted Carl Franks, who had become close to the running back when he coached the position. "He really doesn't take himself too seriously until he steps on the football field."

Rhett's attitude and zest for life were amazing considering his childhood. He was raised by his mother and older brother. There was no father figure in his life. From the time he could walk, he played football with the other kids on the streets of

Facing page: Errict Rhett was the main character both on and off the field and one of college football's finest running backs.

Carvers Ranches, one of the toughest sections of Broward County, learning to avoid tacklers by first dodging cars in the street. "You think astroturf is hard," he stated, "get tackled in the street someday." Rhett said few kids play football in those streets anymore since gangs, guns, and drugs replaced running into cars as the primary hazard.

Rhett said he always wanted to be different. The norm, or following a mold of what people think a college kid should be, would have killed him. "Sort of like the way my name is spelled," he observed. "My mom wanted a different Eric." She got one.

Not that he's never serious. When Spurrier took the job at Florida, Rhett wasn't real pleased. He had signed with Florida when Galen Hall was head coach, planning to follow in Emmitt Smith's huge footsteps. He saw Smith getting twenty-five to thirty carries each game, and he figured that would be fine with him, too. When Hall was fired and Spurrier hired, Rhett thought the pass-happy coach's wide-open system would ruin his chances to carry the football more than a few times a game. One day in his office, Spurrier straightened out his future star. "Errict, let me give you a little history lesson," Spurrier began. "We had a thousand-yard rusher almost every season I was at Duke. Do you think we just threw it on every down? Don't worry, you'll love my offense."

For the most part, Spurrier was right. Rhett carried 148 times for 845 yards in 1990 as a freshman, 224 times for 1,109 yards as a sophomore, and 250 times for 903 yards as a junior. Aside from games like the loss at Auburn, Rhett was satisfied with his work-load, but he was no different from every other running back who wants to carry the ball thirty times a game. Under Spurrier's system the fullback almost never carries the football. Florida also didn't have a good backup tailback in those years. So when the Gators ran the football, Errict Rhett ran the football.

The system's running game was finesse, built around sprint draws, counters, and misdirection plays. The more Florida passed, and defenses entered each game knowing that Spurrier loved the passing game, the more effective Rhett became. He also developed into an excellent receiver out of the backfield, catching 117 career passes in his first three seasons, more than any other true receiver in the SEC. That was one of the things that impressed NFL scouts.

"I love this system," Rhett said. "I think it's better for me than the old system under Coach Hall because if you run the ball every play, the defense is looking for it. Emmitt sometimes got his yards when three linebackers knew he was going to get the ball. This way, those linebackers keep dropping and dropping [into pass coverage] and bam! . . . there's a huge hole there."

Rhett showed up in August about ten pounds lighter than he had played in 1991 and 1992. He figured he could cut and change directions better at 205 pounds than at 215. Coaches had told him that was the one thing he needed to improve, his open-field running. He instinctively preferred to take a defensive back or linebacker head-on in the open field rather than try to make the tackler miss and gain more yards. It wasn't that he wasn't elusive, he just never thought not to try to run over people. "He told me he is going to break some long runs this year," Spurrier announced before the start of the season. "I think he will. Usually he does what he says he will."

Before the season, Rhett was saying a mouthful. "I have to make this my best year at Florida," he said two weeks before the season opener. "This is my last year. I could tell you I want to gain fifteen hundred yards and score twenty touchdowns and all that but that's not important. . . . I have some personal goals, don't get me wrong, but these team goals we set are more important to me. I've tried to be low key out there, but that's just not me. I just talk, talk, talk on the football field. Sometimes, I don't even know what I am saying."

After the first six games, Rhett had rushed for 784 yards on 122 carries for a 6.4-yard average. No other back in the conference was within a hundred yards of him. But he saved his best for his final Georgia game. Not many backs in the nation would have withstood the pounding of forty-one carries and still gained 183 yards. Rhett ran to the locker room afterward. Why? Only Errict Rhett would provide this answer: "I was hungry. The coaches told me to eat light because it was a noon kickoff. Then at halftime, I was changing into dry socks and shoes, and I forgot to eat a banana. You know how tough it is to be out there when you are hungry? On the sideline, all I could think about was getting something to eat."

That night on ESPN, analyst Lee Corso jumped on Rhett's bandwagon, calling him the best back in college football. San Diego State's Marshall Faulk and Michigan's Tyrone Wheatley had received most of the national attention during the season, which agitated Rhett as much as anything. "I don't know why I don't get the national attention . . . maybe it's because people around the country just think we throw the ball all the time," he complained. "Am I as good as Marshall Faulk and those guys? What do you think?"

Spurrier didn't need to be asked the day after the Georgia game. "I saw where Lee Corso mentioned last night that he thought Errict was the best all-around back in the nation and I certainly agree with that. I guess the big question next year will be, What are the Gators going to do when Errict Rhett leaves? His record speaks for itself."

Actually, Rhett hadn't set many school records, but that was about to change. The Georgia game presented him with the chance to do what he had set as a goal when he was a freshman. He wanted not only to break Emmitt Smith's school rushing record of 3,928 yards, but he wanted to do it at Florida Field. The game would be stopped and Rhett would take the football over to the sideline for safekeeping. The fans would stand for minutes, saluting him with a standing ovation. It would be perfect.

It also was remarkable, Rhett thought to himself, that such NFL stars as Neal Anderson, John L. Williams, and Smith had graced Florida Field with their talent, and now he would become the all-time leading rusher in the university's eighty-five years of football. Yet he didn't like talking about the record because it made him appear selfish. Rhett didn't care much for selfish players. Still, everybody knew he, of all people, was a team player.

When Smith was in his final season at Florida, he apparently ignored the freshman running back. Then when he announced he was leaving college for the NFL after his junior season, Smith told everyone that he was turning the position over to Willie McClendon, a high school superstar who never developed as a collegiate running back. Rhett listened and seethed. "He never even mentioned my name," he had observed in 1992. That's why breaking Smith's record meant so much to him, even though he told sportswriters it meant nothing.

"There is one record I am concerned with," he announced, "and it's not Emmitt Smith's record. It's the record of this team. Who cares about rushing records? It doesn't mean that much to me right now. Maybe someday, when I am finished playing football, I can look back on it and it will."

If there was one lesson Rhett learned from Smith, now a star with the Dallas Cowboys, it was how to respect people. He vowed that when he became a senior that he would treat freshmen, no matter how low on the depth chart, as he would other seniors. It was part of the reason that he was the most popular player on the team.

"I want those guys to feel at home, to feel like we're all brothers, to feel we are one big happy family from the time they get here," he noted. "Someday they will be seniors, too. I remembered how the seniors here used to treat the underclassmen and it wasn't with much respect. When I was a freshman, the older guys were always so high on themselves. They would only talk to juniors and seniors. I just made a promise to myself that wouldn't happen when I became a senior. If you are on this team, you are a part of it from the time you sign that letter. . . . You are a Florida Gator."

The day before the homecoming game against Southwestern Louisiana, Smith sent his congratulations through a statement released by the Cowboys. "I knew that when I left there that my numbers wouldn't stand up forever," he began. "I think it's great that he is setting records. I really think Errict is the best back in college football. He's the complete package. He's got strength and speed and good hands."

During the week of the game, Rhett said that he and Smith get along fine now when they bump into each other. There were no hard feelings. At times, Rhett wouldn't take much credit for the record he was about to own. "Why shouldn't something like this happen? I've got a damn good offensive line, a damn good fullback [Kelvin Randolph], and a damn good coaching staff," he declared. Then he would acknowledge that his countless hours of hard work were paying off. "You know, it never came easy for me. For some of these great athletes, it comes easy. I just had to work a little harder than everybody else to get here."

Spurrier, who once said he always votes for one of his players for the Heisman Trophy, thought Rhett was having a Heisman year. By midseason every voter had pretty much penciled Florida State quarterback Charlie Ward onto their mental ballots. "I think Errict should be considered," Spurrier suggested. "He helps our team as much as Charlie Ward and those other guys do for their teams. He runs, he catches, he blocks. We wouldn't be the offense without him."

The football team's homecoming theme was Another Level. After playing football in the streets, playing hundreds of pranks over the years, and running over tacklers since he arrived in Gainesville, Rhett finally was ready to reach another level of his own. There was a game to win and a record to break.

"I just wish it would start a little later," Rhett said. "All these noon and one o'clock kickoffs. . . . I like to sleep in on Saturdays. I am not a real good morning person. I can't eat that huge breakfast. There ought to be a new rule: no games before four o'clock."

This time, Errict Rhett wasn't joking.

10

A TROUBLESOME HOMECOMING

FOR ITS ANNUAL HOMECOMING game, it seems every football power has resorted to scheduling either teams that are perennially mediocre-to-poor or schools that are financially strapped. Usually, the definitions coincide. After all, the alums have to see a win when they return to campus, right?

Florida didn't make the rules, the school just played by them. The university could pay a nonconference opponent from $175,000 to $200,000 for a game because Florida Field would be filled with eighty-five thousand fans paying eighteen dollars apiece to be there. Therefore, Southwestern Louisiana was as good or, more appropriately, as bad as anybody to come to Gainesville and be Gator meat for the Florida homecoming.

The Ragin' Cajuns of Southwestern Louisiana had a history against Southeastern Conference teams, namely an 0–36 win-loss record. Florida had a 20–2 record in its twenty-two previous homecoming games, including wins by scores of 77–14 over West Texas State, 59–0 over Akron, and 52–9 over Kent State. One of the two losses since 1971 resulted from a scheduling flaw that placed the Auburn game on homecoming in 1988. Someone forgot about the homecoming scheduling rules on that one, and Auburn won 16–0.

That surely wouldn't happen this season, even though the Cajuns, a new member of the Big West Conference, had a 6–2 record. It should have been a relaxing, laid-back week for Spurrier and his staff, a week to prepare the team emotionally for the following week's game at South Carolina and the stretch run for the SEC's Eastern Division championship. No such luck for the Gators. A strange and public string of distractions was about to make this a tumultuous seven days.

SEC commissioner Roy Kramer had grown tired of Spurrier's verbally bashing his officials, and he sent the coach a letter clarifying for him who was the boss and who was the coach. Kramer took exception to Spurrier's comments following the Auburn game in particular. One more verbal blasting of conference officials, and Spurrier could be suspended for a game. If that had happened, it wouldn't have set a precedent for Spurrier, who once had been suspended by the Atlantic Coast Conference for complaining about officiating while he was head coach at Duke.

"I probably deserved it," Spurrier replied the next day. "It's really no big deal. I said what I had to say." In reality he had said more than he had to say. Kramer's letter only referred to the coach's comments after the Auburn game and was sent before the Georgia game, after which Spurrier hinted that his team had been on the receiving end of more terrible calls. The big question was, Would his comments after the Georgia game constitute his second offense and therefore warrant a suspension? After receiving the letter, Spurrier said he still intended to compile a video of incorrect calls made against Florida and send it to the SEC office. "It probably won't do any good," he admitted.

Was Spurrier just another paranoid coach who wanted to find an excuse for a team that lacked discipline on the field? Or was there a bit of truth to what he was saying? Were SEC officials actually targeting the Gators?

Conference officials couldn't be biased against Florida, as Spurrier had hinted. If anything, like basketball officials, an official or two may grow tired of the sideline badgering and respond by watching that particular coach's team a little more closely. Football coaches develop reputations the same as basketball coaches. Like it or not, Spurrier was known as a complainer. But that was only a part of Florida's problem.

College football officiating is not a full-time job. Officials are lawyers, bankers, insurance salesmen, and teachers from Monday through Friday. They are paid by the game, not the season. Next to basketball, football is the most difficult sport to officiate. Likewise, holding and pass interference are two of the most difficult calls to make, and Florida's style of play is conducive to committing each infraction.

Technically, holding could be called on every play, especially for the Gators since they throw the football more than most teams. For example, Vanderbilt, an option team, probably is called for holding fewer than ten times per season. The same goes for Mississippi, Nebraska, Wisconsin, or any team that builds its offense around the running game. Pass interference, too, is a tough judgment call. Florida's defense had ranked very high against the run under Spurrier and very low against the pass. Therefore opposing teams were going to throw more than they run against Florida. Furthermore Florida, along with Tennessee and Alabama, probably owned the lead during games more than any other team in the conference. When the opposing team trailed, what would it do? Pass, naturally.

Also the new celebration-taunting rule became a widespread controversy during the season. A team that has something to celebrate, such as a touchdown, probably will be penalized for it more than, for example, Vanderbilt. Florida had led the SEC in touchdowns each season since 1990. As far as taunting, Dennis Erickson, Bobby Bowden, and Spurrier wouldn't agree, but the Sunshine State had taken the lead in finger pointing, intimidation, celebrating, and taunting. Miami's reputation, which peaked in the late 1980s, as a bunch of bullies in football helmets had improved slightly under Erickson. The Hurricanes still are worth at least one good fight per

149

season, and they had already had a good bout with Colorado in September. FSU had been in a few scuffles, too. Florida hadn't been in a real fight under Spurrier, but the Gators did commit their share of celebration-taunting penalties. A confident and sometimes cocky attitude went hand in hand with winning, and that attitude permeated all three football programs in the state. It was a Florida "thing."

Spurrier was most likely correct when he claimed that college football officiating wasn't as good as officiating in the NFL. But the NFL's wasn't great. There were 106 major college football teams with more than 90 schools playing on any given Saturday in the fall. Forty-five games would require 315 game officials to be working at the same time (7 officials per game). Out of those 315, perhaps 250 were competent to very good, but as the cliché says, the sum is only as good as its parts. One part, or one official in this case, can easily hamper a group's overall performance. One missed call or a call that should not have been made can affect a game more than even officials realize. Football officials are not held accountable to a stadium full of fans as much as basketball officials, who are in the open, making the call in close proximity to the irate fans. Football officials report their infraction to the referee, who signals the penalty. No fan or coach, unlike in basketball, can see every part of the field to realize if a call is correct or incorrect.

By the finish of Monday night's practice, Spurrier said enough was enough. He had received his warning. It was time to move on. "I can't talk about the officials any more," he announced. "I've made my point. Everyone knows how I feel."

On Tuesday, he turned his attention to the defensive line's lack of a pass rush. Zeier had thrown sixty-five passes and was sacked only once, not a good measure of pressure by the defensive linemen. The problem was puzzling since the line had appeared to be solid before the season. Every starter returned, including senior William Gaines from a knee injury. "We can't block them during practice," Spurrier asserted. "But in the game people say to me, 'Why are you holding the line back?

150

You ought to let them go after it.'" The line had fifteen quarterback sacks in seven games, but five came against lowly Arkansas State in the first game.

Spurrier also defended the team's nonconference schedule. A topic like this usually pops up during homecoming week. Arkansas State and Southwestern Louisiana were two sacrificial lambs, for sure. But the final nonconference opponent, rival Florida State, was ranked number one. "We don't need to apologize for our schedule," Spurrier added.

As far as the players were concerned, Wuerffel wasn't apologizing for suddenly finding himself number two on the depth chart. He had thought he had the starting quarterback's job for the season and still didn't feel he played poorly enough to lose it. After all, he attempted only nine passes against Georgia in weather that usually precedes ark-building.

"Its not the most tickling experience," he indicated about being benched. "It's just a part of football, and I've got to deal with it. I can't get down on myself. I am going to practice the same . . . if not harder."

Rhett, who had a sore shoulder from the pounding he took against Georgia, wasn't practicing at all. He didn't return to the practice field until Thursday, when the team had already finished its heavy work for the week. Still, Spurrier said he would play on Saturday. Rhett wouldn't miss it, intending to break Smith's record at home.

Spurrier's reprimand by the commissioner was quickly forgotten by Friday night's homecoming celebration. The University of Florida may not always have the best football, basketball, or baseball team, the finest marching band, the prettiest cheerleaders, or the most expensive facilities—although they are close to the top in each category—but the school ranks far and away number one with its annual homecoming party.

Called Gator Growl, the megaevent has become one of the most popular traditions in the state. It certainly is the largest party, with the eighty-five-thousand-seat stadium filled the Friday night of homecoming weekend. Growl, as it has come to be known around Gainesville, is a three-hour entertainment show of skits, jokes, and music centered around the introduction of the football team's seniors. Usually, some name comic like Richard Lewis or Garry Schandling hosts the event. This year it was Dennis Miller. Rocker Tom Petty, a Gainesville native, and the Heartbreakers would play across the street at the O'Connell Center. The football team usually attends the Gator Growl together and then returns to the Holiday Inn West, the team's hotel the night before home games.

Senior receiver Willie Jackson, who played at the same Gainesville high school as Doering and was not recruited much either, had become a legitimate star in his four years. He led the conference with fifty-one receptions as a sophomore and sixty-two as a junior. Big for a receiver at six-foot-two and 205 pounds, Jackson and his strength gave smaller defensive backs trouble. Even more than that, he led the team in determination and heart. He had the same kind of inner drive as did Rhett. If he wanted something, for example, a first down, and he had to break a few tackles to get it, he usually got it. The NFL scouts were paying attention to him very closely, but Jackson's competitive nature caught up with him at Gator Growl and guaranteed that everyone would be reading about Jackson over the new few weeks. Unfortunately, it had nothing to do with catching passes.

During Growl he left the team section in the stadium to go to the restroom. When he tried to return to his seat, he was stopped by a university police officer, Ed Mignone. "He said, 'Willie, where's your ticket? I can't let you in without a ticket,'" Jackson recalled. That would be a problem since players weren't given tickets to the event. They entered and left the stadium as a team. Jackson tried to convince Mignone to admit him. "I could see the coaches from where I was standing," he said. "But [the officer] wouldn't go get one of them. He even knew who I was the whole time."

Then the discussion became an argument, and the argument turned physical, resulting in Mignone's trying to handcuff

Jackson. It was as much a mismatch as if Jackson were facing single coverage on a fade pattern. He resisted, swinging his arms away from the officer as other campus police approached. "All I did was snatch my arms from him and tell him he couldn't grab me like that," Jackson said. "I never threw a punch, never attacked, never did anything but pull away from him."

In less than a minute six policemen were trying to bring Jackson down and suddenly identifying with a host of SEC cornerbacks and safeties who'd tried to do the same thing over the last three seasons. Jackson was tough to tackle. "They were attacking me like sharks. They were all pushing me, and I had my hands behind my back, and they were pushing my face against a wall," he recalled. "One of them tried to grab my legs and flip me so I would fall down."

He never did go down. One policeman, Paul Clendenin, fell to the ground during the scuffle. He was later treated at a hospital for a bruised shoulder and face and released.

At one of the university police substations within the stadium, chief Everett Stevens met with Jackson, Mignone, and Foley, who had been summoned from his seat in the stadium. The handcuffs were removed and Jackson was allowed to return to the team and was introduced to the crowd with the other seniors minutes later. Few realized there had been an altercation.

The next day, while the team was playing Southwestern Louisiana, Stevens recommended a charge of resisting arrest with violence be filed with the state attorney's office. The charge, less than assaulting a police officer, was a felony and carried a maximum penalty of a $5,000 fine and/or a five-year jail sentence. Spurrier listened to Jackson explain his side of the story and decided he should play the game. He was convinced the player had been treated unfairly.

The poor Southwestern Louisiana defensive backs must have thought Number 22 was a black Hulk Hogan in a football uniform. They knew nothing about an altercation. Jackson scored two touchdowns and had eighty-one receiving yards, while the game was just as much a mismatch as expected.

Jackson's second touchdown reception gave Florida a 40–0 lead with 9:39 remaining in the first half. At that rate, Florida would win 120–0, but Spurrier cleared the bench and the final score was 61–14. Florida's defense didn't give up a point. One of Southwestern Louisiana's touchdowns came on a fake punt, the other on an interception return of a pass from third-stringer Eric Kresser that bounced off his receiver's hands. After the interception, Zook turned around on the sidelines and said, "He'll probably blame me for that one, too." Everyone understood who "he" was. Later in the locker room, he boasted, "Write what you want, but the defense had a shutout today."

The defense held Southwestern Louisiana to 210 yards and twelve first downs. "The coaches have been substituting a lot of guys and sending a message that if you are not going to perform, you are not going to play," senior linebacker Ed Robinson stated. "You have a lot of guys with jobs on the line." Speaking of the line, starters Kevin Carter and Ellis Johnson were benched for the game, replaced by David Barnard and Johnie Church. "That was me going over there," Spurrier claimed. "I was challenging them to play with more effort." "Over there" referred to the defense.

"Over here," on offense, Dean, in his first start since the miracle at Kentucky two months earlier, was spectacular. He completed twenty-six of thirty-eight passes for 448 yards, one yard shy of Wuerffel's school and SEC record set against Mississippi State. His six touchdown passes, however, set an SEC record. To put that into perspective, LSU's Bert Jones, Alabama's Joe Namath, Richard Todd, and Ken Stabler, Ole Miss's Archie Manning, and Heisman Trophy winners like Auburn's Pat Sullivan and Spurrier himself were among the great quarterbacks who had played in the SEC. None had ever thrown six scoring passes in one game.

UNIVERSITY OF FLORIDA SPORTS INFORMATION

Willie Jackson made one big reception after another during his career. Unfortunately, he missed three games in his senior season, one to injury and two because of a suspension for an incident at homecoming.

Dean, who would be named the conference's offensive player of the week, played the game in the shotgun formation, as Southwestern Louisiana blitzed and blitzed. "We were thinking this week about how they blitz," Spurrier explained. "So we felt the shotgun would give us a little extra time to get a lot of passes off. Terry had an excellent game. He made some super throws. It seems we are setting some sort of record around here every week."

This was the new Terry Dean. No more strutting. No more cockiness. He suddenly was a humble kid who just wanted to play football. "I think the key today was that the receivers made some great catches," he noted. "You can't throw six touchdown passes without receivers catching them."

Southwestern Louisiana coach Nelson Stokley wondered how Auburn ever defeated the team he had just seen dismantle his team. "They are as aggressive a football team as I've ever seen since I've been in coaching," he commented. "Some people, like Tennessee and Georgia, had some big plays on them throwing the football . . . so I wasn't sure. Now I am sure."

It was the third straight game the Gators had played in the rain, following the third straight week of sunshine from Sunday through Friday. Something about Saturdays in Florida was filling the sky with clouds. "It does seem like we are playing in a lot of water," Spurrier observed.

The old saying goes that the calls usually even out in the end. If that is true, Florida could chalk up two officiating calls for its side. On one play, a Southwestern Louisiana tight end was tackled as a pass headed his way. There was no pass interference penalty, forcing Coach Stokley, a former LSU quarterback, to confront an official. He was hit with a fifteen-yard unsportsmanlike penalty. Later, one of Dean's touchdown passes to Jack Jackson that gave the Gators a 33–0 lead had bounced off the grass about a foot from Jackson's feet. "He caught it clean, didn't he?" Spurrier quizzed the media after the game. Everyone in the room groaned, but the coach smiled.

Spurrier wouldn't talk about Jackson's clash with the police during his postgame press conference, but news of the incident filtered through the press box about two hours after the game. Police spokeswoman Angie Tipton, a true professional accustomed to dealing with incidents involving athletes, explained that Jackson wasn't detained or held overnight because "we didn't know all the facts then. We know Willie Jackson isn't going anywhere. We know where he will be on Saturdays and during the week."

There may have been one player more upset than Willie Jackson, if that was possible. Rhett's dream of breaking Smith's record at Florida Field had been a nightmare. While Dean was breaking one of the most prestigious SEC records because of Southwestern Louisiana's blitzing style of defense, Rhett's day was ruined by it. When a defense blitzes on every play, it is difficult to gain yards by running. So Spurrier practically ignored Rhett when it came to calling plays. A week after carrying a school-record forty-one times, Rhett carried twelve times for only forty yards. He entered the game needing eighty-eight yards, which appeared to be a simple task considering the opponent. When it didn't happen, Rhett stormed out of the locker room without even showering to avoid reporters. It was his best run of the day.

"He's upset and you can't blame him," assistant coach Carl Franks noted, "but what could we do? We couldn't try to keep running the ball. If we leave him in the game, he could get hurt and he already has a sore shoulder." Spurrier didn't understand the problem. "He carried it forty-one times last week and he'll carry it thirty times or more again some day," he added. "He'll have a lot of opportunities to get that record."

Sunday morning's *Gainesville Sun* carried a huge front-page story on Jackson's arrest, even quoting a relative of the receiver about his supposed feelings. The story focused on the decision not to detain Jackson. The coverage angered Jackson, perhaps even more than the incident itself. Spurrier defended his decision to allow Jackson to play. "I gave some thought to suspending him until I heard his side of the story," he said. "I have a clear conscience about it." Asked if he thought his player had been provoked by the police, he replied, "If I decided he could play, yes, you could assume that. There are two sides to every story. We'll just let the legal system takes its course and go from there."

The last thing Angie Tipton wanted was to get into a verbal tennis match with the most popular man in Gainesville. "I am not going to second-guess Coach Spurrier, but we feel comfortable we are recommending the proper charges," she commented.

The charges were one thing, the publicity was another. Jackson was stunned when he read Sunday's article. The incident was taking on a life of its own. "It came out in the papers the way it did because other officers who weren't even there were accusing me of getting preferential treatment because I'm an athlete," Jackson observed. "It was a political thing. I hate politics. The stories came out in the papers that I hit an officer and he gets hurt and goes to the hospital. That's not what happened. The thing that aggravated me more than anything was the media coverage. They don't realize how that can affect your career. You become a marked man."

Spurrier knew a little about that, although in an entirely different context. Again he had to defend his play-calling, this time because it had prevented Rhett from setting the school's rushing record at home. This made him a little angrier than having to defend his decision to play Jackson. "I have never got into putting a player back in the game simply to get a record," he explained. "Our concern is not individual records. He had hurt his shoulder [against Georgia] and hadn't practiced much all week. It made no sense to put him back in there when it was 40–7." Besides, Spurrier knew he would need his star tailback to be healthy to win at South Carolina.

11

THE COMEBACK OF
THE SEASON

S PURRIER HADN'T HAD A CHANCE to study South Carolina by early Sunday afternoon. He did know that since he had taken the head coaching job, Florida was 0–9 against ranked teams in road games. Where do sportswriters come up with these statistics? he wondered. Still, he was curious. "South Carolina isn't ranked, are they?" he asked. The Gamecocks didn't even have a winning record, having lost five of nine games, let alone a ranking.

Spurrier usually had a ploy of some sort to get his team fired up to play when he felt they needed it. Bulletin Board Comments, as they are called, would be posted near the Gators' locker room before each game. With South Carolina as the opponent, there were no problems finding such comments. Quarterback Steve Taneyhill supplied them by the truckload, or newspaper-load in this case. After Florida had held on to beat the Gamecocks 14–9 the previous season, Taneyhill said that Florida wasn't a good football team. The Gators were lucky to win, he added. They weren't among the most talented teams in the SEC, he contended.

"They didn't have many nice things to say about us last year, did they?" Spurrier asked. "We just didn't impress them too much, I guess. Taneyhill said we didn't deserve to be in the [SEC] championship game."

In high school at Altoona, Pennsylvania, which produced 1976 Heisman Trophy winner Tony Dorsett, Taneyhill was one of those kids most parents wanted to backhand. He would score on the basketball court and then run down to the other end, gesturing to the other team's bench. He would pull imaginary six-shooters from the side of his pants and blow away the imaginary smoke. Alabama refused to offer him a scholarship following a recruiting visit because of his demeanor, which was embellished by his long flowing red hair and an earring.

But he matured a little after he reached Columbia, South Carolina. He left his six-shooters in Pennsylvania. Now when the offense scored, he stepped back and took an imaginary baseball swing before raising his arms as if he had just won the World Series with a grand slam. It was all amusing to Spurrier and the Gators.

"He hasn't hit many home runs this season, has he?" Spurrier asked. "That loudness is cool when you are winning, but when you are losing it's not so much fun."

Taneyhill did have talent. As he watched South Carolina's annual spring game during his senior year in high school, he stated flatly, "I will be their quarterback next year. Nobody on this team can beat me out." As it turned out, he was correct, taking the job from senior Wright Mitchell. Taneyhill had a fine freshman season once he won the job, but only after South Carolina had lost its first five games. At that time, a player mutiny had threatened Coach Sparky Woods's job, and Taneyhill came to the rescue. The Gamecocks won four straight behind Taneyhill until losing to Florida. South Carolinians were caught up in the Taneyhill mania, even wearing caps with a fake ponytail pouring from the back. The hats became the hottest-selling item in Columbia. But that was last season.

This season it seemed that Taneyhill had used up all his magic. He had been intercepted nine times and had thrown only four touchdown passes. By comparison, Wuerffel and Dean combined had thrown twenty-eight touchdown passes. Taneyhill's pass efficiency rating was 107.2, ninth-best in the SEC. "It's been a mixture of things, I guess," Taneyhill explained Tuesday. "All I know is that this year has been pretty rough." After two seasons of being the most recognized guy in Columbia, Taneyhill was growing tired of the attention. He said he hated it when someone recognized him "from behind," presumably because of his long hair. When that happened and they asked if he was who they thought he was, he would answer no and continue walking. "Sometime's it's fun," he said, "and sometimes it bugs me."

Off the field, Taneyhill's season wasn't much better. He had been arrested for underage drinking at a campus party hours following the season-opening game, a 23–21 upset of Georgia in Athens.

"That bothered Steve more than anybody was aware of," Coach Woods observed. "It just wasn't a good start for him. You've got to remember that he is just a true sophomore. Most of our receivers are freshmen and sophomores. We haven't been able to run the football much and that makes it difficult for him. We lost four offensive linemen from last year. Then we had several of them get injured. Those people that were buying the wigs [in 1992] are the ones saying, 'Well, you need a haircut.'"

From the appearance of Tuesday's practice, so did all of Florida's scout-team quarterbacks. Yellow locks flowed from underneath their helmets, which gave everyone a needed chuckle. The players had worn wigs to make their imitation of Taneyhill more realistic.

While the scout-team quarterbacks were having fun, Dean was in pain. It was becoming more obvious that he would not be able to play in Saturday's game. His right shoulder, originally thought to be slightly bruised, was deeply bruised and he could barely lift his arm. He had crashed to the ground, landing on the shoulder on his final pass of his

South Carolina quarterback Steve Taneyhill, long hair and all, was having a miserable season on and off the field.

UNIVERSITY OF SOUTH CAROLINA SPORTS INFORMATION

record-setting day. "I landed on it pretty hard," he acknowledged. "It's just sore. I'll have to wait and see if it gets better by Thursday or Friday." Wuerffel, meanwhile, was preparing to start again. "If we were playing today, Danny would start," Spurrier announced.

In a rare move on his special teams, Spurrier decided to bench Larry Kennedy as the punt returner in favor of sophomore Sorola Palmer. "He's been dropping one every week," the coach noted. "We can't have him back there if he's going to keep doing that. It may cost us a game someday."

In the Jackson case, local state attorney Rod Smith wanted a prosecutor with no ties to the university. Smith was a graduate of Florida's law school, so he asked Baker County state attorney Paul Usina to investigate the university police's claim. Greg McMahon, Smith's assistant and also a Florida graduate, admitted that the department had no choice. "This is a very high-profile case and we think it's fair to everyone to do it this way," he declared on Monday. "It should take less than a week. Paul is a good investigator and he has no loyalties that could be challenged." Smith had had his share of public attention, handling the charges of Danny Rolling for the murder of five Florida students in August 1990. Rolling later pled guilty, avoiding a highly publicized trial.

Jackson's father, one of the first blacks to play for the Gators when the team was integrated in 1970, hired Gainesville attorney Alan Parlapiano.

Foley received some good news on Tuesday. The school's independent investigation into Gerald Owens's accusations that defensive line coach Jerry "Red" Anderson had given him money five years earlier determined that there had been no payment. Or at least no evidence of any payment. "Nothing substantiates Gerald's allegations," Foley said. "Coach Anderson's name has a stigma to it, which is unfair. Red's just happy to have it behind him."

This was one of those weeks that made athletic directors weary. Investigations of rules violations one day; wide receivers getting into scraps with police officers the next. What would be next?

If there were a rags-to-riches success story at the University of Florida, Jeremy N. Foley was it. He had never played college football. He didn't come from a giant university that had major athletic teams. He had graduated from tiny Hobart College. After he received a master's degree in sports administration from Ohio University in 1976, the only job he could find was as an intern in Florida's ticket office. Six promotions and sixteen years later, Foley was named athletic director when Bill Arnsparger left to become defensive coordinator of the San Diego Chargers. Foley had practically run the department since Arnsparger left his head coaching job at LSU in 1987 to move to Florida. He had thought he had a good chance at the job when it was given to Arnsparger, but he did-n't get it for another five years. If Florida's president hadn't promoted him to the highest athletic position that time, Foley probably would have left the university.

"I would have had to look around," he said. "It was a crossroads where either I got the job and knew where I was going to be or I owed it to myself and my career to look else-where." It wasn't necessary. In a year and a half as athletic di-rector, Foley had displayed the sensible leadership and control that the school's athletic department had lacked since the mid-1980s. He had a great business sense, operating the $25 mil-lion budget like it was a simple checking account with a $500 balance. He had helped make $35 million in capital improve-ments, including the expansion of Florida Field that added an upper deck to the north end zone section, increasing the sta-dium's seating capacity from seventy-two thousand to eighty-five thousand.

In a period when university presidents were under pres-sure to reduce emphasis on athletics, mainly since more than 60 percent of the nation's athletic budgets were in the red, Foley's athletic department was giving money back. The Gators' athletic department had given the university $2 million to support the library system and an AIDS institute. If Foley lacked anything, it was experience. At the age of forty, he was one of the nation's youngest athletic directors, but his pro-gressive thinking and work habits overcame any mistakes at-tributable to his youthfulness. While most athletic directors in the SEC came from the old school of thinking, Foley was cre-ating new ideas and usually thinking one step ahead. A natural workaholic, he often put in twelve to fourteen hours a day in his office at Florida Field. "Why not? I love this job," he said. "It's the perfect job for me. I love this school. I can see myself here for twenty more years."

On Thursday, one Gator received surprising but splendid news. Kicker Judd Davis, who had made four of four field goals in the slop against Georgia and thirteen of fifteen for the season, was named one of four finalists for the Lou Groza Award. Davis was joined by UCLA's Bjorn Merten, Oklahoma State's Lawson Vaughn, and Alabama's Michael Proctor. The award was only in its second year; the winner would be announced December 2.

The team arrived in Columbia Friday afternoon just hours after Smith announced the completion of Usina's investigation of Jackson's scuffle at Gator Growl. The wide receiver was told the bad news before he boarded the team bus heading for the airport. He returned to his apartment, not looking forward to watching the game on television.

Jackson was charged with resisting arrest with violence and was offered a diversionary program. If he agreed to the program, he would have to serve twenty-five hours of community service and issue a public apology. He also would be on probation for six months, but he would have no criminal record. Jackson's attorney, Parlapiano, talked his client into accepting the deal.

"This is tough, because I don't agree with the decision to file a charge," Parlapiano announced. "But we are going to do it. We have to. It would make no sense to go ahead and go to court. Willie knows that. But I don't think he was guilty of much."

Nevertheless, Spurrier and Foley had no choice now. They had to suspend Jackson for Saturday's game. They announced the penalty as a one-game suspension and added that the Student Judicial Affairs Office would review the case next week. When Foley walked into the lobby of the team's hotel in Columbia, he said he was worried that student affairs would want to further penalize the receiver. "Their investigation is completely independent," he said. "We'll wait and see what they decide."

Having Jackson home in Gainesville during such a crucial game was not an ideal situation for Florida's offense. As long as he, Jack Jackson, Chris Doering, and Harrison Houston were healthy, defenses had trouble double-teaming any of them. One, two, or even three of them were likely to get open on any play. The next day, Florida would be playing in front of a hostile crowd of more than seventy thousand fans in a game that was crucial to the SEC Eastern Division championship.

The Gators' only remaining conference game was at home against lowly Vanderbilt the following week. They hadn't lost at home in four years, so for all intents and purposes beating South Carolina would guarantee they would face Alabama in the conference championship game for the second straight year. "This *is* our most crucial game of the season," Spurrier remarked. "If we lose this one . . ."

If Florida lost this one, Tennessee would waltz into Birmingham to play the Crimson Tide for the SEC championship. The two teams had tied on the same day Auburn upset Florida. "I haven't given up hope yet," Tennessee coach Phillip Fulmer said on the SEC's weekly teleconference call. "South Carolina could do it. Let me put it this way—we'll be paying attention to that game." Fulmer should know the troubles the Gamecocks offer at home. A year earlier, they had upset Tennessee to send Florida to the championship game and now they had a chance to return the favor.

South Carolina's goal was simple: win its last two games against Florida and rival Clemson to earn a bowl berth. None of the Gamecocks had ever been to a bowl and the seniors' careers had been mostly dismal, including the death of coach Joe Morrison in 1989. "We need 'em both," Taneyhill said of the last two games. "We can do it." By Friday, Florida's quarterback situation was determined. Wuerffel would start and Dean probably wouldn't be able to suit up.

That night, Rhett and defensive end Kevin Carter sat down at the Columbia Ramada Inn and talked about motivation. At six-foot-five and about 265 pounds of mostly muscle, Carter had one of the most impressive bodies on the team, but he had yet to come close to reaching his potential. It appeared he wasn't motivated on some plays. Coaches knew that if they could put Rhett's heart inside a body like that, they would have another Reggie White or Richard Dent. "Errict made me aware of some things that were true, some things that I needed to think about, some things that I hadn't been exemplifying," Carter said later. "He made me think about myself."

The biggest shock for the Gators on Saturday morning had to be the weather: sunny, seventy-two degrees, and no chance of rain. They hadn't played a dry football game since whipping LSU 58–3 more than a month earlier.

Florida's first possession ended in the strangest way. Wuerffel had driven the Gators to the South Carolina twelve-yard line in twelve plays when he dropped back to throw on third-and-ten. Suddenly, he stopped. Defensive end Jahmal Pettiford picked him up by his legs and plowed him into the ground. "What the heck are you doing?" Spurrier asked when Wuerffel came to the sideline. "I heard a whistle," he replied. "Somebody blew a whistle." The officials did not stop play or call a penalty. Then the referee ran over to Spurrier, somewhat apologetic, "Sorry coach. Some guy in the corner of the stadium has a whistle." Judd Davis, fresh from becoming a finalist for the kicking award, missed for only the third time during the season, a thirty-three-yard attempt that sailed wide left.

South Carolina tailback Brandon Bennett had to be one of the nation's most underrated running backs. After fullback Rob Desoer ripped off a run of thirty-one yards, Bennett followed it with a twenty-six-yard burst over left tackle for a touchdown. Nobody had run on Florida all season, but South Carolina rushed for seventy-two of its eighty yards on its first possession. If the Gamecocks could run on Florida, they had a chance to win.

It looked even worse when South Carolina's Frank Adams blocked Shayne Edge's punt five plays later. Then Taneyhill threw to wide receiver Toby Cates to make it 14–0. Florida punted quickly again after Wuerffel threw two incompletions. Reed Morton's field goal gave the Gamecocks a 17–0 lead fifty-five seconds into the second quarter. They had more than the lead, they had hope and confidence, something you never want to give an underdog in its home stadium.

Knowing the game was being televised in the South, Spurrier was thinking how giddy Tennessee was feeling at the moment. They probably were thinking this was the same Gator "choke" from the old days. The road demons had appeared again. Adams, a starting cornerback, went up and down South Carolina's bench telling his teammates, "We need more points! We need more points!"

It was one of those times, as Auburn defensive coordinator Wayne Hall divined a month earlier, that Spurrier would grow impatient and abandon the running game. He did. Wuerffel lofted a beautiful bomb off his back foot, hitting a wide open Jack Jackson in stride for a fifty-nine-yard touchdown. Davis then missed the extra point. First a field goal, now an extra point. Lou Groza wasn't smiling on this kicker.

On the next South Carolina play, linebacker Dexter Daniels made an amazing one-handed interception of a Taneyhill pass. Wuerffel then threw twenty-five yards for another touchdown to Harrison Houston, but his ensuing pass for the two-point conversion was intercepted. Just like that, the score was 17–12.

South Carolina would make another crucial mistake late in the first quarter. Taneyhill and Bennett fumbled a handoff and defensive end Johnie Church picked it up, trudging to the Gamecocks' four-yard line. After Rhett gained three, Wuerffel jumped over the pile, holding the ball dangerously high. Still, it was a touchdown, and his two-point pass to Aubrey Hill gave Florida a 20–17 lead. "I've told him to get low on those sneaks," Spurrier exclaimed. "But he still holds the ball up there. One of these days, somebody is going to knock it away."

Taneyhill came right back, completing five of six passes including consecutive throws of sixteen and thirty-six yards.

The latter was a nice crossing pattern to Cates, who darted down the left sideline for a touchdown. The Gamecocks had the 70,188 fans back in the game.

In the locker room at halftime, Red Anderson picked up a chair, tossed it, and screamed at the defensive players. The forty-eight-year-old defensive line coach had the most fiery disposition of any of Florida's coaches. Since his orange hair had started to gray, he didn't get mad as often as when he was a younger coach. When he did, however, players stayed out of his way. This time, he was livid. Maybe he was letting off steam after the Owens affair, which had put his character and integrity on the line. A string of obscenities flowed from his mouth like tobacco juice. "He said what needed to be said," Zook stated. "Just an old-fashioned ass chewing." Linebacker Monty Grow loved it. "Coach Red just went wild," he added. "It looked like a championship wrestling match when somebody throws a chair in the ring and all hell breaks loose."

Up in the massive press box of Williams-Brice Stadium, one of the most modern facilities in the SEC, hundreds of writers and officials from both schools were jockeying for positions around the few televisions. Number-one Florida State was playing number-two Notre Dame in South Bend, Indiana, in the latest game of the century. By the time the Gators and Gamecocks took the field for the third quarter, many press box seats were still empty. Everyone was watching the Seminoles lead Notre Dame 7–0.

While Notre Dame was scoring twenty-four unanswered points on the tube, South Carolina and Florida traded field goals. At least Davis had his confidence back, stroking a forty-one-yarder through the uprights.

With 4:05 remaining in the third quarter, Rhett took the handoff and darted up the middle. Middle guard Eric Sullivan slammed him to the ground, limiting Rhett to only one yard. It was not just any yard, but the 3,929th yard of Rhett's career. It was the yard that bumped Emmitt Smith to number two on the all-time Gators rushing list. The game wasn't stopped and no announcement was made. Rhett himself didn't realize after the game which carry had broken the record. Perhaps this is why he wanted it to happen at his home field. There would have been some sort of ceremony, no matter how brief.

The Gamecocks later downed a punt on Florida's two-yard line, putting the Gators into a deep hole. Spurrier then went from being the dumbest coach in the stadium to the luckiest in only seventy-three yards. He called for a flanker screen to Jack Jackson. Anyone who's had Football 101 knows you should never call a screen pass out of your own end zone. "I just wanted seven or eight yards," Spurrier said later. When he saw South Carolina was not playing a zone defense, he cringed.

Wuerffel looked to the left and saw the Gamecocks were playing man-to-man. Jackson figured Wuerffel would change the play at the line of scrimmage. "I thought, he's got to change this," Jackson recalled. Wuerffel didn't, but dropped back and threw the pass. "I probably should have thrown the ball away," he later explained. "I was just hoping Jack could fall forward out of the end zone."

Jackson caught it one yard deep in the end zone and was trapped by safety Norman Greene, but Greene overran him. Then linebacker Mike Landy had a shot at Jackson, but he missed the tackle. Jackson broke free and saw nothing but grass in front of him. He ran down the left sideline. He pulled a hamstring thirty yards later, but continued running before being tackled at South Carolina's twenty-seven. Wuerffel, who had been knocked down after delivering the pass, stood over a yellow flag in the end zone. He picked it up and ran it to the official, who penalized South Carolina another fifteen yards.

The strangest and probably most ill-advised call of the season resulted in one of the season's most important long gains. "It's a risky play down there," Wuerffel admitted. "It kind of surprised me." Jackson, one of the gutsiest and cockiest players on the team, had bailed the Gators out of the mess.

"We should have had a safety, and they get a seventy-yard gain," Sparky Woods reflected. "That was the play of the game."

Two plays later, Rhett dove into the end zone on a sweep for the go-ahead touchdown. On South Carolina's next possession, linebacker Matt Pearson, who rarely played, tipped a Taneyhill pass and it was intercepted by Grow, who had returned from his broken arm. He caught the pass despite having a massive cast on his right arm. "It just dropped into my lap," Grow remembered. "I couldn't drop it." The play set up another Rhett touchdown, which gave Florida a 37–26 lead. Woods benched Taneyhill and South Carolina never threatened again, mainly because Florida suddenly had a pass rush, sacking the backup quarterback three times. Carter had two of them; Rhett's talk must have worked.

Late in the game, Florida sports information director John Humenik burst into laughter on the sideline, pointing to a section of Gators fans where there was a sign: "Ms. Bobbitt says 'Cocks have been nipped." The Lorena Bobbitt story, three months before captivating the country, had entered the realm of college football.

The team's mascot was an embarrassment to some South Carolinians. Gamecocks was one thing, but the most popular nicknames for the sports teams had been shortened, just as Miami fans called their Hurricanes the "'Canes" and Texas called their Longhorns the "Horns." When South Carolina applied that theory to its terminology, it became personal. New athletic director Mike McGee, who had left the University of Southern California for the job, wanted to put a stop to the abbreviation, but he was encountering some resistance. He was discovering it's tough to change traditions, no matter how silly they appear.

It had been easier for Spurrier, who had a new team with a new attitude. Gators teams of the past would have folded when they trailed by seventeen points on the road. The comeback didn't set a school record, but it came close. It was

For the first half of the season junior defensive end Kevin Carter wasn't performing up to his potential. But near the end of the South Carolina game, he became unstoppable, possibly owing to a talk with Errict Rhett.

UNIVERSITY OF FLORIDA SPORTS INFORMATION

Florida's best comeback on the road since 1968 and best overall since trailing Auburn 17–0 in 1986.

"There were no ghosts of memories past today," Spurrier pronounced, beaming. "The Gators came back to win one. I don't think we're the best team in the country, but we've found a way to win a lot of games. This was a big win." Just then, McGee entered Spurrier's press conference. The two had known each other for more than ten years when each worked in the Atlantic Coast Conference. "Hey, there's South Carolina's athletic director. . . . Mike, you got whistles in your stands," Spurrier called out, breaking the room into laughter.

McGee, Woods, and his players didn't feel like laughing. This meant another losing season and no bowl game. "I don't like losing," Woods said. "We had progress at the beginning of the year and then we got hit with injuries in that Mississippi State game. I am really sad for our seniors." In turn, they would be sad for Woods. Three weeks later, McGee fired him.

In Florida's locker room, Zook leaned against a wall and reminded the assembled sportswriters that the defense had set up three of the offense's touchdowns. Daniels's interception, Church's fumble recovery, and Grow's interception preceded Florida touchdowns. "Did anybody notice that?" he asked. "The ball finally bounced our way for once." Spurrier noticed, although he put it another way. "South Carolina's turnovers turned it around for us," he commented.

Rhett plopped up on an equipment trunk and tried to convince everyone he hadn't been angry the week earlier when he stormed out after the Southwestern Louisiana game. "I left because my mom was waiting on me and I hadn't seen her in a while," he said. "I am too much of a team player to worry about all that." Rhett now had 4,001 yards and one very prominent school record. "I don't care about any of those statistics," he declared. "We won the game, that's all I care about. What, you don't believe me?"

The Gators were 8–1 and only Vanderbilt, which had won four games but had beaten only one team with a winning record, stood between them and the SEC Eastern Division championship. The Commodores were Tennessee's final hope for a another Florida loss in the conference. "I thought about how they had to be high-fiving each other when we were behind 17–0," Spurrier said of the Volunteers. The high-fives now were all Florida's.

12

WINNING THE EASTERN DIVISION

NOTRE DAME HAD HELD ON TO defeat Florida State 31–24 and had taken over the number-one position in college football. With the Seminoles' losing, only Notre Dame, Nebraska, Auburn, and West Virginia still had perfect records. Spurrier voted in the coaches' top twenty-five poll for *USA Today* and CNN, but he never discussed his ballot with anyone. Sunday morning he was asked whom he had ranked number one and where had he put the Seminoles. "That's private," he snapped. In any case, his Gators were now ranked number eight by the Associated Press.

Willie Jackson's case was scheduled to be reviewed by the student affairs office, and Spurrier wanted to get that distraction out of the way. "I was told last week it would be a one-game suspension only and then he would be reinstated," he said. He was worried about the position now. Harrison Houston and Jack Jackson each had nagging hamstring injuries. Jackson's affliction came on that great escape from the end zone that avoided sure disaster.

Such effort was common and consistent from Jack Jackson, the Moss Point, Mississippi, native who spurned the home state teams so he could play in a wide-open offense. He was a running back who ran the forty-yard dash in 4.3 seconds in high school. As a receiver at Florida, he was one of the two fastest players on the team, along with backup receiver Daryl Frazier. Jackson had vision problems in high school, but he never wore glasses. "I was a running back just running away from blurs," he said. When he arrived in Gainesville as a freshman, team doctors prescribed contacts. "Once I was able to see, it was a whole new world for me," he remarked. When Jackson had dropped a pass over the middle in the South Carolina game, he had heard a defensive back yell that he was scared. "Truth was," he explained, "I lost a contact the play before. I never did see the ball coming."

Florida's coaches knew that two of Jackson's plays—the hundred-yard kickoff against Mississippi State and the run after the screen pass against South Carolina—were not only worth watching but they may have saved the team from two losses. Jackson led the conference in kickoff returns, averaging 30.5 yards per attempt. He also had more than a hundred yards receiving in three games, but he wasn't getting much attention outside of Gainesville. Alabama's David Palmer, Colorado's Charles Johnson, and UCLA's J. J. Stokes generally were regarded as the nation's best receivers while Willie Jackson was thought of as one of the best in the SEC. "Jack's got the numbers to go with those other guys," Spurrier protested. "He's got all the qualities you look for in a receiver. He's fast. He's got great hands, and he's very tough over the middle."

It was Spurrier's job to make sure his players weren't looking ahead to the Florida State game. To do that, he had to play up Vanderbilt's strengths and make his team forget the Commodores' weaknesses. "Hey, Vanderbilt took Auburn to the wire and beat Kentucky," he warned. "They could beat us if we're not ready." The Gators supposed anything was possible.

Monday night Dean returned to practice and the quarterback derby resumed. Wuerffel had had an excellent game at South Carolina, completing twenty-five of thirty-seven passes for 333 yards. Steve Taneyhill would have died for similar statistics, but gaudy statistics were becoming routine for Florida's quarterbacks in Spurrier's system. Following practice, Spurrier said he would wait to decide who would start against Vanderbilt. "I've kind of gotten used to it," Dean admitted. "That's the way he said it's going to be and all I can do is go out and practice and do what I've got to do to keep the job."

The next day, Spurrier committed to Dean—for the week. "If he's healthy, and it looks like he is, then he'll be the starter," he announced. "It will be his game." Still, it appeared as if Dean wouldn't have any targets to throw to. Receiver Aubrey Hill was added to the injury list with a slight knee sprain. Now Florida had three injured receivers and another waiting for a student disciplinary panel to decide his immediate future.

Jackson recounted his story to the Student Judicial Affairs board, as did Officer Clendenin, who maintained that Jackson had struck the officers. Officer Mignone was less adamant about Jackson's being violent. "They contradicted each other," Jackson commented. "And when I left the meeting I thought that they were going to let me play on Saturday. I was the only one telling the same story every time I told it. I never hit the guy or they never would have let me go in the first place."

The South Carolina game helped Florida work its way back to minus-six in the turnover/takeaway ratio, deemed by most coaches as the most important statistic in football. Florida had been a minus-nine at one point, mostly because of the seven-interception night at Kentucky. The defensive backs hadn't made many interceptions, just four in nine games, while the linebackers had made six. The team also had recovered only seven fumbles. It baffled Zook. He and the other defensive coaches taught the second and third tacklers on the scene to strip the ball. He stressed catching the ball to the defensive backs rather than just knocking it down. "We stress punching the ball out more than anybody else," Zook explained.

Zook was still puzzled from the 1992 season when Florida ranked last in takeaways in the SEC. He had gone through every play on tape over the summer, counting sixteen dropped interceptions and six other fumble recoveries in which officials had ruled the ball dead. "Right there are twenty-two more turnovers we could have had," he contended. "The interceptions . . . we preach and preach and preach about looking the ball into your hands before running downfield with it. I guess sometimes it's nothing more than the bounce of the ball, and we haven't got our share of bounces."

Zook had called former UCLA and Philadelphia Eagles coach Dick Vermeil, whom he came to know after Vermeil became a college football analyst for ABC. Vermeil was the guru of plotting charts and graphs and keeping statistics on every category possible. "Don't worry," he told Zook. "You are teaching the right things. It will even out in the end. It has to."

As long as Spurrier was head coach, the offense probably would be near the top of the conference in turnovers, particularly interceptions, because they passed more than the other eleven teams in the conference. Florida quarterbacks had thrown fifteen interceptions during the season and sixty-eight since 1990, fifteen more than any other team in the SEC. Zook realized that that factor would tend to keep the team's turnover/takeaway ratio in the negative, but what could he do? "Listen," he said, "as a defensive coach, all I worry about are getting turnovers. I can't control the interceptions by the offense."

Spurrier shrugged off the statistics. "When you throw the ball a lot, you'll have interceptions," he commented. "This year, we had seven at Kentucky and only eight since. We're down again in turnovers, and we lead the league in penalties, so it's obvious we don't do a lot of things right. Somehow, we've won eight of nine."

Making it nine out of ten was all that counted now. The national championship seemed like a long shot, so winning the SEC's Eastern Division was the players' immediate goal. Defeating Vanderbilt would reach it for them. Florida State would travel to Gainesville for the annual showdown the following week.

"We've got a lot to play for," Spurrier admonished his players on Tuesday. "Our whole season is on the line this week. We can't even think about Florida State . . . or Alabama."

"Being a senior," Rhett added, "I want that chance to play Alabama again. I want to close out my career here as an SEC champion and play in the Sugar Bowl. [But] all that matters to me right now is Vanderbilt."

Dean had remembered the same situation two years earlier when lowly Kentucky came to Florida Field with the Gators' SEC championship riding on the outcome. The Wildcats had scored three straight touchdowns to get within 28–26 midway through the fourth quarter. Florida sustained a final touchdown drive to win by a final score of 35–26. "We were supposed to kill them that day," Dean recalled. "I think we really took them lightly, but I don't think that's going to happen this week."

Spurrier was trying his best to ensure it wouldn't happen by reminding his players about that game. "Kentucky came within a play of beating us," he explained. "We got to thinking about other things . . . games in the future and other teams we would play."

Florida was a twenty-three-point favorite and had won twenty-two consecutive games at home, dating back to 1989. It's not as if there hadn't been bigger upsets, however. The LSU team that Florida had beaten 58–3 had shocked Alabama 17–13 in Tuscaloosa two weeks earlier. "If we lose to Vandy," Watson concluded, "it would ruin our whole season. We know what we have to concentrate on no matter who we play next week."

Then the first wave of rumors that Spurrier would be interviewed for an NFL coaching job hit the Gainesville campus. Officials from the expansion franchises in Charlotte and Jacksonville had yet to name head coaches, and Spurrier was being mentioned as a candidate for each. "I guess it's flattering that they think you have those kinds of skills," he reflected. Then he joked about his old position that was now vacant.

Duke's Barry Wilson had resigned under pressure a week earlier. "Duke called me and offered me my job back. I told them I was pretty well set where I was."

On Thursday, Spurrier was disgusted with Wuerffel's and Dean's practice habits. Wuerffel was throwing off his back foot again, and Dean's shoulder may have been bothering him more than he admitted. "I guess I need to do a better job of coaching them in the fundamentals," Spurrier remarked. "They need to work more on the mechanics of throwing." Rhett heard some good news; he was named first-team All-American by *Football News*.

Although South Carolina had run well against Florida in the first half, the strength of the Gators' defense was still against the run. Florida's defense trailed only Alabama and Auburn in rushing yards allowed. To beat the Gators, it was obvious that you had to be able to throw the football, andof all major college football teams, Vanderbilt probably was the worst at trying to do that. Larry Woody, a sportswriter who covered the Commodores for the *Nashville Tennessean,* had the best line to describe the team's offense: "Vanderbilt couldn't throw it into the ocean if the quarterback was standing on the beach."

Privately, Spurrier wondered why any coach would want to run the I-bone (three backs in the I-formation) or be so lopsidedly one-dimensional. "You have to do both [run and pass] to win at this level," he remarked.

He was right. When Miami and its wide-open offense had upset Nebraska and its powerful running game in the 1984 Orange Bowl for the national championship, it symbolized the beginning of a new era in college football. The Nebraskas, Oklahomas, Ohio States, and Alabamas wouldn't win another national championship until they developed balanced offenses. The I-bone, flex-bone, wishbone, and all the other bones were fine if you wanted to win six, seven, or perhaps even eight games, but national championships were being captured by teams with balanced offenses. The transition had actually begun in the 1970s.

Vanderbilt was the only team in the nation that had not thrown a touchdown pass in 1993. The Commodores had completed forty-five passes all season, including ten to the wrong team. Third-year coach Gerry DiNardo, the defensive coordinator at Colorado before arriving in Nashville, maintained that building a balanced offense wasn't yet his priority. "You start by building a strong, solid defense," he explained. "You have to be able to stop the run first. Then your offense can evolve. You have to be able to run it before you can throw it, and we haven't been able to run it as well as last year. We'll teach some new things in spring practice." But that wouldn't help Vandy against Florida this week.

On Friday afternoon, as Willie Jackson was about to check into the team's Gainesville hotel, he was startled to hear that he was to be suspended for another game. At least he could attend this one in person, which was a small consolation and, if anything, would only make him feel worse. "It was all bullshit, everything that happened," Jackson claimed. "I hate every part of it. Politics. The media made a big deal out of it, which pressured them to do something."

The penalty was a standard 10 percent of the student-athlete's season. Two games surpassed 10 percent of the season, and Jackson had already been suspended for one game. In a prepared statement, Jackson said, "It's been a learning process for me. I accept that I am accountable and responsible for my actions. Now I just want to play football."

Spurrier wasn't exactly pleased, figuring the wide receiver had already served his penalty. "I don't know what to say about it," he added. "We'll just play with whoever is here."

By 4:00 P.M. Saturday, Spurrier had another problem, the most pleasant problem a coach can have. He was comparing his team's overall performances against LSU and Vanderbilt. Vanderbilt's one-dimensional offense gained eleven yards and no first downs in the first quarter. Spurrier went to his trick plays immediately, having Rhett run left and hand off to Doering. Doering was supposed to run right and throw back to Dean, who was waiting behind a wall of blockers on the right sideline. But Doering dropped the ball. By the time he picked it up, Dean was still waiting. He lobbed the football to the quarterback, who trotted thirty-five yards for an easy touchdown.

"We worked on that play in practice all year," Dean said. "I was ecstatic when I saw it signaled in." Doering added, "I guess I tried to throw it before I had it. It wasn't the prettiest pass you'll ever see." Dean returned to his natural position of throwing footballs instead of catching them, completing touchdown passes of eighteen and four yards to Aubrey Hill, who was playing in place of Houston. The score was 21–0 after one quarter.

Vanderbilt would lose three consecutive fumbles on three possessions in the second quarter, and Spurrier benched Dean after he followed three incompletions with an interception. Wuerffel wasn't much better, although his nineteen-yard touchdown pass to Jack Jackson, who appeared healthy, made the score 31–0 at the half.

Linebacker Ed Robinson scored Florida's first defensive touchdown of the season, picking up another Vandy fumble and running forty-eight yards to give the Gators a 38–0 lead. Meanwhile, the offense was sputtering, and Spurrier was furious. After Wuerffel fumbled, then threw an interception in the end zone, Spurrier went back to Dean. Backup tailback Tony Davis was playing in relief of Rhett at this point. Davis, an excellent all-around athlete, caught a pass for twenty-six yards and ran twice for fourteen to set up a touchdown pass from Dean to Dean. Terry Dean threw twelve yards to tight end Charlie Dean, no relation. Third-string quarterback Eric Kresser finished the scoring with a sixty-seven-yard bomb to Daryl Frazier to make the final score 52–0.

When Vanderbilt's last pass fell incomplete at Florida's thirty-three-yard line, Zook ran around hugging anyone in his path. Florida had its first shutout in more than two years. The Commodores never had a chance to score, moving only as close as Florida's eleven-yard line. "God, I needed that," Zook screamed. "You don't know how bad I wanted that." He hugged Foley, who usually walks onto the field to congratulate the players and coaches following each game. As players and coaches walked into the locker room, they passed under a sign that read: Free Willie. Some enterprising fan wanted Willie Jackson back in uniform.

Vanderbilt had lost six fumbles and thrown two interceptions, correcting Florida's turnover-takeaway ratio in a three-hour period. The Gators were now a minus-one for the season. "One of our goals every season is no turnovers," DiNardo said. "Just the opposite happened. We caused most of them ourselves." Zook didn't agree. His defense had created eleven turnovers in two games. "We figured we'd get a couple," he asserted. "We had guys flying around and ripping it out."

Even several offensive players felt good for their counterparts on the team. "That's the defense I know," Watson announced. "That's the way those guys play in practice, and I've been waiting to see that all year. It makes my heart warm."

Spurrier wasn't about to get that mushy, especially over something "over there" having to do with the defense. He was still disappointed with his quarterbacks. Dean had completed eleven of twenty-two for 128 yards, three touchdowns, and one interception. Wuerffel had completed eleven of twenty-one for 115 yards, one touchdown, and one interception. "Neither one of them played well," he commented. "Dean is looking at his [primary] receiver too much, and Danny is forcing the ball. They could have had seven or eight interceptions today."

A week earlier he had said he didn't want to start "zig-zagging" his quarterbacks during a game. But against Vandy, Dean was zigged to the bench, then Wuerffel was zagged onto the field. Spurrier then benched him and put Dean back in. "I didn't mean it to happen that way," Spurrier explained. "It just happened. I had to be fair. I pulled one. I had to pull the other." He concluded by saying that he was unsure who would start against Florida State. He was sure of one thing, however, the effort against LSU was better than this.

Wuerffel sat on the stool in front of his locker and shrugged. "Whatever Coach wants to do is fine with me. Maybe this option helps us win ball games."

Minutes later Dean emerged from the shower. He felt like a yo-yo. "It's been a strange year, hasn't it?" he mused. "No big deal to me. I am used to it by now, if you can get used to it."

The win also guaranteed that Florida would face Alabama, which had lost 22–14 at Auburn, in the SEC championship game in two weeks in Birmingham. Tennessee would have to be satisfied with the Citrus Bowl. "We couldn't let Tennessee represent the division," Ed Robinson remarked, still excited over his fumble recovery and touchdown. "We wanted the championship. . . . I guess that was our main focus all along."

Florida had run two trick plays against Vanderbilt, including Doering's throwback pass to Dean for the first touchdown. Somebody mentioned to Spurrier after the game that it would have been better to save them for either Florida State or Alabama when he would desperately need them. "How'd I know we'd win 52–0?" he snapped. "We were just trying to win the game first. Besides, you think those are the only trick plays we got?"

One of the rarest sights after the game was the absence of any celebration. Spurrier had made it a team ritual to hold a massive celebration on the field, including having team pictures made in front of the scoreboards, whenever the team clinched anything. The Gators had celebrated in 1990 at Kentucky when they clinched the best record in the SEC; the next year at home against Kentucky when they clinched their first official SEC championship; in 1992 at Vanderbilt when they clinched the Eastern Division championship; and following the Gator Bowl victory over North Carolina State, the school's first bowl victory in five years. "I've always believed if you have something worth celebrating, you celebrate it," he explained.

This time, Spurrier wanted the players to be hungry for Florida State. Allowing them to let off steam for beating Vanderbilt by fifty-two points wouldn't be productive in the long run. Anyway, it wasn't as if they scored a last-minute touchdown like at Kentucky or had a pass dropped in the end zone like the one during the Georgia game. The victory over the Commodores was secured in the first quarter.

"Last year was a major accomplishment because we started with two losses and we came back," Spurrier commented. "We're hoping we can take some pictures later on. Don't get me wrong, this one is nice."

So nice and easy that the coaches and players spent much of the game glancing at the scores from around the country on Florida Field's massive scoreboards. Number four Miami had lost 17–14 to West Virginia. Number five Ohio State had been crushed 28–0 at Michigan. Two hours after Florida-Vanderbilt had finished, number-one Notre Dame was shocked 41–39 by Boston College.

Tennessee had beaten Kentucky 48–0, after which Wildcats coach Bill Curry described the Volunteers as one of the most impressive teams he had ever seen. Spurrier, who rarely mentions the rankings, couldn't understand why Tennessee (number seven) was ranked higher than Florida (number eight). The Volunteers had a loss and a tie and Florida had only a loss. Most important, the Gators had beaten them on the field. "How can Tennessee be ranked above us?" he asked the huge media crowd after the Vanderbilt game. "I definitely think we should be ranked ahead of Tennessee." Then he answered it himself. "We're not getting the respect because we've been in a lot of high-scoring games. I guess we just haven't dominated games as much as other people."

Surely the Gators would jump from their number-eight ranking as they headed into the showdown with the Seminoles. "Now I guess we have a chance to have even a bigger year with all the things happening around the country today," Spurrier said. "It was some day, huh?"

Some week was just around the corner. The Seminoles, led by Heisman Trophy shoo-in Charlie Ward, would arrive in Gainesville ranked number one. "Can we beat Florida State?" Spurrier asked, repeating a question. "I haven't even thought about that game yet. I think anyone would give us a chance because we are playing here in the Swamp."

13

HOME SWEET SWAMP

WHEN UNIVERSITY OF FLORIDA president John Tigert realized in 1929 that this relatively new and physical American game of football was more than a fad, he started searching around the Gainesville campus for the perfect spot to build a stadium. Other schools were doing it, he thought, so he had better build one for the university so fans would have a comfortable area from which to watch the game. A marshy depression in the middle of campus, just south of University Avenue, caught his attention. Alligators lived there. It was literally a swamp.

Ironically, twenty-one years earlier, the school's athletic teams became known as "the Alligators" when a Jacksonville lawyer suggested the mascot to decorate a school pennant. Austin Miller, according to the *Jacksonville Times-Union,* was a Gainesville native enrolled in the University of Virginia's law school in Charlottesville in 1907. His father, Phillip Miller, operated a drug store in Gainesville that was frequented by University of Florida students. One day Phillip Miller was visiting his son and they shopped at a Charlottesville pennant and poster firm to buy pennants for Miller's drug store. The manager showed them pennants of several Ivy League schools and asked the identity of Florida's mascot. Realizing the school had none, Austin Miller suggested Alligators since the reptile was native to Florida. When the pennants with an alligator picture became popular around Gainesville the next year, the name stuck. As the years have gone by "Gators" became more popular.

Tigert went ahead with his plans, having the swamp filled and a stadium constructed with a capacity of 21,769 fans. On November 8, 1930, the Florida Alligators played their first game at Florida Field, losing 20–0 to Alabama. It wasn't the greatest way to christen a stadium.

By 1991 the stadium's seating capacity had reached eighty-five thousand, and Steve Spurrier was searching for a nickname for the massive conglomeration of steel and brick that not only housed his office, but symbolized a huge part of his escape from adolescence. He had completed his first collegiate pass here in 1964. He had kicked that unforgettable game-winning field goal against Auburn here in 1966. He had coached the team to its first SEC championship here in 1991.

Spurrier believed in establishing and sticking to traditions, such as having the team remain on the field following each home game to sing the alma mater with the fans. It's a good thing the lyrics are displayed on the stadium's electronic scoreboard. Otherwise, the players would be bystanders to this new tradition.

Finding a suitable tag for Florida Field would be more difficult. Spurrier and assistant athletic director Norm Carlson kicked around names like the Gator Den and the Gator Pit. "They all sounded silly," Carlson recalled. Once Spurrier heard the story of Tigert's search, "the Swamp" seemed natural. "You know, once you get into the swamps, only the gators come out alive," Spurrier liked to say. "A swamp is a place where alligators live and play."

Officially, the stadium was named Ben Hill Griffin Stadium at Florida Field, a little too awkward and long to impress anyone or intimidate opponents. You can't imagine a Tennessee player telling a teammate, "Gosh, I think we have our work cut out for us this week, we have to go down there and try to win a game at Ben Hill Griffin Stadium at Florida Field."

Ben Hill Griffin, a citrus magnate who loved the university and the Gators enough to donate more than $20 million to the school during his lifetime, died in 1990, a year before Spurrier had tagged his stadium "the Swamp." You have to wonder what Griffin would have thought about Spurrier nicknaming the modern facility with plush sky boxes and state-of-the-art electronic equipment after a marshy depression. At first, even a few players chuckled. "I didn't know what to think when he started calling it the Swamp," Watson noted. "I kind of rolled my eyes and thought it was corny. Then it caught on with everybody. Nobody was calling it Florida Field anymore. Then I started using it."

So did everyone in the state, and the country followed. National mouthpieces like ESPN's Lee Corso and ABC's Keith Jackson used it when referring to the stadium. Nobody called it Ben Hill Griffin Stadium or even Florida Field anymore. Even opponents started referring to the place as the Swamp. In 1992 Spurrier had a large plastic Gator head mounted near the locker room exit and the school had emblazoned "Welcome to the Swamp" in large letters at the north end of the field. Most traditions take years to become entrenched, but after only two seasons, the Swamp was as much a part of Florida football as were the Gators' bright orange helmets.

As Spurrier had declared minutes after the Vanderbilt game, nobody would say Florida wouldn't have a chance against top-ranked Florida State because the game was to be played here, at the Gators' home field. For starters, the Gators had won all twenty-three games played here under Spurrier, compared to a 14–9 road record during the same period. Florida State had been the last team to leave Gainesville smiling, winning 24–17 in 1989. The upper deck addition to the north end zone in 1991 had added twelve thousand more seats, but more important, it also made the place one of the loudest in the nation.

YEAR OF THE GATOR

There is no running track around Florida Field, as at several other stadiums, and that allows the fans to sit just a few feet from the playing field. At times, the noise is unbearable. Florida fans are sophisticated, too, knowing to be noisy when the defense is on the field and to be more subdued when the offense has the ball.

The intense central Florida heat also enhances the home-field advantage. Gainesville, situated in the middle of the state, doesn't receive the same tropical breezes that grace Miami's Orange Bowl. For most games, especially those in September and October, the place is stifling. Imagine what that does to players from Kentucky and Tennessee who had practiced the previous week in fifty-degree weather.

"There may not be a greater home-field advantage in college football," Florida State coach Bobby Bowden said of Florida Field. "They get to doing that Gator Chomp thing, and before you know it the whole place is as loud as it gets anywhere."

Spurrier had directly credited the fans with several wins in the past, notably the 35–0 rout of Alabama and the 14–9 victory over Florida State in 1991. In that game, Florida State had a first-and-goal at the two-yard line with Florida leading 7–3. An offensive lineman couldn't hear quarterback Casey Weldon's signals and jumped early. After the illegal procedure penalty, Florida State missed a field goal. Later, Weldon couldn't change any plays at the line of scrimmage, resulting in three delay-of-game penalties when FSU was threatening in the fourth quarter. Without those penalties, Florida State probably would have scored and won the game.

That game was played before the SEC ruled that the visiting team's fans must sit behind the visiting team's bench. Called the Florida Rule, it was implemented after all the trouble brewed during the Florida-Tennessee game in 1991.

"They threw batteries at us, and we had to wear our helmets for the whole game," Florida State cornerback Clifton Abraham remembered. "It was so loud you couldn't hear

Florida Field, or the Swamp, is the largest, hottest, and loudest place in Florida.

yourself think . . . loudest place I've ever played." Linebacker Derrick Brooks, then a freshman, said, "It got so bad that day that we had veteran players who were getting intimidated. I was really surprised at that."

"I don't sit in the stands, but I know it is very, very loud down on the field," Tennessee coach Phillip Fulmer commented. "Since they added that upper deck, it's gotten even louder."

Heading into the showdown with the Seminoles, Florida had beaten a number-three-ranked team (Florida State in 1991), two number-four teams (Auburn in 1990 and Tennessee in 1991), and a number-five team (Tennessee in 1993) during the twenty-three-game streak. And the Gators hadn't just won in the Swamp; they had dominated the opposition, winning by an average margin of twenty-four points.

"We really do believe we can beat anybody in the Swamp," Spurrier claimed. "Our fans are the big reason, really.

It's a good, comfortable feeling when we are playing here and I am sure the other teams feel uncomfortable here."

Spurrier hadn't been a psychology major at Florida, but he knew how to get inside his players' heads as well as any coach. He tried to ingrain confidence in them, especially leading them to believe that no team could come to Gainesville and leave with a win. "Florida won here before Coach Spurrier came along," Chris Doering explained, "but he has put it in our minds that we are not going to lose here."

Jack Jackson thought that the Florida crowd was tremendously effective at reversing momentum shifts against the Gators. When an opponent would play well against Florida, the crowd noise would grow even louder, and the admonition usually stimulated the team to overcome the visitors. "When you are on the road and the momentum changes," Jackson added, "the crowd isn't there to get it back for you. People really don't realize how hard we play in this stadium until they come here."

If the Gators upset the favored Seminoles, it wouldn't take too much imagination to see the winning streak at the Swamp stretch to thirty by the 1995 season. In 1994 Florida was scheduled to play at Tennessee and at Florida State. Only Auburn would be a legitimate threat to upset Florida at home, that is, after the Seminoles left town.

"I don't want to be a part of the team that lets this streak end," senior linebacker Ed Robinson declared. "It would be even worse when we look back on it thirty years from now. People would say, 'Hey, he was on that team that lost at the Swamp for the first time.' I don't want that to happen to me." No Gator did, but beating Florida State was easier said than done. "The Seminoles have to come to the Swamp," tight end Charlie Dean said, "and prove themselves to us."

14

PLAYING THE "GIRLS' SCHOOL"

ROBERT CLECKLER BOWDEN ROLLED out of bed November 30, 1986, at 6:00 A.M. and wondered why he ever entered the crazy, heartbreaking profession of coaching football. He had only had a few hours' sleep, and it was a gloomy, rainy, dark Sunday in Tallahassee. No matter how the sky darkened, it couldn't compete with Bowden's mood. He didn't feel like eating breakfast with sportswriters, as he always did on the Sunday following a home game. He didn't feel like taping his television show. And he didn't feel like going to church, which was always one of the most pleasant hours during his hectic week.

He knew he had another year of pure hell in front of him. The irate phone calls would begin tomorrow. The obscene letters would begin pouring onto his desk by Tuesday. Life, in general, would be miserable for another year. All because of a single football game. Bowden's Florida State Seminoles had lost to the Florida Gators. Again. For the sixth straight year.

"If everybody wouldn't remind me of it, I'd be OK," Bowden complained. "But I *will* be reminded of it every day. I've got 364 more days to go to get through this thing. In the old days, men used to say that when things weren't going your way, there's one answer—booze." He then picked up his coffee cup and added, "Can a man start drinking at the age of fifty-seven?"

Such are the effects of the Florida-Florida State rivalry. In a state of fourteen million people and counting, some may not care for the beach, some may not love the Keys, some may not give a hoot for Disney World or Busch Gardens, and some may not even drink orange juice. But you had better believe that everyone has an opinion on Florida-Florida State, even University of Miami fans.

No game means more to the alumni, the boosters, and the fans simply because they live, work, eat, and exist together. Two bankers sitting side by side in Orlando may be a Gator and a Seminole. A prosecutor and the counsel for the defense facing each other in a Tampa courtroom may be a Gator and a Seminole. Two contractors bidding for the same job in West Palm Beach may be a Gator and a Seminole. The dichotomy pervades the state.

University of Florida football began in 1906 and existed peacefully in the state through the Great Depression and World War II. There had been the occasional game with Rollins College, the University of Tampa, Stetson University, and even a Jacksonville club team, but the Gators owned Florida, rarely losing to another team in the state until Miami was added to the schedule in 1938.

Nine years later, the Florida State College for Women in Tallahassee was renamed Florida State University because men were being allowed to enroll. Suddenly, the "girls' school" was coeducational, and naturally, with male students, there had to be a football team. Florida State started out playing the likes of Cumberland, Millsaps, and Erskine until moving up to such teams as Miami, Mississippi Southern, and Georgia Tech in the mid-1950s. The 1954 team won eight of eleven games to earn its first bowl berth, a 47–20 loss to Texas Western in the Sun Bowl. The Gators, whose program was half a century old, were stumbling through mediocrity at the time.

It was natural for the alumni, students, and the football players from each school to want to play each other. Florida's administration and coaches held out, thinking they had everything to lose by playing Florida State and little to gain. They didn't need FSU. Rather, FSU needed them and they knew it. A state senator even tried to pass a bill that required the two schools to meet on the football field. It failed in 1955. The following year, Florida officials succumbed to intense pressure, but the series had to wait two years until the Gators could make room on their schedule.

On November 22, 1958, at Florida Field in Gainesville, Florida State's Bobby Renn returned a kickoff seventy-eight yards and the rivalry was born. More than forty-three thousand fans watched the Gators beat FSU 21–7. Florida won four of the next five games, with the 1961 meeting ending in a 3–3 tie, Florida State's finest moral victory.

As they were reluctant to begin the series, Florida's administrators were also determined that the Gators would never play in Tallahassee, at least not until FSU enlarged its stadium, which at the time held about twenty thousand fans. When Florida State added twenty thousand more seats, the Gators agreed to travel to Tallahassee for the 1964 game. Florida's team, led by a talented sophomore quarterback named Steve Spurrier, initiated the slogan "Never, FSU, Never."

"Nobody should never say *never*," FSU coach Bill Peterson said. The Seminoles won 16–7, their most important victory in their brief history, to finish 8–1–1 before defeating Oklahoma in the Gator Bowl. The "girls' school" had arrived as a football presence, and what was a shell of a rivalry suddenly became real.

On Florida's next trip to Tallahassee, a game official caused what would remain the most talked about play and game of the rivalry. Spurrier led the Gators to a 22–19 advantage late in the game when FSU All-American receiver Ron Sellers headed to the sidelines with an injury. Little-known Lane Fenner came into the game for Sellers. His name would become infamous. With less than one minute remaining, quarterback Gary Pajcic threw long to Fenner, who made a twisting, over-the-shoulder catch at the goal line. Official Doug Moseley started to signal a touchdown but then changed his mind and ruled Fenner had caught the pass out of bounds. Photographs in every Florida newspaper the next day showed Fenner's catch: he was in bounds.

Peterson was so angry he never admitted that the Seminoles lost the game. The Gators won nine of eleven games and Spurrier won the Heisman Trophy that season. Florida State stumbled to a 6–5 finish. The play was debated throughout the state for days, weeks, months. And it still is. Twenty-eight years later, it is referred to as the Lane Fenner Game.

By 1977, a decade and a year following the Fenner game, Florida had won sixteen of the nineteen games between the schools; only one had ended in a tie. The Gators were entrenched as the dominating, powerful SEC team that annually beat up on the "girls' school" to the northwest. FSU alumni weren't feeling too good about their football team.

Then the Seminoles hired an innovative forty-seven-year-old coach from West Virginia named Bowden. After the Gators, coached by Doug Dickey, beat Bowden's first team 33–26, things started to change in Tallahassee. Bowden's next four teams finished 10–2, 8–3, 11–1, and 10–2 and had beaten Florida four straight years, from 1977 to 1980. "I thought, Hey, this beating Florida stuff is easy," Bowden said later. "I can do this. These Gators aren't so tough."

In 1981 Charley Pell followed Bowden to the Sunshine State. He had played for Paul "Bear" Bryant at Alabama, had earned a reputation as an aggressive coach at Clemson, and was Florida's new head coach. Pell suddenly assembled some impressive talent in Gainesville. His recruiting was second to none, and the Gators turned the series around again with a 35–3 rout of FSU in 1981. The Gators defeated the Seminoles every year from 1981 to 1986, including an embarrassing 53–14 debacle in 1983.

"Now they were saying, 'Bobby Bowden can't beat Florida,'" Bowden recalled. "I couldn't. I tried everything . . . one approach after another. Nothing worked."

When it was later discovered that Pell had violated NCAA rules to gather much of the Gators' talent—including stars such as Neal Anderson, Louis Oliver, John L. Williams, Wilber Marshall, Lomas Brown, and Jarvis Williams—Bowden was furious. "Old Charley had been stacking the deck against me," he declared. "I respect people who play by the rules."

The Seminoles had accumulated six years of resentment and frustration when Bowden awakened that November morning in 1986. The Gators, under Galen Hall, Pell's successor, had won again, 17–13. But the next year, Florida State started a streak of its own, winning its first of four straight against Florida. Then the Gators, a year after Spurrier had returned to his alma mater, put a stop to this latest streak with a 14–9 win in 1991.

"There is no reason we can't compete with them," Spurrier claimed. "We have all the facilities here . . . the resources to compete with anyone in the nation. We just have to do things right . . . win games and graduate our players."

By the numbers, Florida leads the series 23–12–1. But as anyone in the Sunshine State knows, you can't judge the Florida-Florida State rivalry solely by numbers and statistics. The colors, the character, the heritage, the traditions, the players, the coaches, and the people have made this rivalry something special. It's Orange and Blue versus Garnet and Gold. It's old versus new. It's "We are the Boys of Old Florida" versus "The War Chant," the Gator Chomp versus the Tomahawk Chop. And it is Spurrier versus Bowden, two of the finest and most innovative coaches in the nation.

Contrary to public opinion, there is no law that states the two schools must play each other in football. Several legislators have tried to push such a bill through, but they have always failed. "We should always play them, and they should always play us," Bowden has said. "Of course, we would have a better chance to win national championships without them on our schedule."

Ditto for Florida. The SEC schedule is difficult enough without a perennial power like Florida State waiting at the end of the season. Since 1987 the Seminoles have a 76–10 record and have never been ranked lower than number four at the end of the season. And it appears that that won't change as long as Bowden has an office at the Moore Athletic Center on Pensacola Street in the state's capital city.

In recent years, Spurrier has had trouble understanding how FSU continues to sign top recruits. Bowden has won most of the head-to-head bids with Spurrier for blue-chip players. On national signing day in February 1993 he expressed his frustration: "I'll say this about FSU . . . they've got the best re-cruiters in college football the way they can convince those kids they can go up there and beat out all those high school All-Americans they already have. I don't know what FSU is telling them up there."

The disputes between the schools have been many, from Florida's reluctance to play FSU in the first place to recent scheduling conflicts caused by the expansion of the SEC. When the SEC decided it would expand from ten to twelve teams in 1990, the conference courted Florida State like a love-starved boy after the prom queen. The Seminoles had a well-rounded athletic program, including a solid basketball program and perennial contenders for national championships in base-ball and football. While there was no doubt that the addition of Florida State would give the SEC the strongest football con-ference in the nation, Florida officials were lukewarm to the idea at best. The state wasn't big enough for *two* schools in the mighty Southeastern Conference.

Finally, the Seminoles elected to join the eight-member Atlantic Coast Conference, figuring the school's academics matched up better with the ACC, and the basketball program would be elevated to national status. The Gators didn't care that much that FSU had chosen the ACC, but the other SEC brethren were insulted that the former girls' school had turned them down. The SEC responded by adding South Carolina from the Metro Conference and Arkansas from the Southwest. The new schools would join the conference football schedule in 1992, as the SEC planned for an unprecedented conference championship game.

The Gators usually faced a killer schedule to end each season as it was. Whereas Florida and Florida State typically had two weeks to prepare for playing each other from the 1980s through 1991, the Gators now found themselves staring into Florida State's facemasks one Saturday and the SEC Western Division champions the next, if they were good enough to win the SEC's Eastern Division. Thus far under Spurrier they had shown that they were good enough, winning their division both years under the new format and figuring to continue to claim the eastern crown for some time to come. Thus, their two most important games of the season would fall on consecutive Saturdays. That's a coach's greatest nightmare.

When the SEC announced its plans for expansion in 1990, Florida athletic director Bill Arnsparger and his successor, Jeremy Foley, tried to convince FSU athletic director Bob Goin to move the game to September, possibly as the annual season opener for both teams. But Goin wasn't interested in discussing the proposal until the current contract expired, which will be after the 1995 season. The Seminoles had no scheduling problems by facing Florida and then having a month to prepare for a possible bowl game.

While Foley understands Goin's stance, he has felt some pressure from Spurrier to get the game moved. After Spurrier publicly expressed his displeasure with the Seminoles over the matter at the annual SEC Football Media Days in August 1991, Goin exploded. "I've told those people down there time and time again that I will talk to them about this when the time comes," he replied. "Their football coach doesn't seem to understand scheduling very well. He should stick to what he knows."

One thing Spurrier knows is his records, be they of his playing or coaching days. When he discovered an error in Florida State's 1990 media guide in the section detailing his playing days, he immediately called FSU assistant sports information director Donna Turner to complain. It stated: "Spurrier had a 2–2 record as a player against FSU." It should have been 2–1, since freshmen weren't eligible to play in 1963. It also noted that "during his Heisman Trophy winning season of 1967, his UF squad lost to FSU 21–16." Every Gator knows that Florida won 22–19 in Spurrier's Heisman Trophy year of 1966; that was the Lane Fenner Game.

Apparently Spurrier lacked some tact during the call, amusing the FSU staff enough to "accidentally" let the same mistake in Spurrier's biography slip by the following year. To them, he was known as "Stevie Wonder." They either wondered what made Stevie tick or they were admitting that Spurrier had worked wonders with the Florida program in just a short time.

Spurrier had lost two of his first three meetings with Bowden, losing 45–30 and 45–24 in Tallahassee, sandwiched around the 14–9 win in Gainesville. In the thirty-five years of the rivalry, none of the meetings would be as important as the upcoming game. Florida had a 9–1 record, was ranked number seven, and had its twenty-three-game winning streak in the Swamp at stake. Florida State had a 10–1 record and was ranked number one. This time much more was on the line than just state bragging rights.

15

THE GREATEST FLORIDA STATE TEAM EVER?

WHILE THE GATORS HAD NEVER come close to winning a national championship, several of Bowden's teams in his seventeen years at Florida State had come within a play or two of winning the big trophy. The 1979 and 1980 teams won twenty-one games and lost just three, including two to Oklahoma in the Orange Bowl. The 1981 Seminoles team helped give Bowden a reputation as a "King of the Road," as the school's sports information people called him. The team had played consecutive road games against Nebraska, Ohio State, Notre Dame, Pittsburgh, and LSU, winning three. The 1987 team came within a two-point conversion of winning the national championship, which went to Miami. The Seminoles went on to beat Nebraska in the Fiesta Bowl that year. Since then FSU has had 11–1, 10–2, 10–2, 11–2, and 11–1 records. Bowden has had the nation's longest bowl-winning streak, having won a bowl game each season since 1985.

By comparison, Florida had never won eleven games in a season and had won ten only once. The Gators hadn't won on New Year's Day since 1967. It seemed the girls' school had passed tradition by.

Of their well-known futility when it came to winning the national title, the 1993 season would be different, Seminoles fans proclaimed. This season would be the one. FSU would march through its twelve-game schedule and then win a bowl game, as usual, to take its first national championship. From August 28 through November 13, nobody was arguing with them over the matter. The Seminoles dismantled everybody in their path, starting with a 42–0 rout of Kansas in the Kickoff Classic in East Rutherford, New Jersey. They won by 45–7, 57–0, 33–7, 51–0, 28–10, 40–14, 54–0, and 49–20 before facing the ghosts of Rockne, Leahy, and the Four Horsemen in South Bend, Indiana.

On the same day that Florida rallied in Columbia, South Carolina, the Seminoles fell 31–24 to Notre Dame. Following the game, Florida State players pleaded with the pollsters not to drop them any farther than number two, thus guaranteeing that the teams would meet again in the Fiesta Bowl for the national title. Then Boston College ruined the matchup when it shocked Notre Dame the following week, sending FSU back to the number-one ranking in the Associated Press poll, but maintaining its number-two status in the coaches' poll.

"It's a plus, but only if we beat Florida," Bowden announced. "If we didn't have that one ball game left, I'd be jumping up and down. If today was my last day on earth, I'd grab half that [national championship] ring and take off. If this week turns out as bizarre as the last, Notre Dame could be number one again. Both Florida and us have skill running out our ears—runners, throwers, catchers runnin' all over the field. The big difference is we're playing down there in the Swamp. That's why I am so scared."

Not that the Gators' scores had scared anyone. Sure they had embarrassed LSU, Southwestern Louisiana, and Vanderbilt, but they also had beaten Kentucky by four points,

Tennessee by seven, and Georgia by seven. They had trailed South Carolina at the half and had lost to Auburn. Was it any wonder that the Seminoles were installed as an eleven-point favorite over the number-seven-ranked Gators?

By Sunday the Orange Bowl officials were as happy as Boston College's players. The Eagles' upset of Notre Dame practically assured the Miami bowl of hosting the national championship game. All undefeated Nebraska had to do was get by Oklahoma at home. If FSU beat Florida, the Seminoles would play the Cornhuskers in Miami. If the Gators won, undefeated West Virginia would play undefeated Nebraska. The Orange Bowl couldn't lose.

That afternoon Spurrier announced that the Gators would play to win and wouldn't give up until the end, referring to the year before in Tallahassee. Before that game he claimed that he would rather beat Alabama the next week in the inaugural SEC championship game than defeat Florida State. At halftime, trailing 38–17, Spurrier pulled quarterback Shane Matthews to prevent an injury that would have prevented him from playing against Alabama. It was the right move to make under the circumstances, but Spurrier was criticized for it.

"People asked me which game was more important and I answered it," he explained. "I usually hate to give 'no comment' as an answer. Maybe I shouldn't have answered the question. We didn't downplay the game at all. I just felt we didn't have as good a team, and we were playing up there. This is a different situation. We feel we can beat anybody at home. Heck, last year we averaged twenty-four points a game and gave up twenty-three. This time, we will do everything we can to win the game and then prepare for Alabama."

Alabama (8–2–1) had fallen to number seventeen after losing to Auburn, and the Tide had a week off before facing Florida. Alabama's players could rest and let the bumps and bruises heal while the Gators were meeting FSU in what was sure to be a physical game. It always was. "We knew that a few weeks ago," Spurrier said of Alabama's scheduling advantage. "We can't worry about it now."

This was exactly the scenario Foley had wanted to avoid while trying to convince FSU's Goin to reschedule the Florida-Florida State game. "It's an awful situation for us," Foley commented. "But it's not one that's going to change for a while. We're the ones who are stuck. Florida State likes having it as the final game."

There was nothing Spurrier could do about it this season. He had other problems anyway, for example, deciding which quarterback to start. "The best one in practice this week will start Saturday," Spurrier announced.

Monday morning in Tallahassee, about fifteen members of the Florida State band marched into the football offices and played the school fight song for a few minutes. The coaches took it for some sort of motivational ploy. One sign along Tennessee Avenue read "Drain the Swamp"; another, "The Swamp Stomp." That afternoon, Bowden and FSU defensive coordinator Mickey Andrews had his team preparing for both quarterbacks. The practice ran longer than usual since the Seminoles had so much ground to cover. Until 1991 the teams had had an off week to prepare to play each other. "It's like preparing for a test," Bowden observed after practice. "You do better if you have two weeks, but if the other team doesn't have that advantage, it's relative."

Florida players were amused at the point spread, which now favored the Seminoles by ten points. "Never thought I would see that," Doering remarked. "To be picked to lose by ten points at home is kind of upsetting. That shows the lack of respect we are getting around the nation. Everyone has been talking about how FSU deserves a rematch with Notre Dame. No one's mentioned that they have to get by us first. It's disrespect for our program and it hurts us as a team. If I was a gambler . . ."

Nothing made Florida State head coach Bobby Bowden's job tougher than a six-year losing streak to Florida from 1981–86. In 1993 son Terry had already beaten the Gators. Could the old man do it too?

Florida State had not only won ten of eleven games but also had covered the point spread in nine. "Are they ten-point favorites?" Jack Jackson asked. "Good. That puts all the pressure on them. I am not that surprised. They have been big favorites every time they have played. Remember, they were favored to beat Notre Dame, too. I still think we are one of the three or four elite teams in the country." Rhett, who almost decided to play for Florida State, wasn't surprised. "No, [but] I am surprised it isn't more than that," he said. "We've played too many close games this year, and they've blown everybody out. Their second and third teams could beat a lot of college teams."

It was one of those days when Rhett was in rare form. He sat in the Gators' meeting room and cracked one joke after another. "Last year they had guys like Carl Simpson, Dan Footman, and Sterling Palmer. . . . They're all in pro football today," he recalled. "We had two guys out of high school at the most important position [tackles Reggie Green and Jason Odom]. Our guys were in awe . . . they about peed themselves."

Following Florida's Monday Night Football, Spurrier still wouldn't say which quarterback he preferred to play against Florida State. Given FSU's quickness on defense, a sportswriter asked if Dean matched up better because of his own quick feet. "Does he?" Spurrier asked back. "I guess he does have some mobility. Hey, Danny ran the ball in high school. I think whichever quarterback plays will play well. Maybe both will play. Who knows?"

The next day it became obvious the uncertainty was affecting Wuerffel. He had shrugged off Spurrier's indecision to this point, while Dean openly expressed confusion. Now Wuerffel was showing signs of bewilderment. "It's not something you would envision happening before the season," he speculated. "I guess we just have to deal with it." Unlike before the Tennessee game, Spurrier hadn't told either Dean or Wuerffel who would start against Florida State. Maybe he didn't know himself. "I don't care anymore," Dean replied to a sportswriter. "It's gotten old. It's funny how it changes week in and week out. I think it would be easier if he just picked one."

Spurrier was getting defensive again. The constant badgering by the media was wearing on him, too. "There's nothing in the rule book that says I have to announce it yet," he said. "I don't think Florida State cares who plays anyway." A *Gainesville Sun* story featuring Doering's comments on the point spread had caught Spurrier's attention. He wasn't happy. "Since when did Chris Doering become our team spokesman?" he asked nobody in particular.

Cornerback Larry Kennedy was asked if he was good enough to be starting at FSU, where corners Clifton Abraham and Corey Sawyer were being listed by various All-American teams. "Most definitely," Kennedy replied. "Why couldn't I? They're not better than me."

After missing the previous two games, Willie Jackson wasn't in a good mood either. The papers had carried the story of his suspension as if it were a major political scandal. "It's been splashed all over the front pages," he complained. "It's like there is nothing else going on in the world."

In Tallahassee, Florida State linebackers coach Wally Burnham worried about his defense being listless for the game. "We're a tired team," he complained. "You don't play as hard when you're tired. Maybe Thursday and Friday . . . not going to classes will help. Mentally, we haven't been sharp. That worries me."

After practice Bowden had a prediction: "We're going to have to score forty points to win . . . at least forty. It ought to be a great spectators' game."

As the week progressed, the usual trash-talking between the teams through the media was conspicuously absent. By Wednesday there wasn't so much as a prediction from either side other than Bowden's estimate that this was to be a high-scoring game. Apparently Bowden and Spurrier had done a good job of warning their players about providing bulletin-board material for the other team. In past years the players had come across like professional wrestlers ranting about their upcoming bouts. "You talk trash because you feel there is something negative to talk about," Sawyer explained. "Florida hasn't shown us anything to be negative about. I think there really is too much at stake for both teams to get caught up in it."

Wide receiver Kevin Knox speculated that there was too much respect between the teams for that. "This week you can't help but be nice. They're 9–1 and ranked high, and anytime a team has Spurrier, you had better keep your mouth shut. If they are down by forty points, they still have a chance to come back and win."

Still, Knox said, "People say the Florida rivalry has died down a little. I don't know how they can muster the breath to say that. Point-blank, it's the University of Florida. This rivalry started for us in high school, when we decided where we would play."

Another receiver, Matt Frier, who had led the Seminoles' politicking to the pollsters after the loss to Notre Dame, warned that the trash-talking would follow the game—if Florida won. "If they beat us, if they take the national title away from us . . . we'll never hear the end of it," he predicted.

Rhett wasn't thinking about rubbing it in, should the Gators win. He was thinking about driving by the Swamp some day thirty years from now. "When I do that . . . I probably will remember the final game I played here," he commented. "I don't want to think about some loss we had to Florida State thirty years from now. This game means everything to me. I still remember the thrill of beating them in 1991. There has been no equal to that moment in my four years here. [But] winning Saturday could easily surpass it."

There was growing sentiment across the nation that the Seminoles not only didn't deserve to be number one, but they were ranked that high because of Bowden's popularity. *Gainesville Sun* columnist Mike Bianchi wrote: "It's my premise that Bobby is so darn adorable, pollsters have been giving his team the benefit of the doubt the last two weeks. This is not a knock on the 'Noles, who might just be the greatest college football team of this, uh, week . . . if you don't believe me, just ask yourself: If a Barry Switzer-coached FSU team had been beaten by Notre Dame two weeks ago, would the 'Noles have dropped only one spot to number two? . . . No way, no how!"

The column had quoted Iowa State coach Jim Walden, who publicly ripped the polls after FSU fell only one spot following the Notre Dame defeat. "If you get beat, you get beat," Walden noted. "But everybody is so determined to see poor ol' Bobby Bowden win the national championship." Again, Spurrier wanted no part of the controversy, refusing to let anyone know how he voted in the coaches' poll.

In spite of the loss to Notre Dame, some pollsters considered this not only Bowden's best team ever, but the greatest team in college football history. But teams that lose can't have that distinction, other critics complained. That title was reserved for Nebraska's 1971 team or Miami in 1987 or Ohio State in 1968, depending on whose opinion you sought.

"We're America's favorite team," wide receiver Knox bragged. "We're like the Atlanta Braves and the Dallas Cowboys. Every little kid wants to grow up and be a Seminole." Rhett got a kick out of that quote. "Did he really say that?" he asked. "Those guys are getting full of themselves up there." Knox's biased opinion aside, how could it be that this team still was considered great, perhaps one of the greatest ever? Two words answered the question: Charlie Ward.

A shy, quiet kid from up the road in Thomasville, Georgia, Charlie Ward had progressed from a mistake-prone quarterback into one of the most dangerous players in college football history. He had completed 226 of 327 passes (69 percent) for 2,586 yards and 23 touchdowns. When he scrambled, he teased defensive linemen as if he was an uncatchable fly inside their facemasks. Using a cartoon analogy, Ward was the Roadrunner and all defensive players were coyotes. One by one the coaches of the Atlantic Coast Conference took turns showering Ward with accolades and praise after the Seminoles demolished their teams. Several admitted, "Best I've ever seen." But all you had to know about Ward was what Spurrier observed, "You just can't catch him."

When someone asked Spurrier about Ward's "awkward throwing motion" following Florida's Monday night practice, Spurrier interrupted. "Awkward? I don't see any flaw in his mechanics. He drops back and has a nice fluid motion. He zings it in there. I don't see why he can't play in the NFL, but I heard he wants to play basketball instead."

Ward was two weeks away from joining Spurrier's elite fraternity as a Heisman Trophy winner. Spurrier didn't want to attend future Heisman banquets and have Ward throw this particular game in his face. "Charlie's probably going to win the Heisman Trophy and he deserves it," Spurrier added. "We've got to keep him from scrambling out of there and hurting us. You know every team says that, and then he goes out and does it on Saturday."

Of all the problems he had faced this season, Ron Zook knew this one was the worst. Heath Shuler was a one-dimensional, drop-back passer. Same for Stan White and Eric Zeier. Steve Taneyhill was a confused player lacking confidence by the time Florida played South Carolina. But Ward? He could beat you running, throwing, scrambling and then throwing. "He can beat you every way possible," Zook noted. "If you drop back and play zone, the guy will pick you apart. If you play man, he'll take off and run for about twenty yards. We blitzed a lot last year and look what happened. There's no set way to defense the guy. What do you do?"

Nobody had yet answered that question correctly, although Miami had come the closest. Florida State had beaten the Hurricanes 28–10, but the Seminoles' offense had gained only seventeen first downs. The 'Noles' defense, which scored one of the four touchdowns, had won the game for them. The Hurricanes had dropped into zone coverage on most plays and tried to keep Ward in front of them, and for the most part that worked. Once the Hurricanes fell behind, mainly because their offense was ineffective, they had to blitz.

That had given Notre Dame defensive coordinator Rick Minter the idea to have his team blitz Ward early in the game. The Seminoles marched right down the field and took a 7–0 lead, forcing the Irish to change their defense into a deep zone. Notre Dame's running game kept the ball away from Ward and the offense, and once the Irish had the lead, Florida State had to throw.

Zook scratched his head and went over the key points to stopping Florida State. "First of all, we have to stop the run. If we don't do that, we are dead meat . . . dead Gator meat. If we do that, then we can't give up the big play . . . the bomb or the long run by Ward. We have to get a few turnovers."

At practice on Thursday morning, Thanksgiving Day, Wuerffel was giving thanks energetically. Spurrier had decided to start him against Florida State, saying that there was no particular reason to start Wuerffel over Dean, just a gut feeling. "If there's any, it's that Danny's played in much of the action this year," he explained. "Terry will come ready to play, and we're planning to get him into the game." Dean had heard that before. Spurrier gave the players the afternoon off so they could watch the NFL games on television. Some players' families had traveled to Gainesville two days early.

In Tallahassee the Seminoles were enduring a deafening noise blaring from their stadium's loudspeakers as they prepared for the noise at Florida Field. Bowden had believed in preparing this way for road games in large stadiums; Spurrier didn't. "Most of that's mental," Bowden claimed.

On Friday, Nebraska settled its half of the Orange Bowl and national championship picture by defeating Oklahoma 21–7. All the Seminoles had to do was beat Florida to secure the matchup with the Cornhuskers. The Gators probably didn't realize it, but the Cornhuskers' win and West Virginia's 17–14 victory over Boston College had knocked Florida out of the national championship race. Even if the Gators defeated FSU *and* Alabama *and* won the Sugar Bowl, undefeated West Virginia would play undefeated Nebraska for the title. And there was always Auburn. Even though the Tigers couldn't play in a bowl because of NCAA probation, they had finished 11–0 and surely would be ranked ahead of Florida.

"Even if we don't have a chance at it," cornerback Kennedy suggested, "this is the biggest game I've ever played in. Most of these guys would say the same thing."

The largest crowd ever to attend a sporting event in the state—85,507 fans—showed up for Saturday's noon kickoff.

The game started early so ABC could televise it nationally. Keith Jackson and Bob Griese were in the broadcast booth. Griese and Spurrier weren't strangers to one another. While Florida assistant athletic director Norm Carlson was mapping Spurrier's publicity campaign for the Heisman in 1966, Purdue was doing nothing for Griese. Some maintain that Griese still rankles over Spurrier's winning the award. If not, it must have been only coincidence that he had ranked Florida number eleven and Tennessee number four on one of his November ballots for the Associated Press poll. Jackson and Griese had witnessed the Gators' 41–34 victory over Tennessee in September from the broadcast booth and would have known firsthand who deserved to be ranked higher. By 12:01 P.M., Jackson was telling the nation, "We're here at the Swamp . . ."

Anthone Lott, the focal point of the Gators' defensive secondary's problems early in the season, intercepted Ward's first pass of the day, but the Gators couldn't gain a first down in two possessions. Then Ward showed the Gators' defense what all the hype was about, completing six of seven passes for short gains and marching his offense down the field. Zook had called for the defense to play zone coverage, hoping to prevent any long gains. On third-and-goal at the five-yard line, Zook decided to blitz. Ward recognized the pressure up the middle and rolled to his right as defensive end Kevin Carter chased him. He then threw back across his body to receiver Tamarick Vanover, who was covered by Larry Kennedy. Kennedy slipped as Vanover jumped for the reception. Touchdown.

Freshman kicker Scott Bentley, whom the Seminoles had recruited from Colorado to solve their much-publicized kicking problems of recent seasons, converted a twenty-three-yard attempt on the first play of the second quarter to make the score 10–0. He added a twenty-two-yarder on the next possession, and Florida State had a 13–0 lead with 7:20 remaining in the half.

The Gators' offense had little to be proud of: two first downs, fifty-nine yards, and zero points. Wuerffel warmed up on the next series, completing passes of seventeen yards to Jack Jackson, sixteen to Willie Jackson, and twenty-nine to Harrison Houston. On third-and-goal from the eleven, Wuerffel pump-faked the safety and hit Jackson in the back of the end zone to cut the lead to 13–7. It was Wuerffel's twenty-second touchdown pass of the season, an NCAA record for a freshman. It was also his final pass of the season. He had twisted his right knee and limped to the sideline.

Terry Dean took the field, and although he didn't realize it at the time, he would be the Gators' quarterback for the remainder of the season. Finally, but in the most excruciating manner for Wuerffel, the quarterback saga that had started on a cool night in Kentucky almost three months earlier came to an end.

Ward's statistics at the half were awesome, although FSU had scored fewer than two touchdowns. He had completed twenty-five of thirty-five for 220 yards; the Seminoles had held the ball for almost twenty of the thirty minutes. "The way our offense was playing, we were lucky to be that close," Spurrier remarked.

Ward was even hotter in the third quarter, immediately driving FSU sixty-five yards to another score. His seven-yard pass to Ken McCorvey made the tally 20–7, and then he hooked up with McCorvey for another touchdown, a sixteen-yarder with only twenty-one seconds left in the third quarter.

The score was 27–7. FSU's band was booming the War Chant from the north end of the stadium. The team's fifteen thousand or so fans were chopping the Tomahawk Chop. The battle appeared over, at least as far as the Gators were concerned. They had never lost under Spurrier in the Swamp and now it appeared they were going to be blown out. "I never got comfortable," Bowden said later. "Their offense is too good."

Specifically, Dean was too good to count out, although he had been just that several times during the season. He was at his best when he improvised and moved around in the pocket. Dean had excellent agility, and against FSU's fierce pass rush, he needed every bit of quickness he had. With Wuerffel on the bench, he somehow pulled off four of the most remarkable plays of the season to get the Gators back into the game.

On the first, a fourth-and-seven play from FSU's forty, Spurrier chose to go for the first down even though thirteen minutes remained. "We had to gamble," he explained. "If we give it right back to them, it's over anyway." Dean dropped back as a Florida State defensive linemen broke free, but the Florida quarterback ducked low to the ground, slipping the tackle. Then he stood up and threw a twenty-four-yard pass to Willie Jackson, who took the football away from Clifton Abraham. Five plays later, Dean passed thirteen yards to Willie again to score and cut FSU's lead to 27–14.

Ward responded by completing five straight passes and running for ten more yards to take the Seminoles to the Florida nine-yard line. Fullback William Floyd, seeing a hole over left tackle that would have clinched the game had he scored, forgot something en route to the goal line, namely, the football. Linebacker Monty Grow stripped the ball from Floyd, and free safety Lawrence Wright recovered it at the six. Spurrier turned and yelled to the offense to get on the field. He felt the magic of the Swamp taking over.

Dean was sacked on second down. On third-and-fifteen he dropped back into the end zone and threw sixteen yards to Houston on a crossing pattern. He followed that conversion with three ugly incompletions that were nowhere close to his receivers. On fourth down, yet another do-or-die play, Dean scrambled and connected with Willie Jackson over the middle, who broke two tackles and gained forty-two yards on the play.

Jack Jackson helped make the fourth amazing play of the rally. On first down at the Seminoles' thirty-one, Dean threw a high pass to the right corner of the end zone. Defensive back Mack Knight tipped it and should have intercepted the pass, but Jackson managed to bat the ball up in the air with his left hand. He bobbled it as Knight fell to the ground. Finally, he clutched it to his chest with one hand. The stadium exploded in one simultaneous roar. Davis's extra point made the score 27–21 with 5:58 remaining.

As Florida players waved their arms and towels on the sideline, FSU players looked at each other blankly, fearing the worst. "We were thinking about the mystique of the Swamp," linebacker Derrick Brooks recalled. "They were out of it. Then boom! They were in it again."

Spurrier ordered an onside kick. During a television time-out he noticed that the Seminoles were expecting it, having sent their "good hands" team onto the field. Spurrier called Davis back and changed the play, ordering the kicker to kick the football deep.

With a first down at the twenty-one, the Seminoles were hearing the full effect of the Swamp. The noise was deafening. Ward's pass on first down was tipped and almost intercepted by Wright. Kevin Carter knocked down his second pass. It was third-and-ten. One more incompletion and Florida would get the ball back with a chance to win the game. The constant roar from the stands made it seem as if the ground were shaking. Even Spurrier put his fingers in his ears. "That was the loudest I've ever heard any crowd in my life," he noted.

Only Charlie Ward Jr. could silence the Gator faithful. He dropped back as defensive tackle Ellis Johnson charged him. Sidestepping Johnson and rolling to his left, just avoiding Johnson's large paw, Ward lofted a soft pass over linebacker Ed Robinson's head. It landed perfectly in freshman running back Warrick Dunn's hands at the thirty-one. Dunn cut to the

Florida State quarterback Charlie Ward went on to win the Heisman Trophy in December. But first he teased the Gators and finally broke their hearts with an amazing effort at Florida Field.

sideline as Lott headed for him. Suddenly, Lott was pushed from behind and his momentum carried him past Dunn, who sprinted untouched to the end zone. There was no penalty. "I saw Anthone about to make the tackle, and he got hit from behind," Zook recalled. Spurrier, not wanting to blame this loss on the officials, said it was "just a little push."

Sawyer intercepted Dean to prevent another amazing rally. The final score was 33–21, Florida State.

"What if we had gotten the ball back then?" Spurrier wondered. "Maybe we should have kicked the onside kick. Who knows what would have happened?" For him, these were haunting questions that would remain unanswerable.

After the game, Ward hugged Dunn, who was playing high school football in Baton Rouge, Louisiana, a year earlier.

The freshman had lost his mother, a policewoman killed in the line of duty, earlier in the year, and Ward had asked the coaches if he could room with him when he arrived on campus. This may have been Ward's best play on his best day. He had completed thirty-eight of fifty-three passes for 446 yards, the most yards by an opposing quarterback in University of Florida football history.

As Ward was led around the field by an assistant sports information director to an interview with ESPN minutes after the game, the Gators milled about wondering whether they had to sing the alma mater. They had never lost at home since Spurrier started the singing tradition. "Are we going to sing this thing or not?" one player asked another, who shrugged. Nobody felt like singing, and soon all the players slowly filtered into the locker room.

Knox and Vanover paraded behind Ward with the sign "State Champs '93." Finished with the interview, Ward slapped hands with Seminoles fans outside the tunnel entrance and headed into the locker room. Cornerback Corey Sawyer looked around. "People said we couldn't beat them in the Swamp," he boasted. "Now we're going to pull the plug and dry it up."

Overshadowed by the loss, Willie Jackson had played the game of his life, catching seven passes for 140 yards in his first game in three weeks. He made one-handed receptions, leaping receptions, and some when he yanked the ball away from FSU defenders. When one writer approached him after the game, he said, "Screw you. Get the hell out of my face." Obviously, he had yet to forget about his treatment by the media over the Growl incident.

Across the room, Ellis Johnson shook his bald head, frustrated by not getting to Ward on that final third down. "I thought we were going to stop them and then win the game," he stated. "I was able to scrape around the outside, but I just couldn't reach him. If he had held it for just another second,

I would have gotten there." Safety Michael Gilmore, who had dived at Dunn's feet on the sideline and missed, said, "The first thing I noticed about Charlie Ward was his poise. He could have rattled at that point it was so loud. He didn't."

Rhett dressed for the final time following a game at Florida Field. He knew he had just played the worst game of his career, at least statistically. He had been held to seven yards on seven carries and caught only one pass.

FSU's defensive coaches had pleaded with the Seminoles throughout the week to stop the Gators' running back. "If Rhett doesn't get a hundred yards, it's over. It's simple mathematics," FSU linebacker Ken Alexander had announced. He was right, Florida held a 19–1 record when Rhett gained a hundred yards or more. That was more than coincidence.

Rhett never had a chance on this day. He was swarmed every time he touched the ball, and when Florida fell behind by twenty points, Spurrier had little choice but to place the running game on the shelf. "I just didn't know they would come that hard," Rhett said of FSU's defensive linemen. "Because they blow so many people out, when you watch them on tape, you don't know whether they're that good or the other team is that bad. Well . . . they're that good."

Spurrier wasn't about to promote the Seminoles in the rankings. If they were ranked number one or two the next day, they would play Nebraska for the national championship. "I'll let everyone else vote on that," he commented. "Leave me out of it."

To his credit, Spurrier was so impressed with Ward that he almost hinted that he would not vote for one of his own players for the Heisman for the first time. Former Heisman winners are given votes, as are more than nine hundred members of the media. "Certainly, he's the Heisman winner," he said. "He's the best scrambler I've seen. That final play killed us."

As Zook stood in the middle of the locker room, he had no trouble putting Ward's talent into perspective. "I've coached, how long? . . . about fifteen years . . . Charlie Ward's the best I've ever seen. Ever!" he added.

Ten minutes later, standing in front of his locker, Dean was alone. Wuerffel had already dressed and limped out on crutches. Dean didn't realize the severity of the freshman's knee injury. "This game is over and now we have bigger things in mind," he declared. "We want to be SEC champions again and get those rings."

Grow's locker was next to Dean's and Wuerffel's. For three years, Shane Matthews had dressed next to him, so he was used to being crushed by the massive media circus. "I won't miss this," Grow complained, winking. "Microphones, cameras . . ." He signed an autograph for a young fan and walked away.

The mood was rare for a losing locker room. It's not so much that it wasn't quiet or gloomy, but the atmosphere was full of optimism. Following the Auburn game, the Florida players had milled around the team bus as though they were waiting for the hearse to leave for the cemetery. This time, some players even smiled when they talked. It wasn't the end of the world. It wasn't even the end of the season. They realized that nothing Florida State had done to them would prevent their beating Alabama and winning the SEC championship.

"I think we can bounce back," Spurrier suggested. "There's no reason why we can't. I think we match up with Alabama because they don't have a quarterback like Charlie Ward." Then again, who did?

16

TURNING THE TIDE

A N UNDERGRADUATE AT THE University of Alabama in 1968, Nancy Dean was in a hurry to catch the beginning of a class one day as she searched for a parking space on the Tuscaloosa campus. Suddenly, a hulking man in a houndstooth hat walked out from between the parked cars into the path of her car. She slammed on the brakes, bringing her bumper to a stop just inches from the man's legs. Paul Bryant tipped his hat, grumbled an apology as only the Bear could, and walked away. "What if I had killed Bear Bryant?" Nancy said. "They would have hanged me."

Three years later, she gave birth to Terry Douglas Dean. On a Saturday twenty-five years after her near-collision with the man who became generally regarded as the greatest coach in college football history, her son would try to prevent Alabama's extending its Southeastern Conference dominance, something that Bryant had established years before. Nancy Dean thought it was funny how these little ironies in life turn out.

Out of a sense of homage, the Bear's name was every-where on the Alabama campus. When Dean dropped back to pass, players who slept in Bryant Hall would try to sack him. Defensive backs who played home games in Bryant-Denny

Stadium would try to read his eyes at the line of scrimmage. Linebackers who visited the Bryant Museum would blitz him.

Most football players today aren't history majors, however. The Gators, now 9–2, were no different. Their knowledge of Alabama's steeped tradition reached as far back as their recruiting days, when they were deciding where to attend college.

Bryant was only a name to them, the same as other legendary coaches like Knute Rockne, Woody Hayes, or John Heisman. To Terry Dean, he was the great man whom Mom almost plunked with the car. Nobody on Florida's team knew or rightfully cared that Bryant's Crimson Tide teams had won thirteen SEC and five national championships. Gene Stallings's team was the only Crimson Tide they had to worry about. And his team had won the national championship last year.

The Gators did have a firm, deep grasp of Florida's history of ineptitude in trying to win the SEC championship, not because they had paged through the football history books, but because everyone had reminded them of it from the time they had signed a letter of intent with the Gators. "Florida can't win the SEC. . . . Florida will choke. . . . Florida will find a way to lose." It was a feeling, a perception, a sense of the future reinforced by the past. The Gators had been in position dozens of times over the years, needing to win a game here or there to be SEC champions, but it never happened before Steve Spurrier became coach.

Changing the mental approach and knocking down those psychological barriers was Spurrier's biggest challenge when he took the job. Somehow, he had to make them think and act like winners before they had ever won. No psychologist in the world would ever convince them that they could beat the SEC's old guard of Auburn, Georgia, or Alabama until they did it themselves on the field. Spurrier had preached to his players to forget the past, flaunting the philosophy that one who ignores history is doomed to repeat it. And it worked. In Spurrier's three-plus seasons, his teams had won three of four against Auburn, four of four against Georgia, and two of three against Alabama. Now they believed. If they wanted tangible evidence that they could win the SEC championship, they just had to walk by the school's trophy case and look at a two-year-old large silver trophy.

The seniors, juniors, and redshirt sophomores had played on that championship team in 1991. This time, however, they would have to win the championship on the road rather than simply beat Kentucky at the Swamp as they had two years earlier.

The SEC championship game was a novel and progressive idea by Roy Kramer, the conference's commissioner, and it was profitable. The inaugural game between Alabama and Florida in 1992 had earned $7 million. The NCAA had mandated that conferences could stage a championship game only if they had twelve or more members. Commissioners in other conferences like the Big Eight, Big Ten, Pac Ten, and Southwest watched the SEC's guinea pig closely while considering expansion themselves.

Kramer and the conference representatives had considered holding the game in Orlando, Tampa, and Atlanta before agreeing on the self-proclaimed Football Capital of the South, Birmingham, which also housed the SEC's headquarters. What better place was there to host the game than eighty-three-thousand-seat Legion Field? Some loved the choice; some hated it. One thing was certain, if either Alabama or Auburn were playing for the championship, they would have a distinct home field advantage. Crimson Tide coach Gene Stallings still denied that his team had any advantage before the 1992 championship game, and he lost some credibility in the process. "It's of no advantage to us," he said repeatedly. "It's not our home field." The Tide played two or three games at Legion Field during the regular season, not to mention the team's large fan base in the city, but they played most of their games at Bryant-Denny Stadium in Tuscaloosa, fifty miles southwest of Birmingham.

At the same time there was no other city that could guarantee a sellout crowd, especially if neither Auburn nor Alabama played in the game. One of the two surely would be favored to win the SEC's Western Division almost every season, but who would show up if Mississippi played Kentucky? Or Mississippi State and Vanderbilt? The thought was a financial nightmare for the conference's athletic directors. So far, thanks to Alabama and Florida, the SEC hadn't had to worry about that. The two teams had played in front of a sellout crowd in 1992, and Saturday's game was nearing a sellout too.

The inaugural championship game couldn't have been any more splendid for the SEC. In fact, it was perfect. It not only was a winner at the ticket office, but the action on the field helped make it a television ratings success. Most important, the right team won—and won in a thriller. Alabama had marched through the regular season with ease, entering the game with a perfect 11–0 record. In past years, before the championship game, the Crimson Tide would have taken their perfect record and danced all the way to New Orleans for a national championship matchup with Miami. But now, one more hurdle remained to be cleared.

What if Florida, an 8–3 team coming off a 45–24 loss to Florida State, upset Alabama and prevented the SEC-friendly Sugar Bowl from hosting the national championship game? This innovative and lucrative concept would have backfired in Kramer's face and in the collective faces of the SEC. "We realize nobody wants us to win the game, but ourselves," Spurrier had noted in 1992. "We just have to believe everything, including the officiating, will be fair up there."

It was. The game was tied 21–21 with less than four minutes remaining, and Florida had the football as Kramer and the Sugar Bowl executives paced nervously in the press box, trying to appear as neutral as possible for Florida's sake. Then quarterback Shane Matthews made the worst mistake of his record-setting career, throwing a sideline pass that All-American cornerback Antonio Langham intercepted. Twenty-seven yards later, Langham was in the end zone and Alabama was in the Sugar Bowl with a perfect 12–0 record. Kramer and the Sugar Bowl committee members beamed as if they had hit the lottery.

It wasn't one of Spurrier's better moments. With another SEC championship lost for the school, in the postgame interview Spurrier lashed out at Matthews for throwing the pass. The next day, when he studied the tape, he determined that receiver Monty Duncan had not come back for the ball properly. He then criticized Duncan publicly and tried to apologize to Matthews. In reality it was a poor decision by Matthews and a poor route by Duncan. But it was an even greater play by Langham, who had worked his way around Duncan from the outside to make the interception.

A year later, as the two teams prepared to meet again, Matthews was a third-string quarterback with the Chicago Bears, Duncan was a graduate assistant coach at Florida, and Langham was recognized as the nation's best defensive back.

On Monday, two days after the loss to FSU, receiver Jack Jackson recalled the details of Langham's play like it was yesterday. "I've thought about it off and on for a year," he began. "First of all, the throw shouldn't have been made. They were in a tight coverage, seven or eight yards deep, and we ran a six-yard route. We should have won that game, but it wasn't Monty's fault." He wasn't surprised by Spurrier's criticism of Duncan, the scapegoat for the loss. "I know the dude," Jackson commented. "It was definitely unfair criticism, but he's tough on all of us. . . . We're used to it by now."

The consequences of the loss to Alabama were gloomy, resulting in a trip to Jacksonville's Gator Bowl, about sixty-five miles from campus. The bowl had been less than exciting for the players, who had practiced in the rain and fog most of the week. On New Year's Eve, three years to the day after Spurrier was hired, the Gators defeated North Carolina State 27–10. Fans, however, had trouble seeing the game, which was played in a thick fog that obscured punts and passes for the players. This time the Gators wanted nothing to do with Jacksonville until they returned the following October to play Georgia.

Whether they wanted to or not, that was where they would play again, on New Year's Eve of all nights, if they lost to Alabama again. New Orleans or Jacksonville. Those were their options. "We ain't going back to Jacksonville," Monty Grow declared. "Write it down. Underline it. Put it in headlines. We ain't going back to Jacksonville." Doering added, "The Sugar or Gator . . . those are two extremes. Nobody wants to go back to Jacksonville." The complaints even got somewhat picky. "The sponsor was Outback Steakhouse, right?" Jackson said sarcastically. "Not one time did we eat at an Outback. Yeah, they treated us real well."

When the Jacksonville newspapers carrying these comments hit the sidewalks the next morning, many Jacksonville merchants may not have wanted the Gators back. They weren't exactly helping tourism. Spurrier regrettably hadn't lectured his players about keeping their insults to themselves. Since the Gator Bowl had contracted with the SEC for the conference's third-place team, Spurrier knew his team could possibly find itself in Jacksonville once every few years; Florida couldn't win the SEC championship and go to New Orleans every year. Or could they? "Nobody there is going to want us again," Spurrier warned. "I wish these guys would quit criticizing the place."

The so-called neutral site issue was bound to come up again during the week, especially after Stallings repeated his comments from a year earlier. Florida would have fifteen thousand fans at the game; Alabama, sixty-five thousand. "Calling it a neutral site . . . that's the silliest thing I've ever heard," receiver Jack Jackson commented. "Ah, who cares? If we lose this game, the season's been a wash anyway."

Knowing the running game would have to reappear for Florida to beat Alabama, some of the offensive linemen maintained they had done their jobs against Florida State. They couldn't figure how Rhett had gained only seven yards. Others couldn't understand why he had only seven carries. "The holes were there," center Gantt Crouch recalled, "and we didn't get many yards. It's not going to work if we keep going away from it."

About twenty minutes into Monday night's practice, Spurrier moved the team to Florida Field since the grounds-keepers didn't have to prepare the field for games for another nine months. Assistant athletic director Norm Carlson, a close friend of Spurrier's who attends each practice, walked into the stadium and remarked, "I think we are going to play our best game of the season this week. I just feel it."

After practice, Willie Jackson summarized his senior season this way: "My season was overshadowed by everything else. . . . I just didn't get as many TDs. I had expected more." Jackson was third on the team with forty receptions for 561 yards and six touchdowns. Jack Jackson had scored ten, and Doering seven. Willie Jackson and Rhett were invited to play in several postseason all-star games. Houston, also a senior and the quietest player on the team, had thirty-three receptions, an eighteen-yard average, and six touchdowns. Someone walked by and asked if he had any all-star invitations. He just smiled and shook his head.

Standing in the south end zone, Spurrier, who was scheduled to coach in the annual East-West Shrine Game in Palo Alto, California, declared, "Harrison's not in any all-star games? Maybe we can get him in the Shrine game. He deserves to be in at least one the way he's played. He's been as consistent as anybody." Then he fidgeted and asked the gathering of sportswriters about the weather forecast for Birmingham that weekend.

The next morning Antonio Langham was the topic of conversation around Florida's locker room. "Is it true?" one player asked another. "Have you heard about Langham?" another asked. Two weeks earlier, Alabama had received a letter from

Alabama cornerback Antonio Langham had won the 1992 SEC championship for the Tide by intercepting Florida quarterback Shane Matthews in the final seconds of that game, but he would miss the rematch.

UNIVERSITY OF ALABAMA SPORTS INFORMATION

Darryl Dennis, a sports agent, stating that Langham had signed an agent-player contract just hours after the Tide's national championship victory over Miami in New Orleans on January 1, 1993. Signing with an agent automatically terminates an athlete's eligibility, according to NCAA rules. If the contents of the letter were true, Langham's collegiate career would be finished. Alabama submitted its evidence to the SEC office and declared Langham ineligible on Tuesday but asked the NCAA to review the case and, if possible, reinstate Langham before Saturday's game.

NCAA assistant executive director David Berst told athletic director Hootie Ingram that a decision would be made by Friday. Langham had admitted signing a document and taking $400 from the man, but he said he didn't know it was an

228

agent's contract. Things didn't look good for the Crimson Tide, which had slumped to an 8–2–1 finish of the regular season.

As news of Langham's troubles spread, Danny Wuerffel was on an operating table at Shands Hospital. An MRI on Monday determined that he had ligament damage in his right knee, and his return for a bowl game looked doubtful. "I guess there was more damage in there than we thought," Spurrier noted.

Now that Langham's availability was in doubt, much of Florida's attention turned to David Palmer. Langham and Palmer were not only Alabama's two most dangerous players, but they were legitimate All-Americans. Palmer led the conference in receiving with fifty-eight receptions. He had won games for the Tide by catching passes in double-coverage, returning punts for touchdowns, and even by playing quarterback. He had run for the two-point conversion that tied Tennessee and later completed a long pass to help beat Mississippi. He was the only player who could single-handedly beat the Gators.

"I don't know how he remembers where to line up," Zook said on Tuesday. "I've seen teams double- and triple-team him, and he still comes down with it. I know we'll probably see him at quarterback, too. I just don't know when."

Alabama's starting quarterback, Jay Barker, who had led the team to the national championship the previous season, had sprained a knee in the Auburn loss and would not play in Saturday's game. This was as crucial a loss as not having Langham. Stallings announced that sophomore Brian Burgdorf would start the game.

Florida was down to one quarterback too, now that Wuerffel was in a knee cast. And that one quarterback had never wanted to play in a game as much as he wanted to play in this one. While his mother had graduated from Alabama, Dean's father was an Auburn graduate and hated the Crimson Tide. "Since I can remember," Dean said, "we would watch Alabama and intensely want them to lose. This game means more to me than any other. Dad's an Auburn guy who has hated Alabama since he was a kid. I want that ring. He said he would buy me anything I wanted if we beat them . . . and I want a new car."

Wheels or no new wheels, Dean had come full circle. He went from ballyhooed starter to the bench. He had returned to help win the Georgia game and then almost pulled out the FSU game. Now he was starting again in the most important game of his life.

"I started the season as the starter and now I am back as the starter as it ends," he reflected. "What happened in between I couldn't control. But I guess it doesn't matter anymore. This is my chance to redeem myself. I can have a good feeling about myself and at least know I've accomplished something."

Spurrier, for once, liked Dean's attitude, although he didn't realize his quarterback had said that he still might not return for the 1994 season. Dean continued to talk about transferring to a Division II school to play football or enter graduate school since he would receive his bachelor's degree in the spring. He wouldn't return just to watch Wuerffel play. Dean was watching more tape and, seemingly, was more tuned to the mental aspect of playing quarterback and less tuned to making outrageous statements. "He asked me the other day which tapes of Alabama to watch," Spurrier remarked. "I was surprised. I guess he was just frustrated at times. That's his nature."

When asked about the possibility of playing Alabama without Langham in the secondary, Spurrier cracked, "I know if this were high school, all those games he played in would be forfeited, and we'd be playing Arkansas on Saturday."

In the meantime, Spurrier had a much less serious incident to address. Jack Jackson had been involved in a fight with a Florida track team member hours after the loss to Florida State. The two were eating at a campus restaurant and started to argue over a girl. The argument became physical. "I won't suspend him for it," Spurrier announced. "Boys do fight about girls. They apologized to each other and that was the end of it."

Stallings wished he could end Langham's problem like that. He followed Spurrier's weekly luncheon with a teleconference call to Florida's media, and he wasn't in a good mood. "We knew about this and self-reported it to the SEC office," he commented. "The NCAA did not suspend him. The way Antonio explained it to me, a guy had put pressure on him to come out early [for the NFL] the night after the Sugar Bowl. What he signed or didn't sign wasn't what the agent showed us later."

On Thursday, Judd Davis, who was not named to either the first or second All-SEC teams, was named the winner of the Lou Groza Award as the nation's finest kicker. Davis, a walk-on who once considered quitting the team, had won the job by default when scholarship kicker Bart Edmiston was injured. Davis had made fifteen of nineteen field goals and forty-seven of forty-nine extra points, but he had never won a game with a kick. "It's kind of crazy . . . three months ago, I didn't even know if I was going to be our kicker," he said. "Now I've won the Groza Award."

The day was another downer for Willie Jackson, who had let traffic and parking tickets pile up. Spurrier said that Jackson wouldn't be suspended this time, but he would be disciplined somehow.

Early Friday afternoon, after both teams had arrived in Birmingham, Spurrier and Stallings walked into a ballroom at the Sheraton Civic Center to promote the game. Stallings quickly turned sour when someone asked when he knew of Langham's alleged signing. "What you should be doing is trying to find out who leaked this . . . who made this public," he replied. "We were handling the matter privately and somehow it got announced to the world. I'd like to know who did it. This whole thing has been a large distraction to us. It has broken our concentration." Two hours later Stallings was even angrier when he learned that the NCAA had denied Langham's appeal. The Crimson Tide would have to finish the season without their best defensive player.

It was raining hard on Saturday morning when the teams awakened, and the wind was gusting between fifteen and thirty miles per hour. If there are two things Spurrier didn't want, it was rain and wind. Especially wind, which plays havoc with the passing game. This wouldn't bother Alabama as much since the Tide's offense was run-oriented.

Assistant coach Carl Franks stood in the tunnel from the locker room, surveying the weather an hour before the 2:30 P.M. kickoff. The rain had stopped at noon. "I think the wind is dying down somewhat . . . it shouldn't be a problem," he said. A minute later, Franks joked, "We're pretty healthy though. Good thing we don't have any players that the agents are coming after. Signing for four hundred bucks doesn't make much sense."

It was obvious from the first play that Stallings planned to use every trick play he had and that Alabama felt it had nothing to lose. The Crimson Tide was loose and fired up. On the first play, Palmer took a pitch and started to the right. As most of the defense pursued, he stopped and threw back to Burgdorf, the quarterback, who had slipped out of the backfield for a twenty-yard gain. Burgdorf passed to fullback Tarrant Lynch for nine yards. Chris Anderson gained twelve on a pitch to the right. Two plays later, Burgdorf passed to Palmer for ten more.

The old, familiar penalties then came to haunt the Gators, as they jumped offside on two consecutive plays. Palmer gained two yards on a rollout before Lynch ran over right guard for the touchdown. Just four minutes and forty-seven seconds into the game, Florida trailed 7–0.

Langham's absence made a huge difference late in the first quarter. With a first down at Alabama's thirteen-yard line,

David Palmer—Alabama's versatile quarterback, receiver, and punt and kick returner—couldn't do it all against the Gators in Florida's 28–13 victory in the 1993 SEC championship game.

backup cornerback Willie Gaston was covering Houston. Spurrier made the perfect call—a hitch-and-go pattern to Houston. Dean pump-faked as Gaston broke for the ball, or where he thought the ball would be. Houston cut up the sideline and was all alone in the right corner of the end zone. The score was now 7–7.

Dean played almost perfectly late in the second quarter after Michael Proctor's forty-five-yard field goal gave Alabama a 10–7 lead. He passed twelve yards to Willie Jackson to set up first-and-goal at the Crimson Tide's three-yard line. By now the rain had started again and was drenching the fans at Legion Field. Spurrier, thinking Alabama would be expecting Rhett to carry the ball, called for a quarterback bootleg. Dean faked to Rhett, who had run left, and trotted around right end for an easy touchdown.

At halftime, Stallings decided to bench Burgdorf and let Palmer play quarterback for the remainder of the game. On a third-and-thirteen at Florida's twenty-eight, Palmer showed his elusive brilliance, breaking two tackles and forcing several other Gators to miss him on a twelve-yard gain. He made the first down on a quarterback sneak on the next play, but Florida held Alabama to another field goal and maintained a 14–13 lead.

Less than two minutes later, with forty-five seconds left in the third quarter, the Gators faced fourth-and-eight and the momentum was beginning to swing Alabama's way. The Crimson Tide fans were now singing in the rain, literally. Of all the amazing plays during the long season—the Wuerffel-to-Doering miracle that beat Kentucky, Lott's game-saving time-out against Georgia, and Jack Jackson's seventy-three-yard gain on the screen pass from the end zone that doomed South Carolina—none were as crucial or as improbable as what happened next.

Punter Shayne Edge, 176 pounds soaking wet, which he now was, jumped to snag a high snap from center. Alabama's Michael Ausmus charged up the middle as Edge caught the snap and ran to the right. He kept running, heading along the Gators' sideline as his teammates waved him by. By the time he was smacked to the cold artificial turf, Edge had gained twenty yards and a first down. Dean dropped back on the next play and threw a bomb that Jack Jackson caught with his fingertips. The forty-three-yard touchdown gave Florida a 21–13 lead and some needed breathing room.

One play later, Palmer tried a bomb of his own, but safety Michael Gilmore intercepted at Florida's forty-six-yard line. Dean and Willie Jackson then took control of the game. They connected on passes of four, thirty-three, and seven yards. On the final reception by Jackson, it took three Alabama players to bring him down. One grabbed his facemask, giving the Gators a first-and-goal at the three-yard line. Rhett scored on the next play to give the Gators a comfortable 28–13 lead. That was the way it would end.

After Dean kneeled to the ground to run out the clock and end the game, Watson and defensive tackle Ellis Johnson hoisted Spurrier onto their shoulders and carried him onto the field. The coach pumped his fist and even gave a number-one salute. The rest of the team gathered around, celebrating the school's second SEC championship in sixty-one years. For the next twenty minutes they frolicked on the field like schoolchildren at recess. They carried the school's flag, jumped on each others' shoulders, and had their picture taken in front of the scoreboard. Spurrier hadn't let them celebrate after clinching the Eastern Division, and they were making up for it now.

Dean trotted around the field, posing for photographers and stopping to chat with sportswriters. "Hey, this is the first

UNIVERSITY OF FLORIDA SPORTS INFORMATION

It wasn't punter Shayne Edge's leg that helped win the Alabama game, but rather his legs. His twenty-yard scramble from punt formation helped turn the momentum back to Florida.

time I've played four quarters," he noted. "Wow! It feels good." Grow pumped his helmet into the air, yelling, "Bourbon Street, Bourbon Street here we come!" That would be Florida's next stop, a January 1 date against unbeaten West Virginia in the Sugar Bowl. Alabama was headed to the Gator Bowl to play North Carolina.

Zook, whose defense had held the Crimson Tide to 279 yards, ran around hugging whomever he could find: first Jeremy Foley, then Grow, then Larry Kennedy. Spurrier hurried down to salute the section of Florida fans. "They were louder than all the Alabama fans put together," he observed. He was satisfied, relieved, and ecstatic. They couldn't say that Florida choked away SEC championships anymore. "I felt pressure all week because we were supposed to win," he added. "Everyone picked us. When the season started, our goal was to get back to this game and win it. We're going into the record books as the SEC champions. We've had a good year, but this win makes it a big year."

Shayne Edge was at the center of the celebration. His improvisation had impressed everyone on the team. "I had to take off," he claimed. "They would have blocked the punt. It was just a matter of getting around the corner. Once I did that, I knew I had the first down."

An hour after the game, in the corner of a large tent arranged for postgame interviews, Terry Dean satisfied the television and newspaper reporters who remained. He had completed twenty of thirty-seven passes for 256 yards. "It is an incredible feeling I can't describe," he admitted. "I was born here. I grew up here. Now to win a game here after all the ups and downs I've been through . . ." Ten feet away, Frank Dean held a game ball while waiting for his son to finish. "He's not getting a car," he commented. "He may deserve one for beating Alabama, but he's not getting one."

Facing page: It was the biggest game of Terry Dean's life. His stats weren't astronomical, but leading the Gators past Alabama was the high point of his season.

17

THE MOUNTAINEERS AND TAMPA

T HREE HOURS AFTER SPURRIER was lifted into the air by his players and carried onto the field, the team's chartered flight landed at Gainesville's Regional Airport. In between, Stephen Orr Spurrier had to feel as high as ever, including that December day in 1966 when he won the Heisman Trophy or the day he was told he would be Florida's next head coach.

The parking lot resembled a Los Angeles freeway at 5:00 P.M. Drivers were honking horns, traffic was gridlocked for three blocks, but nobody seemed to mind. As the players and coaches filtered into the tiny terminal from the tarmac, they were mobbed by Gators fans. "That's the greatest show of support I've ever seen as a coach," Spurrier remarked. "It was wild in there." Assistant athletic director Norm Carlson estimated that it was the largest reception for the team since a 10–6 victory over Alabama, ironically, in 1963.

While Florida fans and players celebrated, West Virginia University officials were completing a power play to send their football team to the Sugar Bowl in New Orleans instead of the Cotton in Dallas. For years, bowl bids were extended at the personal prerogative of bowl executives, known to the college football world as the guys in the colored blazers. They were bank executives or attorneys during the week, but on weekends they would travel the country to watch football games, glad-handing anyone in sight, enjoying a few hors d'oeuvres, talking what football they knew or thought they knew, and promising to roll out the proverbial red carpet for whatever teams they chose to invite to their bowl.

Athletic directors and coaches had tired of the tradition-rich schools playing in the richer and more prestigious bowls when they knew they had undeserving teams. For example, the guys in the bright blazers would work behind each other's backs to seal a deal with Notre Dame three weeks before the end of the regular season. The Fighting Irish might lose their final two games, but they would still end up in the Sugar, Cotton, or Fiesta Bowl with an 8–3 record, while another team with a 10–1 record was forced to take bowl leftovers. It happened almost every season.

That all changed with the so-called Bowl Coalition, supposedly the answer to all the bowl problems. The coalition's format, begun in 1992, was simple. It started with the Orange, Cotton, and Sugar Bowls, which automatically host the champions from the Big Eight, Southwest, and Southeastern conferences, respectively. Whichever of the three teams ranked highest in the final coalition poll—a combination of the writers' and coaches' polls—would earn its affiliated bowl the first pick of an opponent from the Atlantic Coast and Big East conferences and Notre Dame. The Pac Ten and the Big Ten, longtime affiliates of the Rose Bowl, were not involved.

If two teams among the ACC, Big East, or Notre Dame were ranked one and two, they automatically would play for the national championship in the Fiesta Bowl. In the coalition's first year, the formula worked perfectly, matching number-one Miami and number-two Alabama in the Sugar Bowl.

This time, however, not everyone was pleased. The regular season finished in controversy, not over the coalition, but over the poll that comprised the coalition. On the day following Florida's victory over Alabama, the final poll that determined the matchups was released: Nebraska (11–0) was number one, Florida State (11–1) was number two, and West Virginia (11–0) was number three. So Nebraska earned an Orange Bowl berth and the bowl committee selected the number-two Seminoles for the perfect, undisputed package for the national championship, right?

Wrong. West Virginia coach Don Nehlen cried foul, ripping everything from the polls to the Orange Bowl to Bobby Bowden. Ironically, Bowden had coached at West Virginia before moving to Florida State in 1976. "Everybody wants to see poor ol' Bobby win his national championship," Nehlen cracked. "That isn't fair to my players. [FSU] lost a game. They haven't done everything in their power to put themselves in position to win the national championship. We have."

Nebraska coach Tom Osborne, too, publicly sympathized with Nehlen. His sympathy could have been genuine, or it could have stemmed from the rightful fear of meeting Florida State, which according to several experts was the best team to come along in years. Florida State also had beaten Osborne's team three straight times in bowl games.

If the Mountaineers couldn't play for the national championship, they would play for more money. So when the Cotton Bowl, next in the pecking order, invited them to play Texas A&M, they declined. The bowl coalition allowed this by stipulating that a school could turn down an invitation to accept another from a bowl that paid more money. The Sugar Bowl would pay its teams $4.1 million; the Cotton $3.2 million. West Virginia said hello to New Orleans and good-bye to Dallas. The Cotton Bowl wasn't disappointed; the committee could now invite a team that guaranteed excellent television ratings: Notre Dame.

When the coalition dust cleared, Florida and West Virginia were set to do battle in the Big Easy. The Gators, too, were pleased. The Mountaineers may have been 11–0, but nobody wanted to play Notre Dame. The Irish, with three losses, had demolished Florida in the 1992 Sugar Bowl and had a much better team this time around. Spurrier and his coaching staff knew the Gators could defeat West Virginia, which had played five very close games and appeared vulnerable. Miami defensive coordinator Tommy Tuberville called Zook after the pairings were announced. "You got lucky," he said. "You don't have to deal with Notre Dame."

On Sunday, Spurrier went to his office to review the Alabama tapes and join a national conference call for all the New Year's Day bowl coaches. When it was his turn to speak, he said, "We're certainly excited to have won our conference championship yesterday in Birmingham and have the opportunity to go back to the Sugar Bowl. I congratulate Don [Nehlen] for the big year that West Virginia's had. I feel like they deserve a chance at the national championship. Anybody that can win eleven of them . . . that's quite an accomplishment."

Nehlen responded with the usual glowing compliments of Spurrier, the Gators, New Orleans, and the Sugar Bowl. He was asked about the polls. "To be honest, I've probably talked about that too dadgummed much already," he replied. "We all know Florida State is a great, great team but they stubbed their toe. Nebraska didn't. We didn't." Writers continued to grill Nehlen on the subject, while Spurrier cupped his hand over the phone. Norm Carlson was putting golf balls in the office as Spurrier waited. "They're not asking me any questions," he told Carlson. "They want to talk to Nehlen about the polls." Finally, he signed off, saying, "Don, see you in New Orleans."

The real question, however, focused on Spurrier's coaching chances in the NFL. It was rumored that he might be the first coach of the expansion Carolina Panthers, who could not receive permission from the Washington Redskins to talk to the man they really wanted, Joe Gibbs. Apparently, Spurrier was their second choice.

In a story in the *Charlotte Observer,* Spurrier was asked how he would feel discussing the job with Panthers officials after the Sugar Bowl. "I'll worry about that if it comes up," he answered. "Right now, I am not looking to leave. I've got a wonderful job." It wasn't exactly a strong denial. There was a clause in Spurrier's contract with Florida barring him from taking a position with an NFL team in Florida, which prevented Spurrier's leaving the college ranks for the new Jacksonville Jaguars, the Tampa Bay Buccaneers, or the Miami Dolphins, although Foley admitted the clause probably wouldn't stand up to litigation. A source with the Panthers told the *Observer* that the team would make a strong pitch to Spurrier following the Sugar Bowl.

Such rumors are twofold: they lift a head coach's self-esteem and they hurt recruiting, which begins in December. While Spurrier's self-esteem didn't need much lifting, it is a given that recruits don't want to sign with schools and then have head coaches leave for other jobs. Even if Spurrier planned to stay in Gainesville, competing schools would use the NFL rumors as ammunition against the Gators when vying for the same recruits. If Spurrier didn't issue a strong denial, the topic could prevent the team from securing a strong recruiting class.

Spurrier flew to New York to attend the Heisman Trophy banquet on December 13. As expected, FSU's Charlie Ward was the honoree, the landslide winner of the award. At one point that night, Spurrier cornered Florida State sports information director Wayne Hogan. "Hey, Hogan, remember that little fracas we had before the half in 1991?" he asked. "You were involved in that, weren't you?" Hogan, who watches all FSU's games from the press box, told Spurrier he must have him confused with somebody else. "No, that was you. Some of my coaches told me about it." When Hogan finally convinced Spurrier that he was mistaken, the two started to talk about the FSU-Florida game a few weeks earlier. "You guys made it tough on us, took us to the wire," Hogan said. "Ah, our defense isn't any good. We can't stop anybody," Spurrier remarked.

When the team returned to practice the next day, Spurrier announced that he wasn't going anywhere, except to New Orleans. "I see myself staying here for several more years. . . . It could be ten years or longer. Who knows?" A day later, he added, "Florida shouldn't say that Coach Spurrier can coach here as long as he wants. I think everyone should be held accountable. I want to be accountable to everyone who buys a ticket and sends a dollar to the university . . . but I know you have to have five-year contracts for recruiting purposes."

Committing coaches to long-term contracts was part of Foley's progressive approach to maintaining Florida's athletic success. Of course, Spurrier was at the top of that list. Foley and Spurrier's attorney, Bill O'Neil, were finalizing the details on a contract that would bind the head coach to Florida through the year 2000. His base salary would be about $140,000, with the total package, including endorsements and television and radio shows, reaching $500,000 annually. The deal would make Spurrier among the top five college coaches in the country. "It's not a huge raise," Foley announced, "but it's a slight increase. Steve has told me personally that he isn't leaving the University of Florida."

Spurrier was puzzled when the All-SEC team was announced. The Florida Gators were the SEC champions and yet only three players—Rhett, tackle Reggie Green, and defensive tackle William Gaines—had been named to the first team. Tackle Jason Odom, wide receiver Jack Jackson, and punter Shayne Edge were named to the second team. Tennessee led the conference with seven players on the first and second teams.

Willie Jackson, who led the conference in receiving for the two previous seasons, was omitted. So was guard Jim Watson. And Tony Davis. And Chris Doering. And Larry Kennedy.

Kennedy had expected to be an All-American by now. He had made one big play after another as a freshman and then slowly faded into the background. He remained one of the SEC's best defensive backs, but not many quarterbacks threw his way since the players on the other side of the field were less experienced. When it comes to all-star teams, defensive backs are judged by the number of interceptions they make during the season. Kennedy had none. The final snub was his not making the All-SEC team. "They dogged me on the All-Conference team," he complained. "I can't believe it."

By the time the players reported back to practice, Rhett, Watson, Davis, and Wuerffel were spectators. Rhett and Watson had "turf toes," a painful injury caused by stubbing the big toe on artificial turf. Davis had broken his hand in the Alabama game. And for some reason Spurrier still hoped that Wuerffel would be able to play by January 1. "He's going to try to practice next week if he can get off the crutches," he told reporters.

Two days later the team held its bowl media day, entertaining sportswriters and broadcasters from all over the state and those from New Orleans and West Virginia. Watson initiated the conference by telling tales of how the team had partied too hard during its 1991 trip to New Orleans. "It was a free-for-all for fun," he recalled. "We were on Bourbon Street day and night. At one function, they were serving pitchers and we said, 'What are we going to do? The coaches are here.' Then one person went up and got one, and all of a sudden it was a stampede. There were guys throwing up before practice. Then some guys would go right to Bourbon Street from practice at about noon." Apparently, breaking curfew was common. "I think it was the honor system," Doering said, "and nobody honored it."

Spurrier didn't think the overindulgence had anything to do with Florida's 39–28 loss to Notre Dame. Told of Watson's comments, he asked, "What was our curfew anyway? I don't remember." Neither did the players. "I still think we were ready to play. Shane [Matthews] just didn't have one of his best nights, and then we couldn't stop [Notre Dame fullback Jerome] Bettis." He added, "Ah, well, hopefully that experience of two years ago will help us this time. Maybe we will take it more seriously."

Watson admitted he would take a different approach once he reached New Orleans. "They are going to be strict with us anyway, but I plan to go to Bourbon Street maybe once or twice and then work hard. Since West Virginia's never been there before, maybe it will work to our advantage this time."

Now that visiting Jacksonville wasn't on the Florida schedule until next October's Georgia game, receiver Jack Jackson toned down his remarks. Nothing personal, he said. "We weren't trying to knock the Gator Bowl, we just really wanted to get back to New Orleans. We didn't have a great time in Jacksonville last year."

From the Gator Bowl, which was the first bowl game he had ever won as a coach, Spurrier had learned that taking his players off campus helped them to focus on practicing and studying tapes. The Gators had held camp for four days in Jacksonville before Christmas 1992, and Spurrier credited the move with helping them beat North Carolina State. Once final exams were over, he wanted to do it again. Only this time, the team would move to Tampa, where the weather would be about ten degrees warmer than in Gainesville. Then he would give them three days with their families at Christmas before meeting on December 26 for the flight to New Orleans.

"It worked for us last year," Spurrier observed. "There's not much going on around campus, and nobody's here once final exams are done. It's sort of depressing around here. We need to get out of town and get ready to play a good ball game. I've lost the Sugar Bowl as a player and then as a coach. We need to win the thing."

On December 19, a Sunday morning, the team arrived in sunny Tampa and checked into the Wyndam, a plush resort on a small island. The minicamp would cost the athletic department $40,000. As they headed to practice, Kennedy was set on declaring himself eligible for the NFL draft even though he had another season of eligibility remaining. He had requested a draft rating from the NFL's new system for underclassmen contemplating such a move, but he hadn't received a reply. Kennedy's thinking puzzled the coaches. He hadn't made an interception that season and was left off the first and second All-SEC teams and yet he wanted to turn pro.

"He'll change his mind once he finds out where he'll be drafted," Spurrier noted. "I think he just wanted his name in the headlines for a few days. Then when he decides he's staying, his name will be in the headlines again."

Unknowingly, Spurrier was a big reason for Kennedy's wanting to leave early. He had tired of the head coach's treatment of the defensive players and Zook. He felt like a second-class citizen. "Besides, nobody throws my way anymore," he contended. Zook, who had helped recruit Kennedy to Ohio State four years earlier—Kennedy didn't enroll—said that he would talk him into staying for his senior season, but that conversation would wait until after the Sugar Bowl. "Now is not the right time," Zook added. "If I go tell him he's gotta stay now, he's going to resent me for it. Believe me, he's staying. I guarantee it."

More than three hundred fans showed up to watch the team's first practice at the University of Tampa. That night, Spurrier and tight ends coach Carl Franks walked into a restaurant next to the team's hotel. Spurrier noticed the Colts and Eagles were on television. "That ought to be a shootout," he joked. A few of the team's freshmen were eating at a corner table. Seeing them, Spurrier and Franks left.

Cornerback Larry Kennedy had All-American written all over him as a freshman, but two years later quarterbacks had stopped throwing his way and he went unnoticed.

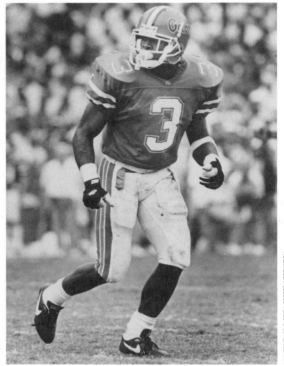

Spurrier had wanted a beer, so the two headed next door to another restaurant

The next day, following practice, Dean announced that he would stay at Gainesville for his senior season. "I will probably enroll in a graduate program and try to become a Rhodes Scholar candidate," he added. "I won't be happy sitting on the bench again, so that just means I'll do everything I can to win the job." Spurrier said Dean would have to. "Nothing is going to be given to anyone," he warned. "Terry realizes he is going to have to work for it like any other position on this team."

On Tuesday, Tom McEwen, long-time columnist for the *Tampa Tribune,* asked about the NFL rumors. "I always ask myself, How could anyone want more than to be the head coach at a great university like Florida . . . ," Spurrier replied. "Where the fans fill the big stadium every Saturday, where the weather is good, where the golf courses are good, and where great athletes are raised in your back yard. Lee Trevino once said that when he was a poor little boy he yearned for the day he could make enough money to move to Florida and play golf." It was a perfect answer for Spurrier, who loved his alma mater, warm weather, golf, and the opportunity to succeed, but not necessarily in that order.

Following each of the practices in Tampa, fans gathered outside the gates and waited for the players to sign autographs or pose for pictures. "Hey, there's Monty Grow, Dad! There's Monty Grow!" one teenaged fan yelled as the linebacker stopped to sign autographs. Nobody on the team appreciated a moment like this as much as Grow.

Monty Ray Grow was not even mentioned with the other players in the team's media guide, a three-hundred-page compilation of pictures, charts, records, and player biographies. Instead, his name was listed as one of the players lost from the 1992 team. He wasn't supposed to play during the 1993 season. He was supposed to be in his hometown of Inverness, getting on with his life after football.

Two years earlier, as a junior, Grow had purchased a bottle of an over-the-counter product named Hot Stuff. The label said the product would add weight and muscle, and at 210 pounds Grow needed all the weight and muscle he could find to switch from safety to linebacker. "I just happened to see it by accident and I thought, What's the harm? I'll try it," he recalled. Grow will never forget his twentieth birthday. It was September 4, 1991, the day that complicated his uncomplicated life. Spurrier had left a message on his answering machine, saying he wanted to see Grow in his office immediately and it wasn't to wish him a happy birthday. "I was scared to death," Grow remembered. "He never calls me. I thought my mom was in a car crash or something." Spurrier told him that he had tested positive for steroids in one of the players' random drug tests administered by the NCAA. He would be suspended for the remainder of the season. Grow appealed to the NCAA and was allowed to play in the first game, leading the team with nine tackles. The next week, the NCAA denied the appeal, and he was declared ineligible.

"I was shocked, I was crushed," he admitted. "I didn't know what they were talking about. I didn't take any steroids." While his teammates won the school's first SEC championship, Grow became a recluse. He had to practice, but he didn't have to socialize with the team, and he surely couldn't stand the pain of watching them play on Saturdays. "I hate those people who go around whining and complaining all the time," he said. "So that's the last thing I wanted to do. I just kept to myself and went home on the weekends. I didn't want to see anybody. I didn't want to talk to anybody. I didn't feel like a part of the team. I guess I just existed . . . wasting a year of my life."

Grow was allowed to return for the 1992 season, leading the team with ten tackles behind the line of scrimmage and a total of 103, third-best on the team. Before the final home game against South Carolina, he was introduced with the other departing seniors. He figured it was his final game in the Swamp. He wanted more, however, believing the NCAA owed him the season he had lost. He retained an attorney, Stephen Bernstein, who first investigated Hot Stuff, which was not regulated by the Food and Drug Administration. Bernstein and Grow also convinced Foley and other university officials that Grow had not ingested steroids, so the school agreed to back him in another appeal to the NCAA. Meanwhile, Bernstein's investigation led to the recall of Hot Stuff. "You really don't want to know what's in the product," Bernstein warned. "It was twenty bucks a can and it consisted of ground-up cattle brains and gizzards among hundreds of other things. The stuff was nothing more than a good laxative." The contents, it was determined, would test positive in a steroids test.

University attorney Pam Bernard and assistant athletic director Jamie McCloskey helped on Grow's case. They summoned Paul Doering, a pharmacy professor and receiver Chris Doering's father, to testify to the NCAA about over-the-counter products and nutritional supplements. In the meantime, Bernstein filed suit against the NCAA and the university only to get the case heard in a state court before the start of the 1993 season. "We never considered it an adversarial suit," Foley noted. "We were just the vehicle to get it into state court." Grow went about his business of lifting weights and

Linebacker Monty Grow fought for his chance to play college football, winning an appeal to the NCAA to regain his eligibility.

running just as if he was expected back at football camp in August. "I would have been the most fit nonfootball player in the country," he stated. On July 22, four days before he scheduled court date, the NCAA called Foley to say that Grow's eligibility had been restored.

Through the ordeal, Grow felt that he had been labeled as a drug user. He arrived at the team's annual media day in August wearing a shirt that read, No . . . I am not on steroids. "I just stood up for what I believed in . . . that's all a person can do," he commented. "Not many people had won any appeal from the NCAA, so I knew my chances were slim. I don't think too many people had planned to see me here this year. Now I am going to have two senior seasons. Not many guys can say that. I just wanted to play football."

But his broken arm at LSU prevented him from playing against Auburn and most of the next three games. He wasn't healthy until the Florida State game, in which he made a career-high eighteen tackles. He followed that with seven more against Alabama, including two behind the line of scrimmage and one pass deflection.

After what he had been through in the past five years, stopping to sign an autograph or two was just a walk in the park for Monty Grow. "I wasn't a part of that team that went to the Sugar Bowl two years ago," he said, "so you can see why I can't wait to get to New Orleans."

18

THE BIG EASY VICTORY

JAKE KELCHNER SAT IN ATLANTA's Hartsfield Airport and tried to
catch a quick nap before his flight to New Orleans. It was
the morning after Christmas, and the West Virginia quarterback didn't want to start worrying about Florida's defense just
yet. Two of the Mountaineers' offensive linemen thumbed
through the Gators' media guide, prompting one to read aloud:
"William Gaines . . . six-foot-five, 293 pounds . . . All-SEC
. . . nicknamed 'Big Nasty.'" One of them turned to Kelchner
and said, "Jake, this guy's going to be all over you." Kelchner shot
back, "He had better not be. It's your job to keep him off of me."

The flight reached New Orleans at 10:00 A.M. Someone
asked Kelchner what time the Mountaineers were due at practice. One of his teammates interrupted, "Practice? We aren't
practicing today. We start tomorrow. We're going to a nude bar
on Bourbon Street." While Kelchner and his buddies were having fun in the French Quarter, Nehlen and most of the
Mountaineers were arriving on a charter flight from
Morgantown. The politicking began immediately. "I think if we
win this game, then there's going to be co-championships,"
Nehlen said. "I am sure that any team that can become 12–0 is
going to get a piece of the championship."

While Nehlen was holding his first press conference in New Orleans, the Gators were fifteen miles away, running plays and sweating through dozens of sprints inside the massive Superdome. The work habits of the week to come had begun. The Mountaineers, on their first trip to the Big Easy, would party and talk. The Gators would work.

Spurrier was working in a few trick plays. "Hey, watch this one," he yelled to the sideline, where Carlson and some bowl executives sat. Dean pitched to Rhett, who handed the football back to the quarterback. Dean then ran around left end. "Doesn't he know that he's down to only one quarterback?" a sportswriter asked. "If Dean gets hurt on that play, that play won't look real smart." Carlson just shrugged.

The Gators took in the customary lecture from a New Orleans police detective about the dangers of the city, where to walk and where not to walk. The French Quarter had had its share of armed robberies and murders of tourists in recent years. "They'll know how to act," Spurrier said. "They don't have too much money to get into trouble anyway." Each player received $230 for the week, as allowed by NCAA rules.

Spurrier and Franks would spend much of the week on the telephone, since the NCAA declared the week after Christmas a recruiting dead period, allowing only phone calls to recruits. "We say, 'Hey, we're in New Orleans at the Sugar Bowl, and we want you to be here with us next year,'" Spurrier noted.

One recruit he didn't have to call was Peyton Manning, a quarterback from New Orleans that every school wanted. Manning, the son of former Mississippi and New Orleans Saints' star Archie Manning, had narrowed his choices to Florida, Tennessee, Michigan, and Mississippi. Manning and his father stood on the sidelines of the Superdome during two of the team's practices, but Spurrier, observing the NCAA rules, couldn't walk by and say hello. "It's funny," Foley pointed out, noticing Spurrier and Manning about fifteen yards apart. "Steve could stand over there and call him on a portable phone, but he can't go talk to him."

One of the few times senior defensive tackle William Gaines ever stood around. He was a dominating player during the second half of the season.

UNIVERSITY OF FLORIDA SPORTS INFORMATION

Other SEC coaches had no problem talking to West Virginia coaches, sharing information about the Gators. Spurrier knew his team wasn't one of the more popular ones in the conference and this proved it. West Virginia defensive coordinator Steve Dunlap talked with Kentucky defensive coordinator Mike Archer and Auburn defensive coordinator Wayne Hall. Maybe Archer told him he should have three safeties in the end zone, instead of two, should the Gators be threatening to win the game in the final seconds. "Coaches help coaches," Dunlap said. "It's no big deal."

"Alabama did the same thing last year with Louisville before we played [Louisville]," Spurrier noted. "I know you are supposed to pull for the other teams in the conference. I guess it doesn't always work out that way. I don't know that we worry so much about all the other SEC schools, and I am sure they don't worry about us that much."

During an interview session on Tuesday, Watson noticed that Dean was surrounded by microphones. "Terry's matured an awful lot this season," he said. "You can really see a difference in him. He handles himself better off the field and on it. Maybe everything works out for a reason. I wonder what would have happened if Coach Spurrier had stuck with him." Dean wondered, too. "I can't change it though by worrying about it," he replied. Neither could Willie Jackson, sitting across the room from Dean at the Hyatt next to the Superdome. "I felt this year that we were going to win the national championship," he remarked. "It turned out that only a couple of plays prevented it."

Following practice, Spurrier gave a roll call of the missing: guard Dean Golden and backup linebackers Henry Haston and Jason Bartley would miss the game because of academic troubles; backup tailback Tony Davis had left the team and headed back to Gainesville on his own. "He was unhappy about something," Spurrier commented. "Let's just say he left and leave it at that. We'll handle it when we get home."

The announcements angered the team's beat writers. Spurrier had known about the academic troubles for at least a week. When he was pressed about the ineligibilities, he complained, "You guys never asked me about it." One sportswriter fired back, "What are we supposed to do, run down the entire roster?"

The next day, Rob Rubin of the *Miami Herald* asked Spurrier about the NFL rumors. The subject had been put to rest two weeks earlier. "Where have you been?" Spurrier snapped. "We're here to talk about the Sugar Bowl."

Rhett showed up at one of the scheduled press conferences and joked, "Did you see that story on me in the paper today? It was this big." He held his fingers about an inch apart. "I am getting no pub down here." Someone had mentioned that whoever gained more yards between Rhett and

West Virginia tailback Robert Walker, a sophomore who rushed for 1,191 yards, probably would play on the winning team. "I had never even heard of Robert Walker until I got here," Rhett commented.

That was exactly the point, the Mountaineers said. They felt they weren't getting the respect they deserved for their 11–0 season. After all, the Sugar Bowl had held out a hope of inviting Notre Dame to play Florida again. West Virginia could have lost as many as five games, beating Maryland by five points, Virginia Tech by one, Louisville by two, Miami by three, and Boston College by three. The Mountaineers had been on television only twice. Florida had been on the tube seven times. Now the Mountaineers were a six-point underdog. "I don't know how a number-three team can be an underdog [against a number-eight team]," Mountaineers offensive tackle Rich Braham noted. Spurrier did. "Maybe those people who set the lines have a lot of respect for the three Florida schools," he replied. "Look at the line in the Orange Bowl, and Nebraska's undefeated." Florida State was favored by seventeen points.

"Nobody has given us any respect and we're 11–0," Walker added. "If we win and become 12–0, they'll have to give it to us."

Nehlen began toning down his comments about Florida State and the respect issue. "All I'll say is that if we finish 12–0, we should get at least one of the championships," he summarized. "I think some people who write about us don't really know us. Coaches know how tough it is to go 11–0."

Nehlen's team had won all eleven games with two quarterbacks, although unlike Florida's system, it was by design. Kelchner, when he was healthy, was the designated starter. He was a classic drop-back thrower with a cannon of a right arm. He had signed at Notre Dame originally but was kicked off the team by Lou Holtz after being charged with driving while intoxicated. Darren Studstill was a quick, ranging quarterback who could run or pass. He had entered the team's final regular

West Virginia head coach Don Nehlen, upset with the polls, continued to politick for his 11–0 team, right up to the kickoff of Florida's 41–7 victory in the Sugar Bowl.

WEST VIRGINIA UNIVERSITY SPORTS INFORMATION

season game when Kelchner strained a hamstring and rallied the team from a 14–9 deficit at Boston College.

"That is exactly why we want two quarterbacks ready," West Virginia offensive coordinator Mike Jacobs said. "Injuries happen. This is like running the I-formation and having two tailbacks."

In Nehlen's alternating system, he usually wanted Studstill to play at least two possessions in each half. So far, it had worked perfectly. "It gives me a chance to get to the sideline and watch what the defense is doing," Kelchner noted. "He comes in and he has fresh legs and a fresh arm, and he's been very productive."

Some Mountaineers were upset at the national perception of them. They weren't hillbillies from the backwoods, defensive back Mike Collins promised. They didn't live in log cabins with mud floors or wear coonskin caps. "We did wear shoes down here," he added. "We just have to educate people, I guess."

While the Mountaineers fretted about not getting a legitimate chance to win the national title, Spurrier used every chance he had during the week to lecture the media on the benefits of a playoff system for a national collegiate championship. "We're the only sport in the country whose champion is determined by you guys," he quipped. "I've been saying it for four years. It just doesn't make sense that we don't have a playoff to determine who the real champion should be." Spurrier had heard all the arguments against a playoff from other coaches and knew he was in the minority. A playoff would take the players away from the classrooms, add pressure to coaches and players, and eliminate the current bowl system, which has existed for the past sixty years. "I haven't heard a good reason yet," he replied.

Nevertheless, there wouldn't be one anytime soon, and Spurrier had to settle for winning a major bowl game. That wasn't any more important to West Virginia than it was to Florida. The Gators had not won a New Year's Day bowl game in almost thirty years. In that span, Miami had won four national championships while Florida State had won the Fiesta Bowl twice, the Cotton once, the Orange once, and even the Sugar once. That was embarrassing to the Gators since the Sugar Bowl automatically invites the SEC champion. "How long has it been since we won on New Year's Day?" Watson asked. "Twenty-seven years . . . wow!"

Spurrier had quarterbacked the 1966 team to a 27–12 win over Georgia Tech in the Orange Bowl on January 1, 1967. He never figured the school would endure the next twenty-seven years without winning on New Year's Day. His teams had exorcised the ghosts of Auburn, Georgia, and Alabama since he became the head coach at Florida. His teams had won two SEC championships for a school that previously had none. Now he had to teach them how to win a major bowl game. The cover of the team's playbook had been designed to remind the players of the significance of the game, a cartoon with a gator riding an elevator. The caption read, "What level do you want?" The choices were also-ran, contender, or powerhouse.

"We've overcome a lot of those obstacles," he said. "This is another one. We've never won eleven games, and we've never won the Sugar Bowl. Everybody knows that."

Watson saw the game as a chance to pave the way for future Florida teams to visit New Orleans. "We have to move the program forward with this game," he observed. "If we win, it will make it easier for other teams to win on New Year's Day. The pressure won't be there for them."

As the week progressed, Florida's players couldn't help but notice the Mountaineers enjoying themselves at the hundreds of bars in the French Quarter. The Gators toured Bourbon Street, and when they did stick their heads inside a bar, they noticed a preponderance of blue and gold on the bar stools. "At the clubs, it was all West Virginia players," Rhett observed. "I think some of our guys learned that lesson the hard way last time we were here." Even Coach Nehlen admitted he could have held a team meeting one night as he walked down Bourbon Street.

Nehlen planned to take the team, not only out of New Orleans on New Year's Eve, but out of the state. "We're going to some hotel in Mississippi . . . damned if I know where," he said.

During one of the few times players from the two teams clashed on Bourbon Street, Florida receiver Jack Jackson mocked West Virginia cornerback Mike Collins, saying, "I am going to hold a tailgate party and you're invited . . . you'll be tailgating me into the end zone!"

On New Year's Eve, administrators from both schools attended the Sugar Bowl gala at the Hilton, where the Gators were also staying. As a band blared away, Denise Zook sat with the wives of a few other coaches. "Where's Ron?" she was asked. "Are you kidding?" she answered. "He wouldn't be caught dead at a party like this on the night before a game. He hates this stuff." He was upstairs watching tape of West Virginia's offense.

Spurrier showed up briefly to be introduced along with Nehlen. Carlson, Foley, and sports information director John Humenik represented Florida. At the stroke of midnight, everyone toasted, and Carlson whispered, "I think we are going to win . . . we're going to win big. They've been partying all week."

Spurrier greeted 1994 by relaxing and watching several of the afternoon bowl games on New Year's Day. He was amused that Penn State had destroyed Tennessee by a score of 31–13 in the Citrus Bowl in Orlando. The Vols had gone into the bowl season boasting that they should have been ranked higher than Florida throughout the season. Arizona had shut out Miami, 29–0. Notre Dame had narrowly beaten Texas A&M, 24–21, in Dallas. The Irish had needed an impressive win to overcome Florida State's claim to the national championship should the Seminoles beat Nebraska. Minutes before the Sugar Bowl started, the Cornhuskers and Seminoles kicked off in Miami.

The national championship debate was the last thing the Gators were thinking about that night. As the home team, they could choose their uniforms. They came out wearing their usual attire for road games, orange pants and white jerseys. On the first play, Rhett couldn't hold onto a pass from Dean over the middle and was pounded hard to the turf. He stayed down for about a minute, holding his back. After gaining one first down, Florida punted.

If Kelchner, known to his teammates as "Jake the Snake," was sluggish after a week of hard partying, he didn't show it early in the game. He ran for eight yards on the Mountaineers' first play. Then he passed for fourteen more and another fourteen. Dropping back from Florida's thirty-two-yard line, he lofted a high spiral toward the corner of the end zone. Receiver Jay Kearney twisted Lott around and ran by him. Touchdown! West Virginia led 7–0 just 4:46 into the game.

The play closely resembled some of the dark moments of the Gators' defense during the Tennessee or Mississippi State games. There was a Florida defender backpeddling, but not far enough, then losing sight of the receiver as the pass sailed over his head. God, Zook hated that sight. Spurrier walked down the sideline and screamed into his ear, something about getting the defensive backs deeper, but no one else heard the details. With the touchdown, the thirty-five thousand Mountaineer fans elevated the Superdome's noise to rock-concert level.

Florida gained only one first down on its next possession and punted again. After a personal foul against Florida's defense, Kelchner then passed twelve yards to Kearney for a first down near midfield, and Spurrier visited Zook again. It would be his final visit of the season. Two plays later, linebacker Dexter Daniels and defensive tackle Mark Campbell slammed West Virginia's Jon Jones to the ground for a two-yard loss, and the Mountaineers punted.

On the next Florida possession West Virginia stopped Rhett short of a first down, which would have forced the Gators to punt. But while Rhett was underneath the pile, linebacker Tim Brown repeatedly punched him in the stomach. Rhett jumped to his feet screaming, "He's punching me! He's punching me! Man, why are you doing that?" An official noticed Brown's Evander Holyfield imitation and penalized the Mountaineers fifteen yards.

It was the turning point the Gators needed. Dean completed four consecutive passes, including a spectacular catch by Aubrey Hill. On first down at the three-yard line, Spurrier called for a sweep to the left. When Rhett took the pitch, West Virginia defenders had read the play. Rhett cut back to the right, darted inside, and lunged for the end zone to tie the game. "Errict turned a bad play into a good one simply by reading the defense," Spurrier would say later.

Early in the second quarter, Nehlen inserted Studstill into the game for Kelchner as planned. The rotation may have

Running room was hard to find early in the game, but the Gators' offensive line wore out West Virginia by halftime and Florida tailback Errict Rhett saw gaping holes in the Mountaineers' defense as a result.

worked eleven times during the season, but this time it back-fired. Studstill scrambled out of the pocket and was crushed by Grow from the blind side. Studstill's head snapped back, forcing his mouthpiece to fly to the ground. It was the most vicious tackle of the season, a real decleater that Grow saved for his final game. The Gators' sideline erupted into high-fives. "Monty's hit rattled Studstill," safety Lawrence Wright claimed.

Later, when Studstill dropped back, Grow blitzed from the right side and leveled his helmet into the quarterback's back. Wright jumped to make an easy interception of Studstill's wobbly pass at Florida's forty-eight-yard line. He ran right, then near the Florida sideline he stopped and circled around to the left. He cut right again and into the end zone. "That was unbelievable," Spurrier said later. "He starts turning around and we're all yelling, 'No, Lawrence, run forward!' It was the dangdest thing I've ever seen." It was the team's first interception return for a touchdown in two years.

Dean and Willie Jackson put on an impressive show the next time the offense had the ball. Dean completed passes of thirteen and eleven yards to Jackson, and then, on a blitz, he threw a high pass toward the right sideline. Jackson took the ball away from defensive back Mike Logan and jogged into the end zone to complete the thirty-nine-yard play. Only fifty-one seconds remained in the half with the Gators leading 21–7.

The second half wouldn't be as close. Florida's pass rush, absent for the first half of the season, was unblockable now, as Kelchner was running for his life each time he dropped back to throw. Rhett then scored the two quickest touchdowns of his career, running in from two yards and one yard in a two-minute span. In between, West Virginia's Mike Logan had fumbled the kickoff return, and Florida's Shea Showers recovered at the Mountaineers' fourteen-yard line. With 8:58 remaining in the third quarter, the Gators had a comfortable 35–7 lead and hundreds of West Virginia fans were leaving the Superdome. Rhett was still getting the brunt of West Virginia's frustration. "I

BARRY J. MORGAN

The play of the game. Redshirt freshman free safety Lawrence Wright's interception didn't match his spectacular return for a touchdown in which he cut right, turned completely around, then headed for the end zone. The play gave Florida a 14–7 lead and West Virginia a hint of what was to come.

don't know why they kept punching me," he said after the game. "They kept hitting me. It kind of ticked me off."

West Virginia never threatened to score again. Studstill played just three more plays, each an incompletion. The work was over and the fun was just beginning for the Gators. Spurrier cleared the bench, bringing his upperclassmen to the sideline to watch the remainder of the game. Willie Jackson finished his tumultuous season and his excellent career with nine receptions for 131 yards. Dean completed twenty-two of thirty-seven passes for 255 yards, finishing the season as sharp as he started it against Arkansas State. Grow was a one-man wrecking crew on defense, harassing Kelchner and Studstill throughout the night. But the most valuable player award was Rhett's. In his final game, he had gained 105 yards and scored three touchdowns. Bushwick would have been proud.

As Spurrier stood on the sidelines, one of the offensive lineman suggested the "hidden-ball play," which calls for several players to gather in a circle in the backfield with the ball. Then they break the huddle running in different directions while the defense has to figure out who has the ball. Spurrier called the play, and fullback Chris Bilkie carried up the middle for nine yards. Later in the possession, Davis kicked a twenty-six-yard field goal with 1:55 remaining to make the score 41–7. The Gators were taking no prisoners on this night.

Two minutes later they were celebrating again. They had won a Sugar Bowl for the first time. They had won eleven games for the first time. Just as they did in Birmingham four weeks earlier, they paraded around the field, high-fived each other, and had their pictures taken over and over again. Then Spurrier led them on a trip to celebrate with the fans who remained in the stadium.

Slowly the celebrating stopped as fans watched the final minute of the Orange Bowl on the stadium's television screens. Nebraska had just kicked a field goal to take a 16–15 lead with only 1:16 remaining in the game. The Superdome broke out into a simultaneous imitation of FSU's War Chant and

BARRY J. MORGAN

It was that kind of night for West Virginia's offense. Here, Darren Hambrick and another Gators defender smother a helpless Mountaineer.

Tomahawk Chop. It was mockery at its best, and the Gators loved it. Minutes later they saw Charlie Ward lead the Seminoles back for a game-winning field goal and the chanting stopped. It looked as if rival Florida State would be the national champion, but the Seminoles couldn't have been more satisfied than the Gators.

It was 11:20 CST. Dean said, "I don't think anybody on this team truly understands what this means. We're the first team at Florida to win eleven games and the first to win the Sugar Bowl." Watson hinted that this victory signaled a time of change in the Sunshine State, regardless of the final score in the Orange Bowl. "It seems like we've always been chasing Florida State and Miami," he said. "Well, I think we've passed one and we're catching up with the other."

Nehlen, whose argument about FSU and the rankings appeared silly now, made no excuses, saying, "We got whipped. . . . We got whipped big time. What was the problem? Those guys out there in the orange pants were the problem."

Spurrier didn't want to spend much time in a postgame interview session. "I am very proud of our team," he announced, sitting behind a podium on the Superdome's first floor. "Everything seemed to go our way after West Virginia's touchdown. This was a major accomplishment. Actually, the whole season was. This will be something that these players will carry with them for the rest of their lives. We're glad it's over, and it's time to walk up and down Bourbon Street."

That was the players' next destination. Spurrier was soon headed out the Superdome door and into a cool, foggy New Orleans night. It was almost midnight and there was a party waiting, friends to hug, champagne to pour, and a toast to make.

AFTERWORD

U NIVERSITY OF FLORIDA FOOTBALL didn't cease to exist once the Sugar Bowl was won and the text of this book was completed. On February 2, 1994, Steve Spurrier signed another good recruiting class for the Gators, but highly prized quarterback Peyton Manning chose to play for Tennessee rather than Florida.

On that day Spurrier also announced that he would not be making any changes in his coaching staff. He added that Ron Zook "likely" would remain his defensive coordinator, "unless he takes another job somewhere else." "I know he's talking to other coaches out there," Zook said. "So we'll see what happens. I know I can coach. We just needed another year for these kids to mature some."

While college football fans spend Saturdays in the stadiums dressed in their school's colors and either tolerating a few hours' disappointment if their alma mater loses or exulting for days when their team wins, the attachment is precarious at best for those whose lives are most closely touched by the game. Charley Pell demonstrated that to the world in early February when he attempted suicide in Jacksonville. Fortunately he failed. Pell had had the job of his life as the head coach of the Florida Gators from 1979 to 1984. Once he lost that as a result of NCAA violations, he wandered from job to job, hoping to find something to fill the void. He never did.

Three weeks later, on March 3, Spurrier hired former Tulane defensive coordinator Bob Pruett and demoted Zook to special teams coach. "We can't keep finishing last in the SEC in pass defense," Spurrier explained. "I am sick of it. I'm the head coach, and it's my responsibility to have a better defense."

"Hey, it's coaching, it's a job," Zook observed. "I'll come back. I can't quit. I have a wife and two kids at home."

Defensive line coach Jerry "Red" Anderson was reassigned as an assistant to the athletic director. He wasn't happy about the change.

Most people say that football's only a game. A competition. No more, no less. They say the results don't matter. They say it's how you play the game, not whether you win or lose. Tell that to Charley Pell.

The game is about people. It affects their lives. Hurts them. Lifts them. Crushes them. Exults them. Teaches them. Improves them. It is a part of all who coach it, play it, watch it, or write about it.

For some it's only for a day. For some it's a season that ends late on January 1 when the final bowl game clock finishes counting down to :00. For the privileged others—the coaches and the players—the game and its memories last a lifetime.